OECD
ECONOMIC
SURVEYS

1999-2000 WITHDRAW:

ORGANISATION FOR ECONOMIC CO-OPERATION AND DEVELOPMENT

ORGANISATION FOR ECONOMIC CO-OPERATION AND DEVELOPMENT

Pursuant to Article 1 of the Convention signed in Paris on 14th December 1960, and which came into force on 30th September 1961, the Organisation for Economic Co-operation and Development (OECD) shall promote policies designed:

- to achieve the highest sustainable economic growth and employment and a rising standard of living in Member countries, while maintaining financial stability, and thus to contribute to the development of the world economy;

- to contribute to sound economic expansion in Member as well as non-member countries in the process of economic development; and

- to contribute to the expansion of world trade on a multilateral, non-discriminatory basis in accordance with international obligations.

The original Member countries of the OECD are Austria, Belgium, Canada, Denmark, France, Germany, Greece, Iceland, Ireland, Italy, Luxembourg, the Netherlands, Norway, Portugal, Spain, Sweden, Switzerland, Turkey, the United Kingdom and the United States. The following countries became Members subsequently through accession at the dates indicated hereafter: Japan (28th April 1964), Finland (28th January 1969), Australia (7th June 1971), New Zealand (29th May 1973), Mexico (18th May 1994), the Czech Republic (21st December 1995), Hungary (7th May 1996), Poland (22nd November 1996) and Korea (12th December 1996). The Commission of the European Communities takes part in the work of the OECD (Article 13 of the OECD Convention).

Publié également en français.

Table of contents

• • • • •

Boxes

Tables

Annex

Statistical annex

BASIC STATISTICS OF CANADA

THE LAND

Area (thousand sq. km)	9 976	Population of major cities (thousands, 1998):	
Agricultural area (1991, per cent		Montreal	3 424
of total area)	6.8	Toronto	4 586

THE PEOPLE

Population (1999)	30 454 118	Labour force (1999)	15 721 542
Number of inhabitants per sq. km	3.1	Employment in agriculture	410 467
Population, annual net natural increase		Immigration (annual average 1995-1999)	203 640
(average 1995-1999)	138 132	Average annual increase in labour force	
Natural increase rate per 1000 inhabitants		(1995-1999, per cent)	1.5
(average 1995-1999)	4.7		

THE PRODUCTION

GDP (million of Canadian dollars, 1999)	957 911	Origin of gross domestic product	
GDP per capita (Canadian dollars)	31 454	(1999, per cent of total, 1992 prices):	
Gross fixed investment per capita		Agriculture, forestry and fishing	2.5
(Canadian dollars)	6 126	Mining and quarrying	3.6
Gross fixed investment		Manufacturing	18.2
(per cent of GDP)	19.5	Construction	5.6
		Non business sector	17.2
		Other	55.4

THE GOVERNMENT

			Number of seats	
Government current expenditure on goods			House of Commons	Senate
and services (1999, per cent of GDP)	18.8	Composition of Parliament		
Government gross fixed capital formation		(June 2000):		
(1999, per cent of GDP)	2.2	Progressive Conservative	18	39
Federal government current revenue		Liberal	157	57
(1999, per cent of GDP)	18.5	New Democratic	20	..
Federal direct and guaranteed debt		Bloc Québécois	44	..
(1999, per cent of current expenditure)	264.1	Independent	5	5
		Canadian Alliance	57	..

THE FOREIGN TRADE

Exports (1999)		Imports (1999)	
Exports of goods and services		Imports of goods and services	
(per cent of GDP)	43.2	(per cent of GDP)	40.3
Main merchandise exports		Main merchandise imports	
(per cent of total):		(per cent of total):	
Wheat	0.9	Industrial materials	18.1
Natural gas	3.0	Motor vehicles and parts	23.2
Lumber and sawmill products	5.5	Producers' equipment	33.1
Pulp and paper	5.4	Consumer goods	11.3
Other metals and minerals	7.6	Main suppliers	
Motor vehicles and parts	26.5	(per cent of commodity imports):	
Other manufactured goods	30.6	United States	76.3
Main customers		European Union	8.7
(per cent of commodity exports):		Japan	3.2
United States	85.8		
European Union	5.1		
Japan	2.6		

THE CURRENCY

Monetary unit: Canadian dollar	Currency units per US$	
	Year 1999	1.486

Note: An international comparison of certain basic statistics is given in an annex table.

Assessment and recommendations

Canada's recent economic performance has been favourable, underpinned by the sound macroeconomic and structural policies pursued over the 1990s. With improved fundamentals, including a fiscal surplus, activity has rebounded vigorously from the external shocks in 1997-1998. Economic expansion since then has been strong and broadly based, benefiting both from a favourable external environment – buoyant US demand, rising world commodity prices – and improved confidence at home associated with substantial job creation and rising incomes. With real GDP growth averaging over 5 per cent (at an annual rate) since late 1998, slack in product and labour markets has been rapidly taken up. The unemployment rate has fallen to levels last seen in the mid-1970s, and the economy may now be operating at, or slightly above, full capacity, as conventionally measured. Nonetheless, while the sharp rise in energy prices has pushed up "headline" inflation, "core" inflation – excluding energy and other volatile items – has stayed well within the bottom half of the official 1 to 3 per cent target band. At the same time, with the improvement in Canada's terms of trade coming from higher commodity prices, the current account has shifted rapidly towards surplus.

... and
the economic
outlook looks
favourable...
In the period ahead, economic growth is projected to moderate, averaging 3 per cent in 2001 following about 4½ per cent this year, as US demand becomes less supportive and tighter monetary conditions restrain the interest-sensitive components of household and business spending. On the other hand, renewed fiscal stimulus should bolster domestic demand, although households may prefer to take advantage of announced tax cuts to strengthen their balance sheets. Such a "soft landing" scenario would avoid the

emergence of major tensions and imbalances in the economy. Core inflation is expected to rise somewhat but to stay near the middle of the official target range,. Despite vanishing terms-of-trade gains, the external balance should be in slight surplus, as imports slow roughly in line with exports.

... provided activity settles down smoothly to a more sustainable pace

While unexpected developments in the United States would obviously have consequences for the Canadian economy, given the strong trade and financial linkages between the two countries, there are also important risks to the outlook associated with the domestic economy. The principal risk derives from the fact that, during the projection period, the economy may be operating above OECD estimates of non-inflationary capacity, even though the latter build in a considerable acceleration in potential output growth (to over 3 per cent per annum) owing in part to efficiency gains. Yet considerable uncertainty about aggregate supply remains. Continued low core inflation could mean that the sustainable level of output is even higher than estimated, but it is by no means clear to what extent technological advances and restructuring have enhanced *trend* productivity growth in Canada. These uncertainties about the economy's productive potential will put the inflation-targeting framework to the test, the more so since the surge in energy prices could result in higher inflation expectations and consequently increased wage claims.

Careful monetary management is thus required...

Despite the benign inflation environment, the Bank of Canada has become concerned about economic activity picking up too much momentum. While they had held benchmark interest rates steady when US rates were raised during the summer of 1999, they followed subsequent moves by the US Federal Reserve as from November. Canadian nominal interest rates have remained below their US counterparts, however, which might help explain why the Canadian dollar has appreciated less than might have been expected on the basis of commodity price developments alone. With excess supply in the economy apparently eliminated by late 1999, the modest tightening in the monetary stance was appropriate, even though core inflation has so far remained low. Indeed, looking forward, a further tightening in monetary conditions would seem to be warranted. Given the uncertainties mentioned above, the Bank has de-emphasised the output gap as a guide for monetary policy and is placing increasing weight on various indicators of future inflation, including monetary aggregates which have shown strong expansion of late. This implies, however, a considerable degree of judgement required on its part. It is true that its success in maintaining low inflation has established the credibility of its targeting regime. That, combined with the fact that core inflation remains well below the mid-point of the target range, provides it with some room to explore the economy's productive limits. Given the risks of spillover from any pick-up in inflation in the United States and the time it takes for monetary policy to have its impact on activity and prices, it would seem advisable to err on the side of caution and continue to raise interest rates if the strong momentum of the economy persists.

... as well as prudent fiscal policy...

The sharp improvements in federal and provincial fiscal balances towards surplus have resulted in a marked fall in the very high gross government debt-to-GDP ratio, which by end-2000 will have come down by about 15 percentage points after peaking at over 120 per cent of GDP in the mid-1990s (based on the new definition including funded government pension liabilities), and the prospects are good for further declines over the medium term. This has helped reduce risk premia and interest-rate volatility, both of which have had a negative impact in previous years on government finances and on the economy in general. However, while monetary policy is in a tightening mode, fiscal policies, after six years of retrenchment, are now easing, and this trend may be reinforced by the fact that additional revenue beyond budgeted levels – which has been the rule, given prudent planning assumptions – is largely used for funding one-off spending initiatives. Without any slack remaining, in the near term it would clearly be preferable to use these revenues for debt reduction rather than new spending, so as to take pressure off monetary policy. Indeed, accelerated debt reduction continues to offer substantial advantages for Canada. It would allow an earlier transition to lower tax rates, enhance the flexibility policy makers will have in designing appropriate policies, further reduce the country's vulnerability to economic shocks and strengthen the credibility of the government's macro-economic strategy.

... within
a medium-term
framework

In a longer-term perspective, the government's current rule of thumb, which allocates half the budget surplus to new spending initiatives, should be reconsidered, with greater weight being given to debt reduction and tax cuts. Tight control over spending and careful evaluation of new initiatives would, over time, make room for even greater debt drawdowns and more comprehensive reform of the tax system, where there is still scope for improvement despite the recent measures, as discussed below. In this regard, the government's presentation of five-year fiscal projections is welcome, as it facilitates public debate on feasible policy options. However, there is still a need for a more comprehensive medium-term framework, providing a coherent prospective plan for programme spending, tax changes and debt reductions, with priority given to reforms in those areas that produce the most significant long-term benefits for the economy.

Structural reform
has begun
to pay off...

The broadly based structural reform agenda pursued since the latter part of the 1980s has touched on all aspects of the economy as the authorities have sought to improve its efficiency and thereby productive capacity. The benefits were slow to materialise, possibly reflecting the significant excess supply in the first half of the 1990s as economic imbalances were unwinding, as well as the staged way in which reforms were implemented and the time lags between their introduction and eventual impact. However, as noted, signs are now emerging that these reforms are beginning to pay off in terms of higher potential output and falling structural unemployment.

... but the extent
to which the "new
economy"
has arrived
is uncertain

Amidst these positive signs, there are no clear indications of an improvement in *trend* productivity performance. So far, measured productivity growth has not picked up to the extent it has in the United States. In combination with poorer employment performance over most of the decade, this has implied a decline in relative living standards and has led to a debate over whether Canada is getting left behind in the transition to the "new economy". Indeed, the divergence between the two countries' performance reflects the fact that, in Canada, the two industries which are leaders in the "new economy" – electronic equipment and industrial machinery – make up a much smaller share of output and have made slower productivity advances than in the United States. Thus, at the macroeconomic level, Canada cannot expect to see the same contribution to productivity gains emanating from these industries as its southern neighbour. On the other hand, the recent strength in investment in machinery and equipment, led by spending on computers, could spur a rise in labour productivity growth by increasing the stock of capital available per worker. Recent federal budgets have introduced measures aimed at promoting innovation and taking advantage of opportunities presented by the new economy. But a fuller and more rapid exploitation of the possibilities opened up by new technologies is likely to require continued efforts to complete the structural reform agenda.

Policy makers need to complete unfinished business in the labour market...

The authorities have made substantial progress in implementing the OECD *Jobs Strategy* recommendations, but there is unfinished work and a need to maintain the momentum of labour-market reform. Recent developments in Employment Insurance (EI) payments, for example, suggest that incentives to take up benefits for certain groups have not been altered significantly. Thus, it is essential that remaining issues be dealt with, including the large variation in regional generosity. At the same time, any renewed easing of eligibility criteria beyond that already announced should be resisted, since this risks creating casual labour-force participation (and dependence on EI), moving away from the insurance principles adopted in 1996. Improved labour-market conditions also imply the need for a greater focus of active labour-market and social policies on shorter-term, and less costly, adjustment measures. In that regard, evaluations of all interventions should be systematically undertaken and those under way completed quickly to ensure that they are bolstering work incentives and reducing dependency. Encouraging inter-regional labour (and other factor) mobility, with the ensuing efficiency gains, would be greatly assisted by the swift completion of the provisions of the Internal Trade Agreement and Social Union Framework, and indeed, by moving beyond the targets already set therein.

... and address emerging issues in product markets

One area that will require further examination by the authorities is electronic commerce (e-commerce). While estimates suggest that expenditures in this area are relatively small, they are nonetheless expected to soar, holding the possibility of substantially improving efficiency in the distributive trade sectors. Careful attention is required to create the conditions for a vibrant e-commerce marketplace by ensuring that unwarranted barriers which might limit this activity's expansion are relaxed, thereby safeguarding the domestic tax base. However, although the United States does not collect sales tax on many e-commerce purchases, Canada should not move in this direction. On the international front, support for free trade under the auspices of the World Trade Organisation (WTO) remains the cornerstone of Canada's trade policy. Commitment to the rules-based trading system has led Canada to agree to implement the recent panel decision on the Auto Pact, which it should do by removing its tariffs on all imports of automobiles and parts. While this may lead to some restructuring of the sector, it would benefit consumers via greater competition and choice in the marketplace.

They should also take greater strides forward on tax reform...

Meanwhile, the latest Budget contains very welcome initiatives to lower the tax burden on Canadians, with the announcement of a five-year tax reduction plan. The most important change is the immediate restoration of full indexation of the income tax system; this puts an end to "bracket creep", which will benefit low-income families the most. The authorities have indicated that, should the budget situation allow it, they intend both to bring forward some of the measures currently envisaged for implementation only by 2004 and to go further in the tax reduction process. Moves in this direction would be beneficial, particularly for corporate taxes where corresponding rates for non-manufacturing and non-resource companies are still significantly higher than in the United States and most other OECD countries. Lowering taxes on service-sector firms more substantially would remove the present bias against knowledge-based activities, thereby levelling the playing field among enterprises, while serving to complement other measures that may help to boost innovation, such as R&D incentives. Bringing forward the envisaged measures in the personal tax field (raising the threshold at which the highest tax rate kicks in and eliminating the surcharge on higher incomes) would also be useful, as they should have positive effects on labour supply. A more certain timetable on when new measures would be introduced could be helpful in locking in expectations. In addition, there are ongoing concerns in the area of capital and payroll taxation. Furthermore, shifting the tax system towards increased use of less distorting indirect taxes, as suggested in previous *Surveys*, together with initiatives that could preserve the quality of the environment should be envisaged.

... while both improving public spending discipline and directing new outlays to areas that enhance productive capacity...

However, as noted above, the ability to move in these directions is constrained by the lack of an effective framework on how to judge and deal with competing, and indeed escalating, claims on budget surpluses. In this regard, it would be desirable to develop a structure for the transparent assessment of the benefits arising from spending initiatives, allowing an appraisal of how these weigh against those generated by tax and debt reductions. A first step would be to ensure that current spending is carefully examined as to whether a re-allocation towards areas that enhance the economy's productive capacity is possible. The latest Budget, for instance, provides for funding for initiatives that, among other things, seek to boost universities' research capacity, improve infrastructure and get the government "on-line" (one objective of which being to promote e-commerce). Since the benefits of such discretionary measures are not always apparent, their implementation and impact should be carefully monitored (including carrying out cost-benefit analysis where relevant) with a view to setting up a list of "what works" in order to target future expenditures efficiently, as well as to better communicate and justify government spending priorities. Claims on surplus funds are most apparent in the area of health care. While some spending increases in this respect might be useful, such claims should be judged in the light of the potential to introduce reforms that could both contain costs and increase service quality. Indeed, changes in the delivery of primary care would help to improve the continuity of services provided to patients, reducing unnecessary interventions, and thereby costs. Physician remuneration remains a controversial area, but Canada could adopt a mixed capitation/fee-for-service model that several other OECD countries have already implemented.

... as well as moving quickly to implement planned financial sector reforms

One area that continues to undergo substantial reform is the financial sector. The government's proposals for over-hauling the industry's framework currently before Parliament have the potential to enhance competition, which would benefit business and consumers alike through a greater choice of products and more efficient and liquid capital markets. Following the necessary interaction with interested parties the legislation should be passed and implemented quickly to reduce uncertainty, assisting market participants in their planning and decision-making. The recently intro-duced supervisory framework appears flexible enough to deal with the likely associated challenges, but in some cases more transparent guidelines might be useful (for instance, in the merger process for large banks). At the same time, policymakers should continue with their efforts to reduce regulatory overlap and duplication, where it exists, in order to minimise the burden on financial institutions as their business environment becomes increasingly competi-tive. Supervisory bodies should continue to be provided with sufficient resources to deal with the potential for increased risk arising from greater competition.

Future growth needs to be environmentally sustainable

Policymakers need to make sure that the higher growth that is expected to result from structural reform and skilful macroeconomic management is sustainable not only eco-nomically but also in terms of its effects on the environment. In an effort both to strengthen the government's perfor-mance in protecting the environment and bring consistency to its policies, legislation has been enacted that requires federal departments regularly to table sustainable develop-ment strategies. In addition, it has established the position of the Commissioner of the Environment and Sustainable Development who plays a key role in monitoring policy progress. As noted by the Commissioner, there is still an "implementation gap" in many areas. It is true that, in Canada, sustainable development policies face a number of specific conditions: the proximity of and economic integra-tion with the United States; the large inter-provincial differences in environmental conditions and resource avail-ability; and last, but not least, the shared jurisdiction between the federal and provincial governments in these areas. Nonetheless, there is scope for enhancing policy per-formance. Improving the mechanisms for decision-making at all government levels, as well as those intended to ensure co-operation among them and to reinforce accountability, would be helpful. Voluntary agreements have not proved up to the task of dealing with the resource and environmental challenges on their own. Thus, more extensive use of economic instruments will be necessary.

Incentives for natural resource development and use raise sustainability concerns...

The sense of "immensity" and Canada's rich endow-ment of natural resources have led to policies favouring their development and use. Although, apart from the Atlantic groundfish sector, the limits of availability of resources have generally not been reached, the sustainabil-ity of such policies is an issue in the long run. Resource-based production is energy-intensive and may in the end cause serious pollution problems, notwithstanding the Canadian environment's substantial assimilative capacity compared with other OECD countries. Support has been especially important for activities based on non-renewable resources (such as oil, gas, metals and minerals), coming mostly in the form of preferential tax treatment. Although the recently announced tax measures will, over time, contribute to levelling the playing field, this has put other sectors of the economy, such as knowledge-based indus-tries, at a disadvantage, while elevating the overall tax burden. The resulting intensive exploitation of non-renewable resources also has environmental consequences in the form of polluting substances release and greenhouse gas emissions.

... while whether water is being well managed has become an issue...

In the same way, overuse of water, because it is under-priced, has become a problem in some regions, despite the abundant supply overall. While the government has been endorsing the principle of "economic pricing" of water for some time, provincial and local governments, which are responsible for water management, are moving only slowly in this direction. In regions with extensive irrigation in particular, the current implicit subsidisation has reduced water availability and increased pollution by boosting chemical-intensive agricultural production. To bring about more efficient water use, provincial and territorial governments should therefore implement the principle of "economic pricing" without delay, while making water rights transferable in problem areas (provided that does no harm to the ecosystem). This requires substantially increased use of water metering, which is still far from universal, and the elimination of quantity discounts. Such a policy would be consistent with the recent decision to ban bulk water removal, thereby preventing exports, which reveals a very high implicit social valuation of water. Nonetheless, a carefully designed export licensing system might allow Canada to reap some benefits from its abundant aggregate water resources, while at the same time preventing harmful environmental effects.

... and dealing with the collapse of the Atlantic groundfisheries remains a policy concern

The Atlantic groundfisheries provide an illustration of how well-intentioned public support, in the face of unexpected environmental developments, may contribute to the overexploitation of a common resource. Although significant progress has been made in reducing the number of license holders in the groundfish sector, the sector is still over-capitalised and has too many fishers. This reflects the difficulty in trading-off the short-term adjustment costs for fishing communities, with their distributional and regional implications, against the longer-term sustainability of the sector. Other beneficial measures taken in Atlantic fisheries management (both groundfish and others) – notably the increase in the share of fisheries based on property rights in the form of individual transferable quotas and measures to foster industry commitment to responsible fishing – are also working towards reducing over-capacity and improving efficiency, which will serve to make activity in this sector both ecologically sustainable and economically viable. However, some labour-market policies, which tend to impede mobility, have been less helpful in achieving these objectives. While the Atlantic groundfish experience has not been typical of the industry as a whole, initiatives that could further improve efficiency and sustainability throughout the fisheries include: increasing the share of individual transferable quotas, reducing discretion in setting allowable catch levels, applying user charges that more closely reflect the costs of managing specific fisheries, further de-linking regional investment support from the fishing industry, and redesigning support to workers in the fishing and fish-processing industries so as to encourage them to search for other employment possibilities. The key challenge for policy makers is to make social and resource management policies compatible with considerations of economic efficiency in order to achieve both conservation and societal goals.

Further progress could be made in addressing pollution problems

Policies and regulatory mechanisms aimed at curbing air, soil and water pollution have been successful in some areas, notably the Great Lakes. However, there is scope for improvement. The polluter-pays principle is not systematically applied, and reliance on voluntary agreements has not been sufficient to achieve environmental objectives (for instance, in the case of the management of toxic substances). No-cost opportunities for curbing pollution are rare, and, a strategy based on voluntary agreements alone cannot be expected to correct completely for the external costs of pollution. Hence there is a need to increase the use of economic instruments (for instance, charges on toxic emissions and waste, and disposal fees for products containing toxic substances) to reinforce the polluter-pays principle.

More action needs to be taken to deal with climate-change issues

The government has been a leading proponent of international action on climate change. However, while an extensive consultation process has been launched, much more concrete action is needed. Meanwhile, greenhouse gas (GHG) emissions are rising steadily and are currently about 13 per cent higher than in 1990. With a government plan forthcoming only later in the year, it will be very difficult to meet the Kyoto Protocol targets agreed in 1997, which commit Canada to reducing emissions to 6 per cent below the 1990 level in the period 2008-12. Even if Canada is able to buy GHG emission quotas on an international market, it will probably have to take steps to accelerate the reduction in domestic fossil-fuel consumption per unit of GDP. In this case, rather than resort to command-and-control-type regulations, it would be advisable to rely primarily on a cost-effective instrument, such as a tradeable permit scheme, and not to exclude specific sectors (such as transport and energy) from its application. Increased taxes on fuel might be helpful to reduce emissions related to transport. In any case, measures will need to be implemented well before the target period in order to allow for a gradual adjustment in the energy-using capital stock.

The economy has turned the corner, but challenges remain for the new millennium

After a difficult and lengthy adjustment period, the Canadian economy ended the decade on a strong note, as policy measures implemented during the 1990s have established a sound foundation for better economic performance. The inflation-targeting framework adopted in 1991 has created a low-inflation environment. Improved budgetary positions of governments have put the high public-debt-to-GDP ratio on a clear downward path. Structural reforms in key areas a decade or more ago, which were complemented by important changes to the unemployment insurance system in 1996, have also enhanced conditions for growth. These policy efforts have begun to pay off, as manifest in the current healthy pace of economic expansion and the decline in the unemployment rate to historically low levels. The challenge for policymakers now is to ensure that these favourable developments are sustained. With the economy possibly operating above its estimated potential, a further tightening in monetary conditions from mid-year levels would seem to be warranted to avoid the emergence of excess demand and ensuing inflation pressures if the economy's strong momentum persists. As to fiscal policy, priority should be given to continued debt reduction while creating room for desirable changes to the tax system, by maintaining tight control over spending. In this framework, extreme care is needed to avoid new initiatives with long-term spending implications in response to short-term revenue windfalls. At the same time, there is scope for advancing the structural policy agenda to enhance economic efficiency and thus provide the wherewithal for an improvement in the standard of living in both absolute terms and relative to trading partners. Finally, greater use of economic incentives and instruments would help avoid environmental degradation and resource depletion to the detriment of current and future generations, thus enhancing environmentally sustainable growth over the longer run.

I. Macroeconomic performance

The Canadian economy is now well into its ninth consecutive year of growth, and activity has been buoyant in recent quarters. Not only is the current expansion already longer than the previous one, but also inflation and balance-of-payments pressures are absent so far, unlike the situation towards the end of the upturn in the 1980s. In part this reflects the fact that excess supply persisted over an unusually long period during the present cycle, as growth in the first half of the 1990s was restrained by the need to unwind macroeconomic imbalances (in particular unsustainable fiscal deficits) and by economic restructuring (in response to market opening). But with improved fundamentals (continued low inflation and the elimination of budget deficits), trend growth has picked up in recent years (Figure 1). While turbulence in world financial markets, together with lingering concerns about the fiscal situation in Canada had led to a marked deceleration in growth in the mid-1990s, the impact of the subsequent Asian and Russian crises was muted, with the economy rebounding relatively quickly from these external shocks.

As trend growth accelerated, per capita GDP, which had stagnated in the first half of the 1990s, picked up too. Nonetheless, relative to an OECD benchmark, it has made little progress, and the per-capita income gap against the United States has widened further in recent years (Figure 1). Moreover, the rebound in GDP per capita reflects to a large extent a rise in the employment/population ratio, which has returned to levels prevailing in the second half of the 1980s. While productivity has posted a cyclical recovery, it is too early to tell whether earlier structural reforms and technological advances have already manifested themselves in terms of stronger trend productivity growth (see Chapter III). The remainder of this chapter reviews, against the backdrop of the major forces shaping economic activity, recent and prospective economic developments in Canada in more detail.

Forces shaping economic activity

As noted, the 1997-1998 financial crisis in emerging markets had a relatively limited effect on economic activity in Canada. The most significant

Figure 1. **Growth performance over the long term**

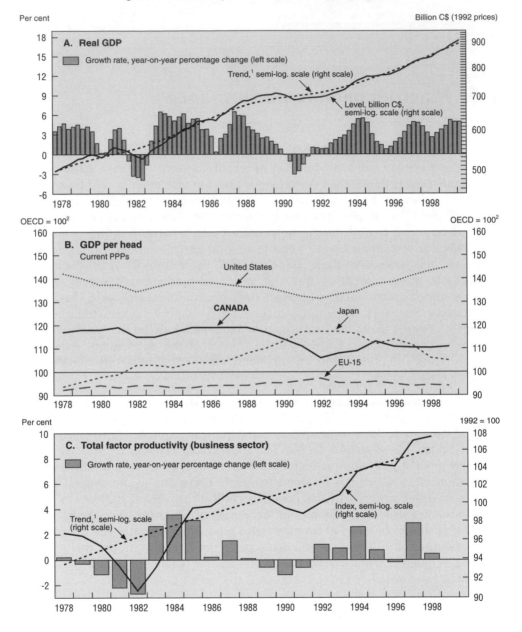

1. Hodrick-Prescott filter, $\lambda = 1\ 600$.
2. Excluding Korea, Czech Republic, Hungary and Poland.
Source: Statistics Canada; OECD, *National Accounts.*

channel through which it dampened growth was the associated sharp fall in world commodity prices. As Canada is a net exporter of commodities, this entailed a substantial deterioration in its terms of trade, which, in turn, depressed profits, undermined business and consumer confidence and adversely affected domestic demand. Export volume growth, however, held up quite well, given the continued expansion in the United States, Canada's major trading partner. Indeed, Canada's export market growth slowed only moderately (Figure 2). In addition, the depreci-ation of the Canadian dollar in response to the decline in commodity prices acted as a shock absorber, facilitating a shift in activity from the primary sector to manu-facturing and other export sectors and providing an additional incentive for these sectors to take advantage of the strong US economy. With the downward move-ment in the exchange rate, overall monetary conditions eased significantly, despite a temporary rise in interest rates in the context of the global financial-market turmoil. At the same time, fiscal contraction, which had exerted a consider-able drag on growth in previous years, diminished markedly.

With the subsequent recovery in commodity prices and a strengthening international economy, activity in Canada regained some momentum in late 1998. By the end of 1999, Canada's terms of trade had recovered their pre-Asian-crisis level, and profit margins bounced back sharply to levels not seen in two decades. This, together with an improving labour-market situation, restored business and consumer confidence (Figure 2). Reflecting continued strong US growth, a rapid recovery in parts of Asia and, of late, accelerating economic activity in Europe, the expansion of Canada's export markets has again reached its previous vigorous pace. Partly offsetting these favourable influences have been more restrictive macroeconomic policies (see Chapter II). Fiscal restraint was more pronounced in 1999 than in the prior year. Monetary conditions have gradually tightened since the beginning of 1999, at first through some strength-ening in the exchange rate in response to rising commodity prices, and more recently as a result of interest-rate increases. In the period ahead, this should, together with slowing export market growth, dampen the expansion of private demand, which has so far remained robust. On the other hand, fiscal policy is no longer acting as a drag on activity.

Strong economic expansion

After slowing to 3¼ per cent in 1998, real GDP growth again reached 4½ per cent in 1999 as a whole, with even stronger gains in recent quarters (Table 1). While the export-intensive manufacturing sector was leading the way, the acceleration in output growth over the past year has been widespread among other industries as well. Although the mining sector still recorded a decline in production in 1999 as a whole, its output increased at double-digit rates through the second half of the year. Broadly based, robust economic growth continued in the first quarter of 2000.

Figure 2.   **Conditions for growth**

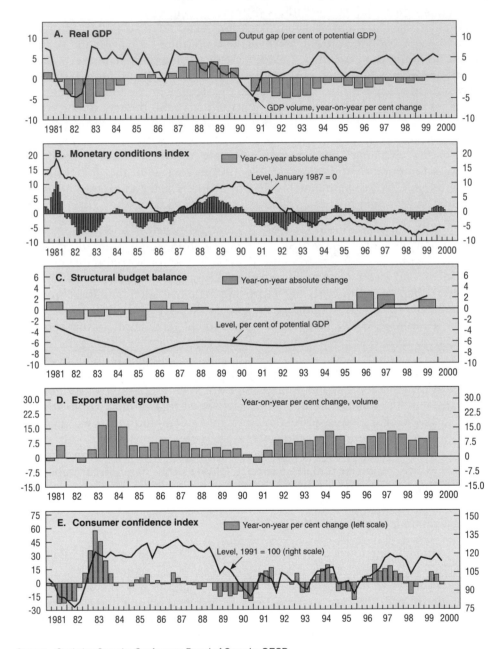

© OECD 2000

Table 1.   **Demand and output**

Percentage change over previous period, seasonally adjusted annual rates, volume (1992 prices)

	1979/ 1973	1989/ 1979	1999/ 1989	1997	1998	1999	Q4 1999	Q1 2000
Private consumption	4.0	2.9	2.2	4.4	2.9	3.5	3.7	3.4
Government consumption	3.7	2.5	0.6	-1.2	1.6	1.3	1.6	0.1
Gross fixed investment	5.0	5.3	2.7	15.4	3.4	10.1	18.7	11.0
Public	0.2	4.9	2.6	-2.4	1.4	15.9	22.4	12.4
Private	5.9	5.4	2.7	18.2	3.7	9.4	18.2	10.8
Residential	3.4	4.0	-1.0	12.6	-2.0	6.6	12.1	9.8
Non-residential	8.2	6.4	4.7	20.7	6.1	10.5	20.5	11.2
Final domestic demand	**4.1**	**3.3**	**2.0**	**5.2**	**2.8**	**4.4**	**6.3**	**4.4**
Stockbuilding[1]	0.1	-0.1	0.0	1.0	-0.5	-0.2	2.0	-1.1
Total domestic demand	**4.2**	**3.2**	**2.0**	**6.2**	**2.2**	**4.2**	**8.5**	**3.1**
Exports of goods and services	3.8	5.3	8.1	8.8	8.9	10.0	10.7	13.9
Imports of goods and services	5.2	6.8	6.9	15.1	6.1	9.4	22.1	7.9
Foreign balance[1]	**-0.1**	**-0.3**	**0.4**	**-1.8**	**1.1**	**0.4**	**-3.6**	**2.5**
Error of estimate[1]	0.0	0.1	-0.1	0.1	0.0	0.0	0.6	-0.7
GDP at market prices	**3.9**	**2.9**	**2.3**	**4.4**	**3.3**	**4.5**	**5.1**	**4.9**
Agriculture	-0.6	2.2	1.6	0.3	2.4	6.4	-0.2	-4.8
Mining	-3.3	1.1	2.2	4.5	-0.3	-2.4	12.7	9.4
Manufacturing	2.6	2.2	2.5	6.8	3.9	6.2	4.0	4.0
Construction	4.5	2.7	-0.4	9.0	0.1	3.7	11.7	9.9
Services	4.4	3.1	2.3	3.2	3.1	3.9	4.0	3.9
GDP at factor costs	**3.5**	**2.8**	**2.1**	**4.1**	**2.9**	**4.1**	**4.6**	**4.2**
Memorandum item:								
GDP per capita	2.7	1.7	1.1	3.3	2.4	3.7	..	..

1.   Contribution to GDP volume growth.
Source: Statistics Canada.

With renewed strengthening in external demand...

On the demand side, exports have remained the mainstay of economic growth. In volume terms, their rate of expansion reached 10 per cent in 1999 as whole (Table 1) and has remained strong in early 2000 (see below). With a favourable competitive position, owing both to exchange rate depreciation in 1998 and continued moderate domestic inflation, the acceleration in export growth has broadly matched market developments. Indeed, according to OECD estimates, the expansion of Canada's export markets for goods and services slightly exceeded the 10 per cent mark in 1999, with stronger demand from the United States and the Asia-Pacific region contributing equally to the pick-up in market growth.

Part of the GDP growth in 1999 as a whole can be mechanically attributed to a rise in net exports (Table 1). This is in stark contrast to the previous upturn in 1997, when the real foreign balance deteriorated markedly in the face of strengthening domestic demand, exerting a drag on economic growth. Two factors may help to explain this. While the components of aggregate demand with a large import content (such as consumption of durable goods and investment in machinery and equipment and in inventories) rebounded, they regained their previous (that is, pre-Asian crisis) momentum only by around mid-1999. In addition, improved international competitiveness following exchange-rate depreciation may have reduced the import propensity, encouraging the substitution of domestic for imported goods. Although imports surged in late-1999 in response to booming fixed and inventory investment, they have slowed again since then. As a result, the ensuing negative growth contribution of the real foreign balance has remained limited (Figure 3).

... and a sharp rebound in domestic demand...

Given the associated interest-rate hikes and confidence effects, domestic demand suffered more from the 1997-1998 financial crisis than did aggregate real exports and GDP (Table 1). The slowdown in domestic spending was widespread but particularly pronounced for residential investment and inventory accumulation,[1] whose contributions to GDP growth turned negative. Partly offsetting the weakening in private expenditure was renewed real growth in public spending on goods and services. The subsequent rebound in domestic demand, which commenced in late 1998, has been broadly based, with interest-sensitive components leading the way.

Compared with other major demand components, the growth in *private consumption* has been relatively stable in recent years. Nevertheless, spending on durable goods has been more volatile, reflecting fluctuations in borrowing costs[2] and consumer sentiment, but generally much stronger than earlier in the decade (Figure 4). The recent strength of private consumption is largely due to the resurgence of personal income growth. Real personal income per capita had fallen from 1990 to 1994. Despite a significant drop in the savings ratio, this restrained spending, especially on durable goods, and created substantial pent-up demand. Since then, most of the previous decline in disposable income has been made up. In addition, improved labour-market conditions have enhanced expectations of continued healthy employment growth and willingness to make major purchases. At the same time, the growth in personal-sector debt associated with the rise in spending on durable goods has been outpaced by gains in assets in a variety of forms (including housing, equities and bonds). As a result, real personal-sector net worth has increased. This indicates that, although the personal sector appears to be saving relatively little out of the measured current flow of income, its rate of overall savings – that is, including capital gains and durable assets growth – has remained strong.

Figure 3.   **Contributions to changes in real GDP**
Per cent changes over 4 quarters

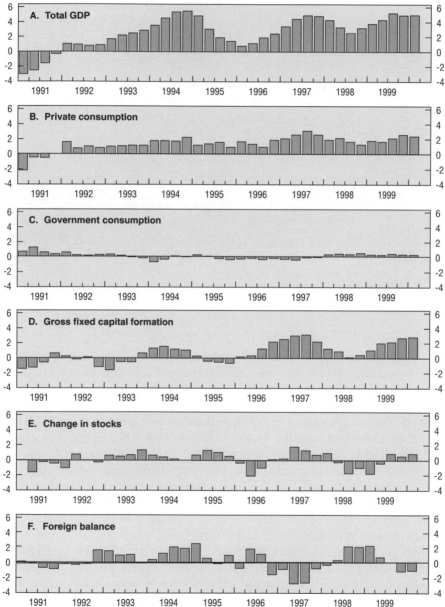

Source: Statistics Canada; OECD, *National Accounts.*

Figure 4. **Household demand**
Year-on-year volume percentage change

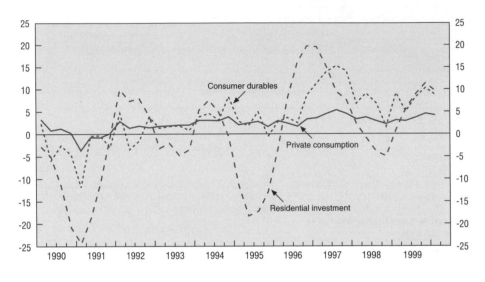

Source: Statistics Canada.

After declining in 1998, *residential investment* has bounced back strongly (Figure 4), reaching levels not seen in a decade. There has also been a strong revival in the resale market, where turnover reached record highs in 1999. Some of the growth in housing demand reflects a rebound in activity held back in 1998 by temporary factors such as the ice storm in the east and construction strikes as well as uncertainty resulting from the Asian crisis. But most of the recent strength in the housing market is due to the same factors that have underpinned current consumption, such as increasing real personal disposable income per capita, falling unemployment rates and rising consumer confidence. Increasing debt ratios may suggest that current levels of residential investment are not sustainable. Indeed, the ratio of mortgage debt to housing wealth has risen markedly. However, despite the higher level of mortgage debt, historically low interest rates mean that mortgage servicing costs (relative to disposable income) are lower than at the beginning of the 1990s, boding well for households' ability to service mortgage debt (even though the impact of unforeseen rate increases could be severe). In any case, estimates of demographic requirements indicate that, following the depressed level of housing starts over most of the 1990s, there is some pent-up demand, and thus room for further growth in residential investment.

Robust *business fixed investment* growth in recent years has pushed its share of GDP (in constant-price terms) to the highest levels in more than four decades (Figure 5). With non-residential construction expanding broadly in line with GDP, this largely reflects buoyant spending on machinery and equipment. Within the latter, expenditure on computers and office equipment has been the driving force, approaching one-third of total machinery and equipment investment. Computer purchases increased by almost 20 per cent in 1998, thereby partly compensating for the weakening in other investment components, and surged by over 40 per cent in 1999. The need to replace computer equipment in response to predicted Y2K problems possibly contributed, although available indicators point to further strong investment in early 2000. Business construction, which was strongly affected by the effects of the Asian crisis and collapsing world commodity prices, has revived as engineering projects have been taken up again. The oil and gas industry, in particular, which had sharply reduced capital spending, is again stepping up exploration and development activity. Partly due to the rebound in world commodity prices, corporate profits have risen to record levels relative to GDP, providing businesses with strong cash flows to finance new investment. Nonetheless, survey indicators provide mixed signals about investment conditions. On the one hand, business confidence has increased significantly, and a record share of firms expect that their financial positions will improve further, making it possible to take advantage of investment opportunities. On the other, intentions surveys indicate a marked slowdown in future investment activity. However, it is likely that recent economic developments turned out stronger than expected by most survey respondents and that investment intentions will be revised upwards.

Inventory investment, which had contributed to the slowdown in 1998, has again become supportive of economic growth over the past year. Nonetheless, with surging final demand, the inventory-to-sales ratio (in volume terms) has declined sharply, more than reversing its temporary rise in 1998 (Figure 6). However, although the ratio has dropped to its lowest recorded level, its downward trend has slowed noticeably. This is somewhat surprising, as one explanation of the trend decline in the ratio since the 1980s has been the increasing adoption of computer technology, which allows for efficiency gains in inventory management. A factor that might help explain recent inventory developments is the pronounced change in economic conditions over the 1990s. Prolonged demand weakness during the first half of the decade may have provided strong incentives for firms to improve the efficiency of their inventory use to improve cash flow. With strengthening demand, the inventory-to-sales ratio appears to have tended to stabilise at the new lower level, in spite of the spreading availability of computer equipment and office machinery in recent years. Other factors that could have dampened the decline in the ratio are lower inflation and real interest rates as well as the changing composition of demand and output associated with the strengthening economic upturn.

Figure 5.   **Business fixed investment**

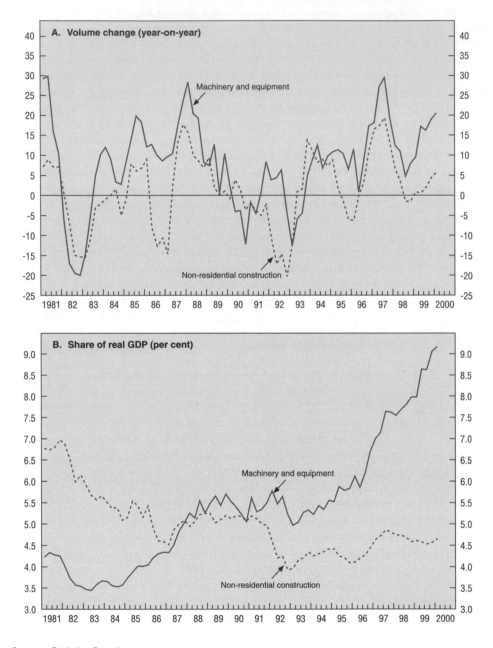

Source: Statistics Canada.

Figure 6. **Inventory-to-sales ratio**
Seasonally adjusted

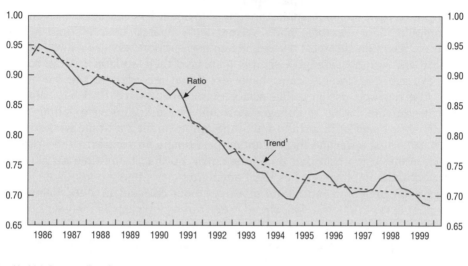

1. Hodrick-Prescott filter, λ = 1 600.
Source: Statistics Canada.

... excess supply has been eliminated for the first time in a decade

As noted, the current business cycle has seen an unusually long period of economic slack. According to OECD estimates, an output gap emerged in the second half of 1990 and seems to have persisted until the first half of 1999 (Figure 2, Panel A). Excess supply would have been even more substantial had the expansion of estimated productive potential not slowed during the first half of the 1990s. Since then, primarily reflecting increased growth of capital and labour inputs (see below), potential output growth appears to have edged up again, exceeding 3 per cent per annum more recently, about the rate prevailing in the 1980s. This prolonged the period during which output could grow without hitting capacity limits. But with the recent spurt in growth, the economy seems to have finally moved into a position of slight excess demand, although estimates of productive potential and the output gap are subject to large margins of error. Other measures of capacity utilisation point in the same direction. Inearly 2000, according to Statistics Canada, the rate of capacity use in non-farm goods-producing industries exceeded the previous peak reached during the late 1980s, attaining a level not seen since the mid-1960s. However, changes in the estimation methodology could mean that this measure over-states the true level of capacity utilisation in the 1990s relative to earlier periods.

Improving labour market conditions

Employment has grown at a healthy pace over the past three years, with its 12-month increases reaching 3 per cent in the first quarter of 2000 (Table 2). Reflecting output developments, manufacturing employment has surged, led by hiring in the computer and electronic parts sector. Partly related to the boom in these industries, scientific, technical and administrative support services as well as transportation and warehousing have sharply increased their workforce. More recently, above-average employment gains have also been recorded in the construction sector. The renewed rise in public-sector employment since 1998 has continued, with considerable hiring at colleges and universities. Improving labour-market conditions are manifest in a shift to full-time employment. Part-time work dropped in 1999, reflecting a decline in involuntary part-timers, in contrast to the previous year, when the increase in part-time jobs outpaced that in full-time employment. Moreover, while employment has risen among all major age groups, older people (55 and over) benefited most from growing labour demand in 1999, followed by young people (15 to 24), who had already seen strong job gains in the year before.

Table 2. **Labour supply and demand**

Per cent change, annual rates

	1979/ 1973[1]	1989/ 1979	1999/ 1989	1997	1998	1999	Q1 2000/ Q1 1999
Working age population	2.2	1.4	1.4	1.4	1.3	1.3	1.3
Labour force	3.2	2.0	1.1	1.7	1.8	2.0	1.8
Employment	2.9	2.0	1.1	2.3	2.6	2.8	3.0
Goods producing sector	1.6	0.6	−0.1	2.8	3.0	2.6	3.8
Service sector	3.6	2.6	1.6	2.1	2.5	2.9	2.7
Public sector	2.8	2.3	0.7	−1.2	1.0	2.4	2.9
Unemployment rate[2]	7.2	9.4	9.5	9.1	8.3	7.6	6.8
Youth (15-24)	..	14.7	15.3	16.2	15.2	14.0	12.8
Older workers (55+)	..	6.2	7.3	7.0	6.3	5.5	4.9
Participation rate[3]	61.7	65.5	65.5	64.9	65.1	65.6	65.8
Youth (15-24)	..	68.9	64.5	61.4	61.8	63.6	64.0
Older workers (55+)	..	28.3	24.7	24.2	24.5	25.1	25.7
Employment ratio[3]	57.3	59.4	59.3	59.0	59.7	60.6	61.4
Memorandum items:							
Labour productivity[4]	1.3	0.9	1.2	2.0	0.6	1.7	1.8
Total factor productivity[5]	0.6	0.4	0.7[6]	2.9	0.5	..	..

1. Not strictly comparable to other columns.
2. Per cent of labour force.
3. Per cent of population 15 years and over.
4. Total economy. Per employed person.
5. Business sector.
6. 1998/1989.
Source: Statistics Canada.

Labour productivity gains have increased somewhat, after slowing in 1998 when the economic expansion weakened while employment continued to rise at a solid pace (Table 2). Using hours, instead of numbers employed, affects the productivity growth pattern only marginally. With performance in recent years close to the long-term average, abstracting from cyclical influences, there is little evidence of a pick-up in the productivity trend, although compositional factors (such the re-entry of young people into the workforce and renewed job creation in the public sector) may have curbed aggregate productivity growth.

Improved job opportunities have led to a renewed gradual rise in the labour-force participation rate as discouraged workers returned to the labour market (Table 2). While this phenomenon has been widespread among age groups, it has been most pronounced for young people, whose participation rate had shown the steepest fall in the first half of the 1990s. Yet, at the aggregate level, the labour-force participation rate is still more than 1½ percentage points below its peak level in the late 1980s. It is difficult to ascertain to what extent this decline reflects structural factors. For example, the changing composition of the population, and in particular the rising share of people over 65 (included in the denominator), is estimated to have reduced the aggregate participation rate by nearly 1 percentage point over the 1990s. In addition, labour-market reforms should have lowered participation somewhat (by tightening eligibility for Employment Insurance benefits). However, rising school enrolment rates, which have reduced youth participation, probably have both structural and cyclical components; the latter should diminish with greater job availability. Thus, while the labour-force participation rate would seem to be approaching its trend level, estimates of the latter are subject to considerable uncertainty.

With labour-force participation rising only gradually, strong net job creation has translated into a rapid decline in unemployment over the past three years (Table 2). By the first quarter of 2000, the unemployment rate had fallen to below 7 per cent, and it has since declined further, to just over 6½ per cent, its lowest level since the mid-1970s. At around 12½ per cent, the youth unemployment rate is close to that recorded at that time, following its pronounced decline in the recent period. According to OECD estimates, aggregate unemployment is now running somewhat below its structural rate, although the latter has also been on a downward trend in recent years. However, given the margin of error around such estimates and the difficulties in gauging the impact of the 1996 Employment Insurance reforms, it cannot be excluded that the structural rate is lower than the OECD estimates and close to, or even below, the actual unemployment rate. Indeed, while there have been some reports of labour shortages, there are few signs of significant inflationary pressures stemming from the labour market, with wage growth remaining moderate relative to productivity gains and inflation.

Moderate wage and price inflation

Compensation per employee (which takes account of non-wage labour costs) increased by 2 per cent in 1999, unchanged from the year before, despite some acceleration in recent quarters (Table 3). Measures of *effective earnings* (based on payroll data) show a similar picture but are very volatile because of repeated changes to the way the data are compiled (Figure 7). A new measure (excluding benefits and premia) from the Labour Force Survey, which is less erratic but only available since 1997, indicates that *hourly wages* increased by 2½ per cent in 1999, up from 1½ per cent the year before, with their year-over-year rise reaching 3 per cent in the first quarter of 2000. This is broadly in line with information from *wage settlement data*, which used to be a good indicator of underlying wage inflation. However, the recent upward trend in private-sector wage settlements has been exaggerated by high settlements involving the Big Three automobile companies in September and October 1999. Past experience suggests that the risks of wage emulation by other sectors following these agreements are low. Moreover, the upward trend in wage increases has been accompanied by a pick-up in productivity gains. As a result, the year-over-year rate of growth of unit labour costs, while rising gradually, reached only 1½ per cent in the first quarter of 2000.

Table 3. **Wages, prices and profits**

Per cent change, annual rates

	1979/ 1973	1989/ 1979	1999/ 1989	1997	1998	1999	Q4 1999/ Q4 1998	Q1 2000/ Q1 1999
Wages								
Compensation per employee	10.2	6.8	2.9	4.5	2.1	2.0	2.3	3.4
Wage rate (business sector)	9.3	7.0	2.9	6.8	4.0	3.0	2.8	4.7
Hourly earnings in manufacturing	11.6	6.1	2.5	0.9	2.1	0.1	0.8	3.2
Major collective settlements	..	6.4	2.0	1.5	1.7	2.3	2.9	2.3
Unit labour costs								
Total economy	9.6	5.7	1.3	1.3	1.4	0.5	0.8	1.6
Manufacturing	9.3	4.8	0.5	−1.2	3.0	0.1	1.0	2.7
Profits								
Pre-tax	14.0	5.3	5.6	9.3	−5.6	23.7	36.5	34.8
After-tax	14.2	4.1	5.0	6.9	−10.6	25.0	42.3	41.3
Pre-tax per unit of output	9.7	2.4	3.2	4.8	−8.6	18.2	30.1	28.4
Prices								
GDP deflator (current weights)	9.5	5.8	1.6	1.0	−0.6	1.6	3.1	3.3
GDP deflator (fixed weights)	10.3	6.0	1.8	1.1	0.0	1.8	3.0	3.3
Consumer price index	9.2	6.5	2.2	1.6	1.0	1.7	2.4	2.7
Private consumption deflator	9.1	6.2	2.0	1.8	1.0	1.3	1.3	1.4
Export price deflator	12.4	3.0	1.2	−0.8	−1.1	0.9	1.2	4.0
Import price deflator	11.6	1.7	1.6	0.2	2.5	−2.1	−5.4	−3.1
New housing price index	..	..	−0.5	0.8	0.9	0.9	1.5	1.9

Source: Statistics Canada.

Figure 7.   **Wage indicators**
Per cent

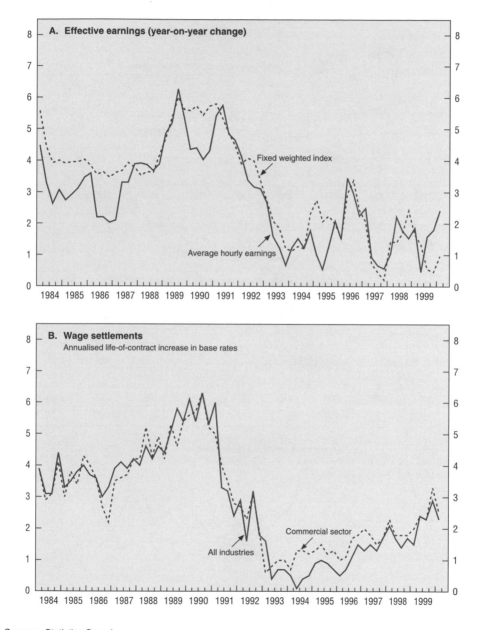

Source: Statistics Canada.

Figure 8. **Inflation indicators**
Percentage change over 12 months

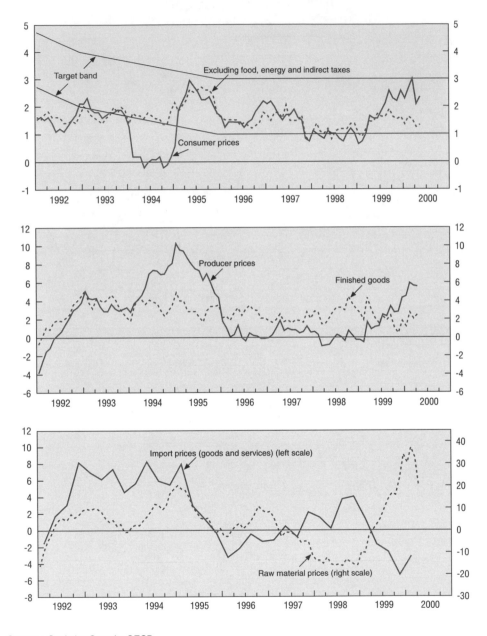

Source: Statistics Canada; OECD.

With little upward pressure from the wage side, underlying inflation has remained moderate, although rising profit margins have added somewhat to price increases. While the annual rise in the overall CPI ("headline" inflation) temporary climbed to 3 per cent, largely due to the surge in crude-oil and other energy prices, "core" inflation (excluding food, energy and the effect of indirect taxes) has remained relatively stable, averaging 1½ per cent following some pick-up in the first half of 1999 (Figure 8). The effect of higher energy prices on core inflation (for instance in the form of increased transportation costs) appears to have been limited so far (about 0.1 percentage point year on year as of March). Some rise in inflation expectations, toward the mid-point of the 1 to 3 per cent official target band, may have contributed to raising underlying inflation. The depreciation of the Canadian dollar in 1998 also translated into price increases in some consumption categories in 1999 (like household furnishings and clothing). However, the exchange-rate pass-through effect on core inflation seems to have been more modest than would have been expected on the basis of historical relationships. This might reflect the fact that some of the 1998 depreciation has been since reversed. Indeed, imported inflation has turned negative overall, as the strengthening in the Canadian dollar since the beginning of 1999 has implied a decline in import prices for manufactures, more than offsetting the impact of sharply higher raw material prices. Increased prices for commodities have, however, led to a rise in the average price of Canadian exports, where the share of non-manufactures is larger than on the import side. This has entailed a recovery in the GDP deflator following its fall in 1998, when Canada's terms of trade had deteriorated.

Broad external balance

After deteriorating somewhat during 1997-1998, the current account has moved back towards surplus (Figure 9). The major factor behind these swings is the fluctuation in Canada's terms of trade, which, in turn, reflects commodity price developments. Following their recovery from early 1999, the terms of trade have returned to around the level prevailing before the Asian crisis. Canada's relative cyclical position, which had exerted a dampening influence on the external deficit in 1998, has changed little since, as demand has expanded broadly in line with that in major trading partner countries. Canada's competitive position has remained favourable. Although relative unit labour costs on a common currency basis have risen somewhat as a result of the renewed strengthening of the Canadian dollar, they remain close to historic lows.

Canada's current account is characterised by a surplus in merchandise trade and a large deficit in investment income flows, reflecting sizeable external deficits in the past. As changes in the invisibles balance have tended to be limited, swings in the current account have mirrored fluctuations in the trade surplus. In 1999, merchandise exports and imports grew at virtually the same pace

Figure 9. **The current balance and its major components**

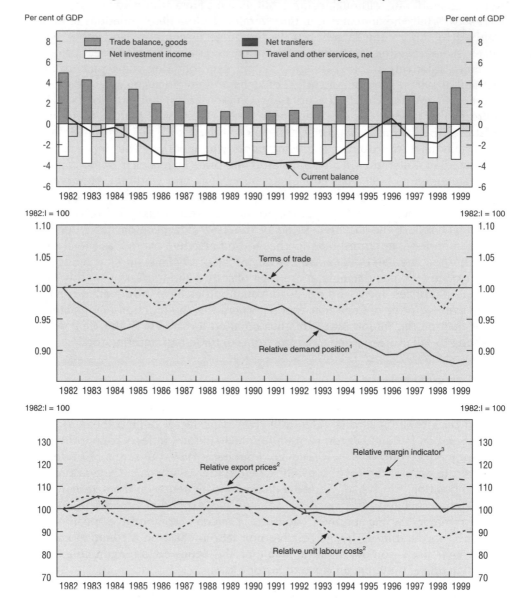

1. Index of Canadian final domestic demand divided by an export share weighted index of final domestic demand of major trading partners.
2. In manufacturing. Common currency.
3. Ratio of relative export prices to relative unit labour costs.
Source: Statistics Canada; OECD.

in volume terms. Buoyant US demand boosted exports, while stronger growth in Canada pushed up imports. The marked improvement in the nominal merchandise trade balance in that period thus stems from the rebound in the terms of trade. As noted, resurgent commodity prices led to a rise in export prices, while declining prices for imported machinery and equipment helped to hold down import prices. Growth in the automotive products sector accounted for almost half of the total export increase in 1999, reflecting higher production capacity in Canada and record sales in the United States. As a result, the share of automotive products in total exports rose to a record level of nearly 27 per cent, exceeding that of primary products, while the share of exports going to the United States reached a record 86 per cent of the total. In early 2000, the merchandise trade surplus has widened markedly again, following a temporary decline in the fourth quarter of 1999, as net exports picked up, leading to a substantial surplus in the current account (Table 4).

The increase in the trade surplus in 1999 was offset to some extent by a rise in the invisibles deficit. After improving noticeably in 1998, when US travellers took advantage of the low exchange rate, the services deficit narrowed only a little. At the same time, the investment income balance, which had been relatively stable in the years before, deteriorated significantly, as profits earned by foreign firms in Canada increased markedly. This trend was interrupted, however, in the first quarter of 2000, contributing together with higher profits of Canadian companies abroad to a substantial fall in the investment income deficit (Table 4). Last year, for the first time since 1992, foreign direct investment in Canada exceeded Canadian direct investment abroad. While the latter declined from the record set in 1998, foreign (mainly American) direct investment surged as a result of several high profile acquisitions of existing Canadian companies. On the other hand, foreign portfolio investment in Canada dropped significantly, to a 25-year low, against the backdrop of lower government borrowing requirements and lower interest rates than abroad. Finally, Canada augmented its official international reserves considerably, with the increase in 1999 second only to that recorded in 1988.

A favourable short-term outlook

Following continued strong economic expansion in the early part of 2000, the pace of activity is projected to ease, with real GDP growth still averaging 4½ per cent in 2000 but then decreasing to 3 per cent in 2001 as a whole (Table 5). This reflects both external and domestic influences. While Canada has so far benefited from its strong trade links with the United States, the projected slowdown in the US economy implies a significant decrease in Canadian export market growth. Nonetheless, exports should continue to expand at a relatively healthy pace, given Canada's favourable competitive position. At the same time, past and

Table 4. **Balance of payments**
C$ billion, annualised

	1996	1997	1998	1999	Q4 1999	Q1 2000
	Seasonally adjusted					
Goods exports	280.1	301.5	322.5	360.6	377.9	396.5
Goods imports	237.7	277.8	303.4	326.8	342.9	348.4
Trade balance	42.4	23.8	19.1	33.8	34.9	48.2
Travel and other services, net	−9.1	−9.4	−7.0	−6.1	−5.7	−5.0
Investment income, net	−29.4	−29.1	−29.2	−32.2	−31.5	−26.4
Transfers, net	`0.7	0.8	0.8	1.0	0.9	2.7
Current balance	4.6	−13.9	−16.3	−3.4	−1.3	19.4
	Not seasonally adjusted					
Current balance	4.6	−13.9	−16.3	−3.4	1.1	3.4
Capital account	8.0	7.5	4.9	5.1	4.6	4.4
Canadian assets (net flows)	−73.3	−61.9	−61.2	−45.3	−91.0	−109.1
of which: Official international reserves	−7.5	3.4	−7.5	−8.8	−17.1	−16.0
Canadian liabilities (net flows)	53.1	70.8	67.5	33.9	76.0	79.3
Financial account[1]	−20.2	8.9	6.3	−11.4	−15.0	−29.9
Statistical discrepancy	7.6	−2.5	5.0	9.7	9.3	22.0
	Seasonally adjusted					
Memorandum items:						
Current balance						
US dollars	3.4	−10.0	−11.0	−2.3	−0.9	13.3
Per cent of GDP	0.6	−1.6	−1.8	−0.4	−0.1	1.9
Net external liabilities						
Canadian dollars	318.2	314.0	326.3	300.3	. .	. .
Per cent of GDP	38.2	35.8	36.2	31.4	. .	. .

1. A minus sign denotes an outflow of capital resulting from an increase in claims on non-residents or a decrease in liabilities to non-residents.
Source: Statistics Canada.

prospective monetary tightening (in line with the United States) is expected to dampen the growth in domestic demand, and in particular its interest-sensitive components such as spending on consumer durables and housing. Business fixed investment is also likely to moderate, owing to slower consumption and export growth. However, the deceleration in domestic spending is expected to be gradual, given remaining pent-up demand (in particular for housing) and high consumer confidence associated with improved labour-market conditions. Moreover, fiscal relaxation should bolster domestic demand, although households may prefer to take advantage of tax cuts to strengthen their balance sheets, especially in the case of a stock market correction.

Table 5.   Short-term projections

Percentage change over previous period, seasonally-adjusted annual rates, volume (1992 prices)

	1996 C$ billion[1]	2000	2001	2000 I	2000 II	2001 I	2001 II
Private consumption	482.4	3.6	2.8	3.5	3.1	2.8	2.5
Government consumption	171.6	1.9	1.7	2.0	2.0	1.6	1.5
Gross fixed investment	143.7	9.2	5.4	8.9	6.5	5.2	4.6
Public[2]	19.2	9.5	4.2	7.5	5.5	4.0	3.5
Private residential	39.5	7.8	5.0	8.6	5.8	4.9	4.5
Private non-residential	85.0	9.7	5.7	9.3	7.0	5.6	4.9
Final domestic demand	**797.7**	**4.5**	**3.2**	**4.4**	**3.6**	**3.1**	**2.8**
Stockbuilding[3]	2.3	0.3	0.0	0.0	0.0	0.0	0.0
Total domestic demand	**800.0**	**4.7**	**3.1**	**4.3**	**3.6**	**3.1**	**2.8**
Exports of goods and services	321.2	8.7	6.4	9.3	7.2	6.3	6.0
Imports of goods and services	287.6	9.5	6.9	8.9	7.6	6.9	6.3
Foreign balance[3]	**33.7**	**–0.1**	**0.0**	**0.4**	**–0.0**	**–0.1**	**–0.0**
Error of estimate[3]	–0.6	0.0	0.0	0.0	0.0	0.0	0.0
GDP at market prices	**833.1**	**4.5**	**3.0**	**4.6**	**3.5**	**2.9**	**2.7**
Industrial production		**5.7**	**3.6**	**5.6**	**4.0**	**3.5**	**3.4**
Unemployment rate[4]		**6.6**	**6.5**	**6.7**	**6.5**	**6.5**	**6.5**
Inflation and wages							
GDP implicit price deflator		2.9	2.3	3.0	2.4	2.3	2.1
Private consumption deflator		2.2	2.1	2.4	2.2	2.1	2.1
Private compensation per employee		3.0	3.4	2.9	3.1	3.4	3.5
General government balance (per cent of GDP)		**2.0**	**1.7**	**2.2**	**1.9**	**1.7**	**1.7**
Interest rates[4]							
Short-term		5.9	6.6	5.6	6.3	6.6	6.6
Long-term		6.3	6.5	6.2	6.4	6.5	6.5
Current account balance (per cent of GDP)		**0.9**	**1.1**	**0.8**	**1.0**	**1.1**	**1.1**

Note: The above projections are an updated version of those published in the OECD *Economic Outlook* 67 which take account of data revisions and new information available by the end of June 2000.
1.   Current prices.
2.   Excluding nationalised industries and public corporations.
3.   Contribution to GDP volume growth.
4.   Per cent.
Source: OECD.

Such a "soft landing" scenario would avoid the emergence of major tensions and imbalances in the economy. Wage growth is expected to edge up but to remain relatively moderate, as rising labour-force participation limits declines in unemployment while structural unemployment falls further. With the economy currently operating slightly above estimated capacity, core inflation is projected to rise somewhat but to stay well within the official target band, as economic growth falls a little below its estimated potential rate of just over 3 per cent. Moreover, headline inflation, which has been pushed up by energy price increases, is expected to fall back to the core rate, reducing the risk of rising inflation expectations that might spill over into wage growth. At the same time, despite vanishing terms-of-trade gains, the external balance should show a slight surplus, as import growth slows broadly in line with export growth.

There are some risks to this outlook, however. One is related to the fact that during the projection period the economy would be operating above the OECD's estimates of non-inflationary capacity. While continued low core inflation so far could mean that the sustainable level of output is higher than estimated, it is by no means clear to what extent technological advances and structural reforms have enhanced productivity performance in Canada. As discussed in the next chapter, these uncertainties about the economy's productive potential will put the inflation-targeting framework to the test, the more so since, with easing fiscal policies and high confidence levels, domestic demand may not slow as much as envisaged. The other major risk concerns developments in the United States. Continued rapid US growth would provide further stimulus to net exports and domestic demand in Canada, adding to inflationary pressures. But such an outcome might also trigger a substantial tightening of US monetary policy that could ultimately lead to a "hard landing" of the US economy. Although the probability of such a scenario is currently assessed as being low, it would obviously have serious consequences for the Canadian economy, given the strong trade and financial linkages between the two countries. It could also significantly worsen the medium-term economic outlook.

A medium-term scenario

An OECD central scenario (Table 6) is that, over the 2000-05 period, real GDP growth in Canada could average just over 3 per cent per annum, about the same rate as projected for the OECD area as whole. This would be a considerable improvement in economic performance. Indeed, since the last cyclical peak ten years ago, growth has averaged only 2¼ per cent (Table 1), and even from the trough in 1991 it has measured not more than 3 per cent per annum. Domestic demand is projected to expand broadly in line with GDP, reflecting in part less restrictive fiscal conditions than over the 1990s. Net exports are not expected to contribute to growth on the assumption of a constant real exchange rate. The

Table 6. **A medium-term scenario**

Average annual percentage change, volumes

	1991-1999	1999-2005
Private consumption	2.8	2.8
Government consumption	−0.0	1.6
Fixed capital formation	4.4	5.4
Stockbuilding[1]	0.2	0.1
Total domestic demand	2.6	3.2
Exports	9.3	6.9
Imports	8.0	7.4
Real foreign balance[1]	0.5	−0.1
Real GDP	3.0	3.1
Output gap[2]	−2.3	0.4
Potential output	2.6	3.0
Labour productivity	1.6	1.5
Employment	1.6	1.6
Participation rate (per cent)	65.4	66.5
Unemployment rate (per cent)	9.7	6.6
Private consumption deflator	1.5	2.1
GDP deflator	1.2	2.3
Private compensation per employee	2.8	3.3
Current balance[1]	−2.0	0.7
General government financial balance[1]	−4.3	2.1
Real exchange rate	−3.7	0.2
Short-term interest rate (per cent)	5.6	5.5
Long-term interest rate (per cent)	7.6	6.4

1. Per cent of GDP.
2. Per cent of potential output.
Source: Statistics Canada; OECD.

current account is nevertheless projected to remain in surplus, a substantial improvement from the deficit position in the past. At the same time, inflation is expected to stay easily within the (current) official target range, even if somewhat higher than in the past given the absence of excess supply. On the assumption of declining but ongoing budget surpluses, the government debt-to-GDP ratio is projected to continue to fall rapidly, which should help keep interest rates low.

The above scenario is based on the technical assumption of gradually closing output gaps. As the economy is estimated to be now in a slight excess demand position, this means that during the projection period growth falls below its potential rate, which in turn is expected to decline a little, to under 3 per cent per annum. This would still be significantly higher than the average outcome in the 1990s. It implies somewhat greater gains in productivity reflecting continued robust increases in fixed capital formation, and also somewhat stronger growth in labour supply. However, as noted, it is still not clear to what extent economic efficiency has improved. It also remains to be seen if the recent strength of investment can be maintained. As to labour inputs, the crucial issue is the underlying trend in the participation rate. Population ageing is likely to produce downward pressures on the aggregate participation rate, although this could be partly offset by stronger labour-market attachment of younger cohorts or a rise in the trend participation rate of older workers. These uncertainties underline the importance of carefully setting macroeconomic conditions, as discussed in the following chapter.

II. Macroeconomic policies

The stronger growth performance of the Canadian economy in part reflects the authorities' commitment to sound monetary and fiscal policies, which have brought about a marked improvement in economic fundamentals. This has been manifest in continued low inflation and a string of budget surpluses. To ensure that the economy continues to expand along a non-inflationary path, the Bank of Canada has raised interest rates several times since November 1999, following similar moves by the US Federal Reserve. In view of the economy's rather different cyclical position, the Bank had held its official interest rates steady through previous increases in US rates from mid-1999. Meanwhile, fiscal policy continued to act as a drag on demand in 1999. However, recently decided tax cuts and spending increases at both the federal and provincial government levels imply a move towards fiscal relaxation in the period ahead, following six consecutive years of budget restraint. The sections below review monetary and fiscal policies in more detail. The chapter concludes with a discussion of the issues soon to be facing policymakers, when the macroeconomic strategy in place will for the first time be put to the test in conditions of full capacity utilisation.

Monetary management

The operational framework

The Bank of Canada targets CPI inflation with the aim of bringing its underlying rate towards the centre of a control range over a horizon of about two years. Since 1995, this target range has been 1 to 3 per cent. By the end of 2001, the government and the Bank plan to determine the ultimate target for monetary policy consistent with price stability. In the short run, the Bank focuses on the CPI excluding food, energy, and the effect of indirect taxes, referred to as "core" CPI. The Bank uses its influence over short-term interest rates to achieve a rate of aggregate demand expansion consistent with the inflation-control target. To this end, it establishes a 50-basis-point operating band for the overnight money-market financing rate, with the Bank Rate being fixed at the top of the band.

The Bank still publishes a Monetary Conditions Index (MCI), which combines movements in short-term interest rates and the effective exchange rate, as a short-hand measure of the policy stance, but has tended to place less emphasis on it. This reflects a number of difficulties with this concept. *First*, although the Bank began to use the term "policy guide" to describe the MCI, and repeatedly pointed out that its desired path has to be constantly reassessed in the light of new information, some observers have tended to treat the MCI as a precise short-term target for policy. *Second*, the markets' search for a rule of thumb has meant that they have tended to treat all exchange-rate movements as portfolio shocks that required an offsetting interest-rate adjustment. However, in contrast to the first half of the 1990s, in the latter part of the decade "real" shocks (such as changes in the terms of trade) seemed to predominate, and an offsetting interest-rate response was not always appropriate for inflation-control purposes. *Finally*, the Bank itself has found it sometimes difficult to make a judgement on the source of shocks to the exchange rate and their likely persistence. In such circumstances, the MCI has not been especially helpful as a communications device to guide the markets.

Nonetheless, given the high degree of openness of the Canadian economy, movements in the exchange rate continue to play an important role in the assessment of monetary conditions. While the Bank has abandoned regular exchange-market interventions, it is prepared to intervene when it feels that this would provide a useful signal to market participants. In this case, to enhance the signal effect, it is committed to announcing the intervention, in the same way as it signals a change in the operating band for the overnight interest rate. In the event, there has been no foreign exchange-market intervention since this approach was adopted in September 1998.

In the inflation-targeting approach used in Canada, the central bank undertakes actions that are projected to bring core inflation to the centre of the control range in six to eight quarters in the future. Given the considerable uncertainty about measures of the output gap, the Bank is placing increasing weight on various indicators of future inflation, such as unexpected movements in core inflation, commodity prices, wage settlements, real estate prices, and the spread between conventional and indexed bond yields. While movements in the money supply have always played a complementary role as a check on forecasts, over the last year the Bank has moved to prepare independent projections derived from the developments of monetary aggregates. Moreover, regional surveys of businesses and associations have become a regular input into the analysis of the future path of inflation.

Most recently, the Bank has taken a further step to enhance its communications strategy. Half way between the semi-annual *Monetary Policy Reports*, it now publishes an update covering recent developments. This initiative reflects the authorities' view that the conduct of monetary policy can be rendered more efficient and effective by ensuring that market participants and the public at large are regularly informed of the rationale for policy moves as well as the Bank's assessment of the current state of the economy.

The recent conduct of policy

Monetary conditions, as measured by the Bank's MCI, reached their point of greatest ease at the end of 1998. Since then they have tightened gradually (Figure 10). Initially, the tightening came from a strengthening of the exchange rate, both against the US currency and in effective terms, as recovering world commodity prices enhanced market confidence in the Canadian dollar. Benchmark short-term interest rates were actually lowered further in the first half of 1999 (by 25 basis points both in March and May) with a view to supporting continued economic expansion while maintaining inflation comfortably within the target range. Indeed, at that time, core inflation was running near the bottom of the target range, and the Bank's measure of economic potential still showed an excess supply gap, which would imply undesired disinflationary pressure.

The Bank held benchmark interest rates steady when US rates were increased during the summer of 1999, considering that monetary conditions in Canada were consistent with the inflation target. Nonetheless, money-market rates moved up, reflecting both the actual and expected rise in US short-term rates as well as market expectations of higher rates in Canada. At the same time, the exchange rate weakened a little, despite an ongoing increase in commodity prices and improvement in the current account, as the re-emergence of negative spreads between Canadian and US short-term interest rates (Figure 11) weighed against the Canadian dollar. Overall, monetary conditions, as measured by the MCI, remained relatively stable during that period.

Later in the year, with excess supply in the economy eliminated by some measures, the Bank became concerned about activity picking up too much speed, although core inflation remained unexpectedly low. Hence, to reduce inflationary risks, it increased short-term interest rates by 25 basis points in November 1999, February and March, and then by 50 basis points in May, following similar moves by the US Federal Reserve. This brought the target rate for overnight money and the Bank Rate to 5¾ per cent and 6 per cent, respectively. As these decisions were anticipated, market rates have firmed somewhat less than official benchmark rates since November. Despite a persistent negative interest-rate differential against the United States, the Canadian dollar initially strengthened a little against its US counterpart, reflecting the continued rebound in commodity prices and improving economic fundamentals, before losing ground more recently.

Long-term interest rates began to drift upwards earlier than short-term rates, implying some steepening in the yield curve through 1999 (Figure 11). The rise in bond yields over the course of the year largely reflected developments in the United States, with little change in the negative Canada/US spread that had emerged when the budget moved into surplus in 1997 and only briefly vanished during the period of financial turbulence in 1998. Apart from the improvement in economic fundamentals, which reduced the risk premium built into Canadian

Figure 10. **Monetary conditions**

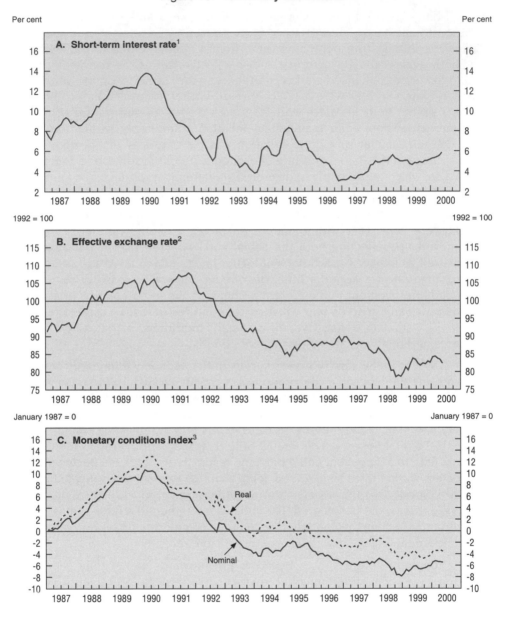

1. 90-day commercial paper rate.
2. Canadian dollar against 6 major foreign currencies (weighted average index).
3. Weighted average of changes in the interest rate ($3/4$) and in the effective exchange rate ($1/4$).
Source: Bank of Canada.

Figure 11. **Interest rate differentials and the yield gap**
Per cent

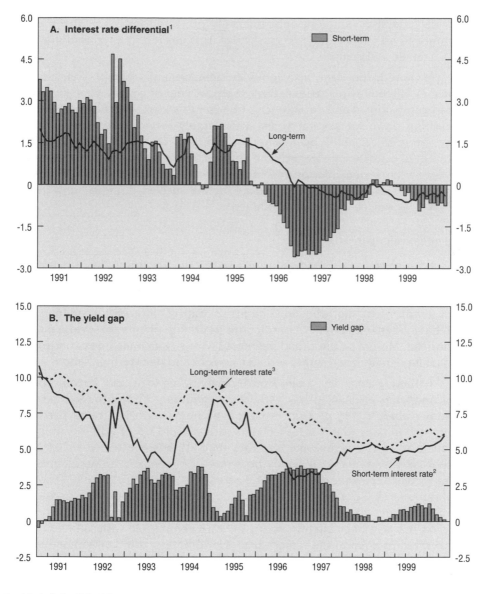

1. *Vis-à-vis* the United States.
2. 3-month commercial paper rate.
3. Over-10-year government bond yield.
Source: Statistics Canada and OECD.

interest rates, the persistent negative long-term spread appears to reflect the markets' perception that pressures on productive capacity in Canada are still less intense than in the United States.[3] More recently, yields on longer-dated maturities have fallen back, as markets adjusted to the prospects of a complete elimination of US federal government debt (officially projected for 2013). Together with the upward trend in short-term interest rates, this has led to a renewed flattening in the Canadian yield curve.

As noted, the Bank also looks at developments in bond yields as an indicator of inflation expectations. Over the past year or so, the yield differential between conventional and "real return" bonds has widened to above 2 per cent, after drifting down for several years. This largely reflects the rise in nominal interest rates, since yields on real return bonds have edged down a little. An adjustment of expectations towards the centre of the inflation-control target range might be partly responsible for this change. However, a difficulty in interpreting this measure is that it is also affected by factors such as liquidity[4] and investor preferences as well as inflation uncertainty.

Money and credit aggregates

Both narrow and broad measures of the money supply have been found to contain useful information about future trends in output and inflation (Atta-Mensa, 2000). In particular, the narrow aggregate M1 has been, in real terms, a good predictor of short-run movements in output. In addition, swings in M1 growth have been found to help predict the trend rate of inflation over a medium-term horizon. Moreover, the broad aggregate M2++ (which includes contributions to mutual funds) has been correlated with current and near-term inflation.

Following a significant slowdown (partly owing to special factors, see 1999 Survey), monetary expansion has gathered momentum during the course of the past year (Table 7). The pick-up in narrow money growth has been particularly pronounced. Initially, this was associated with a build-up of liquidity related to the transition to the year 2000. The fact that M1 has continued to expand at double-digit rates in early 2000 may be a matter of concern, however, given that the Bank considers that, over the long term, this aggregate should grow at an annual rate of 4 to 5 per cent to be consistent with low inflation. The acceleration in broad money growth has been less marked, but the aggregate's recent expansion has also been slightly above the rate compatible with inflation staying close to the mid-point of the target range. Nonetheless, the Bank's money-based indicator models continue to predict that inflation will remain within the target range over the next two years.

Household credit has grown at a solid, albeit not excessive pace (Table 7), indicating continued healthy consumer spending in the near term. With household borrowing rising somewhat faster than disposable income, the personal debt

Table 7.   **Money and credit**

Per cent change over previous period, annual rates

	1996	1997	1998	1999	Q4 1999	Q1 2000
Monetary growth						
Gross M1	10.7	15.5	10.3	7.7	13.4	26.1
M1	11.3	15.2	11.2	3.4	12.8	30.6
M2	3.0	−0.3	−0.2	2.8	6.2	7.2
M3	5.3	4.6	3.8	3.1	6.8	11.7
M2+	4.2	0.8	−0.6	3.9	7.2	7.6
M2++	6.5	7.6	7.7	6.7	9.1	8.6
Credit expansion						
To business sector	5.2	9.0	10.0	4.5	5.7	6.0
of which: Short term	1.9	7.6	11.8	1.2	3.5	11.3
To household sector	4.9	6.6	6.4	6.5	6.3	7.3
Consumer credit	7.3	9.8	10.3	8.3	12.3	13.7
Residential mortgages	4.1	5.5	4.9	5.8	4.0	4.7
Memorandum items:						
Nominal GDP growth	3.2	5.4	2.7	6.2	7.1	8.9
Income velocity (GDP/M1)	−7.1	−8.6	−7.6	2.7	−5.1	−16.7
Income velocity (GDP/M2)	0.2	5.7	2.9	3.3	0.9	1.6
Income velocity (GDP/M3)	−2.0	0.8	−1.0	3.0	0.3	−2.6
Income velocity (GDP/M2++)	−3.1	−2.1	−4.6	−0.5	−1.8	0.2
Debt to disposable income (per cent)	106.0	109.7	112.3	114.6	. .	. .
Interest cost to disposable income (per cent)	9.2	8.6	8.6	8.8	. .	. .

Source: Statistics Canada and Bank of Canada.

ratio has edged up further. Nonetheless, the estimated ratio of interest payments to disposable income is still well below its average for the past 20 years. Growth in business credit has remained relatively modest, as higher profits have limited the demand for external financing, although long-term borrowing has expanded at a robust pace. Altogether, the information coming from financial variables suggests above-potential growth through 2000, in particular when the spread between long- and short-term interest rates is included in the Bank's indicator models.

The fiscal stance

The strategy

Since the deficit was eliminated three years ago, federal fiscal policy has aimed at achieving a "balanced budget or better" to ensure that the public debt-to-GDP ratio remains on a clear downward track. The government is committed to allocating any budget surpluses – the so-called "fiscal dividend" – so that, over the course of its mandate, one-half is spent on new programmes and the other half goes to tax cuts and debt reduction. In principle, it aims for budget balance on an *ex ante* basis. However, in practice, this has implied *ex post* budget surpluses, reflecting the incorporation of contingency reserves and prudent economic assumptions.

In the mid-1990s, the incoming government adopted a narrowly focused two-year time frame for budget planning and began making conservative economic and fiscal assumptions in its budgets. With the deficit crisis successfully overcome, some problematic features of this approach became apparent – notably its neglect of the longer-term implications of some budget measures, and the forecasting bias which made it difficult to judge the credibility of fiscal projections. To address these issues, the November 1999 *Economic and Fiscal Update* unveiled a new approach to budget planning, presenting five-year projections based on current tax and spending policies and average private-sector economic forecasts. The degree of additional prudence, which used to be embedded in revenue and spending projections, is now shown explicitly while the contingency reserve is included primarily to cover risks arising from unavoidable forecasting inaccuracies and unpredictable events. By deducting a prudence margin and contingency reserves from the projected no-policy-change balance, the scope for new budget initiatives is gauged for the coming five years. However, budget decisions will continue to be made on a rolling two-year time horizon.

The provinces and territories have tended to adopt more formal fiscal policy frameworks. Since the mid-1990s, the majority of them have implemented legislated fiscal rules (Table 8). In all but one case, these include balanced-budget legislation with varying degrees of flexibility. Among the largest provinces, such a framework became effective in Quebec last year and will be applied in Ontario from next year. In several jurisdictions the legislation includes a referendum requirement for tax increases. Legal obligations to repay debt are less widespread, although certain jurisdictions have debt reduction targets that are not legislated. So far, targets pertaining to fiscal balances and debt have generally been met or exceeded, so that the penalties[5] provided in some cases for failing to meet legislated requirements have not been triggered.

General government

The slight general government financial surplus that had emerged in 1997 remained broadly stable in the following year, but then widened markedly to over 2 per cent of GDP in 1999 (Figure 12). This was one of the highest surpluses among OECD countries, which on average were still in a deficit position. According to OECD estimates, about one-quarter of the positive swing in the Canadian financial balance in 1999 can be traced to cyclical influences, implying a renewed significant tightening in the fiscal stance following only modest restraint the year before. As a result, the estimated structural primary surplus of general government approached 7 per cent of GDP, the highest level recorded in the OECD area. This highlights the

Table 8. **Legislated fiscal rules**

Jurisdiction[1]	Fiscal rule (year enacted)	Highlights of the legislative requirements
Nova Scotia[2]	Financial Measures Act (2000)	Annual balanced budget from 2002-03 onward; with four-year fiscal plans.
		Includes a one-year carry-over provision and provisions for extraordinary events. Requires that new programmes be financed from existing budgets and reduces foreign currency exposure.
New Brunswick	Balanced Budget Act (1993; amended in 1995)	Balanced budget to be achieved over a four-year period beginning in 1996-97.
		Includes provisions for extraordinary events.
Québec	Act Respecting the Elimination of the Deficit and a Balanced Budget (1996)	Annual balanced budget from 1999-2000 onwards.
		Includes a one-year carry-over provision and provisions for extraordinary events.
Ontario	Balanced Budget and Taxpayer Protection Act (1999)	Balanced budgets beginning in 2001-02; however, deficits of 1 per cent of revenues are permitted if offset in following year.
		Includes referendum requirement for tax increases, provisions for extraordinary events and penalties for failing to meet legislated fiscal requirements.
Manitoba	Balanced Budget, Debt Repayment and Taxpayer Protection Act (1995)	An annual balanced budget from 1995-96 onward.
		Debt Retirement Fund, with payments every five years after 1996-97.
		Includes referendum requirement for tax increases, provisions for extraordinary events and penalties for failing to meet legislated fiscal requirements.
Saskatchewan	Balanced Budget Act (1995)	Balanced budget over a four-year period.
		Debt Management Plan, requiring no specific debt repayment. Contains provisions for extraordinary events.

Table 8. **Legislated fiscal rules** (*cont.*)

Jurisdiction[1]	Fiscal rule (year enacted)	Highlights of the legislative requirements
Alberta	Deficit Elimination Act (1993)	Balanced budget by 1996-97.
	Balanced Budget and Debt Retirement Act (BBDRA) (1995)	Annual balanced budget every year starting in 1996-97.
		Elimination of net debt (excluding unfunded pension liabilities, which are dealt with in a separate plan) before 31 March 2010, with yearly minimum payments (note: the province eliminated the net debt in the first quarter of 1999-2000)
	Taxpayer Protection Act (1995)	Requires referendum for introduction of retail sales tax.
	Fiscal Responsibility Act (1999)[3]	Annual balanced budget; economic cushion of at least 3.5 per cent of revenue; 75 per cent of the cushion for debt repayment and 25 per cent as a contingency reserve for in-year initiatives.
		Legislated 25-year debt repayment plan for the accumulated debt. This Act replaced the BBDRA when the net debt (excluding unfunded pension liabilities) was eliminated.
Yukon Territory	Taxpayer Protection Act (1996)	Prohibits debt accumulation.
		Includes required referendum for tax increases and penalty for creating or increasing an accumulated debt.
Northwest Territories[4]	Deficit Elimination Act (1995; amended in 1996)	Deficit targets leading to a balanced budget in 1998-99.
		Prohibits debt accumulation. Allows one-year carry-over for deficit and includes penalties for failing to meet legislated fiscal requirements.

1. The Taxpayer Protection Act introduced in British Columbia in 1991 was repealed following the election of a new government in 1992.
2. Tabled in April 2000 but not yet legislated.
3. The Fiscal Responsibility Act was amended to permit in-year spending initiatives to exceed 25 per cent of the economic cushion in 1999-2000.
4. Unexpected decreases in federal funding and increases in expenditure prevented the Northwest Territories from meeting the requirements set out in their 1995 legislation. The legislation was amended to be more flexible to unexpected changes in revenues and expenditure while still achieving the objectives of a balanced budget and a reduction in net debt by 1998-99.
Source: Department of Finance, Canada.

Figure 12. **Decomposition of the general government financial balance**
Per cent of GDP (National Accounts basis)

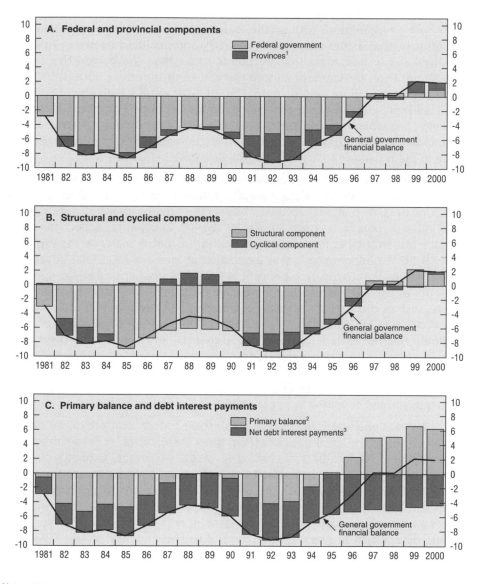

Note: 2000 data are OECD projections.
1. Including territories, local government, hospitals, Canada and Quebec Pension Plans.
2. Excluding debt service.
3. Interest payments are shown with a negative sign.
Source: Statistics Canada; OECD estimates.

progress in fiscal consolidation made since the first half of the 1990s, when the structural primary balance was negative. But it also points to the persisting high debt service burden that resulted from the earlier era of large budget deficits.

The main factor behind the improvement in government finances in 1999 was spending moderation. With all the major outlay components expanding less than national income, the expenditure-to-GDP ratio declined by about 2 percentage points and is now more than 10 points lower than the early 1990s peak of nearly 50 per cent. Easing debt service charges contributed significantly, with net interest payments falling towards 6 per cent of GDP – still a high level by international standards. In contrast to outlays, revenues expanded at a healthy pace as economic conditions improved. However, they were no longer a source of fiscal restraint as tax reductions at both the provincial and federal levels made for a decline in the revenue-to-GDP ratio for the first time in five years.

All levels of government registered an improvement in their fiscal position in 1999. However, while the federal surplus remained relatively stable, at around ½ per cent of GDP (national accounts basis), the small provincial deficit in 1998 turned into a surplus of 1½ per cent of GDP in 1999. Buoyant tax collections associated with the strengthening economy contributed. But a major factor explaining provincial fiscal performance is that a substantial increase in federal government transfers (equivalent to nearly ½ per cent of GDP) has not implied higher spending, at least not as yet. Even after adjusting for one-off influences – notably privatisation receipts, such as the sale of a highway in Ontario (which reduced its capital spending by ¼ per cent of Canadian GDP), and part of the rise in federal transfers – there is no doubt that the underlying position of provincial finances has improved significantly. To a lesser extent this is also true for local government, which has moved into broad budget balance. Moreover, as a result of reforms that included, among other things, an accelerated increase in contribution rates, the Canada Pension Plan has moved into surplus, following five years of deficit.

Tax cuts and spending increases in recent federal and provincial budgets imply an easing in the fiscal stance in the period ahead, after six consecutive years of retrenchment. Nonetheless, according to OECD estimates, Canada's structural primary surplus relative to GDP, albeit declining, would still be one of the highest among OECD countries by 2001. The following sections review developments in federal and provincial government finances in more detail. While the discussion so far was based on national accounts data, it will henceforth refer to public accounts data, which in practice have tended to show somewhat less favourable budgetary balances.

Federal government

The February 1999 Budget, like its predecessor, included targeted tax relief as well as spending initiatives in priority areas (such as health care and innovation), which were, however, to a large extent pre-booked to the fiscal year 1998-99 (ending in March). The Budget projected a continued "underlying surplus" of C$ 3 billion, the amount of the contingency reserve set aside (Table 9). The final accounts for 1998-99 then showed a budgetary surplus of C$ 2.9 billion (0.3 per cent of GDP, slightly lower than the year before), implying a marginal drawdown of the

Table 9.   **Federal government finances: changes since the 1999 Budget**

C$ billion

	1998-1999	1999-2000	2000-2001
1999 Budget underlying surplus (before Contingency Reserve)	**3.0**	**3.0**	**3.0**
Impact of economic developments			
Budgetary revenues			
Personal income tax	−1.2	1.6	2.7
Corporate income tax	−0.4	1.7	2.7
Other income tax	0.0	0.4	0.6
Employment insurance (EI) premiums	0.2	0.7	1.1
Goods and services tax	0.1	0.5	0.8
Other excise taxes and duties	0.0	−0.8	−0.4
Non-tax revenues	0.5	−0.3	−0.5
Total revenues	−0.8	3.6	7.0
Programme spending			
Elderly benefits	0.0	−0.2	0.1
EI benefits	−0.2	−1.7	−2.0
Transfer to other levels of government	0.1	0.6	0.9
Direct programme spending	−0.6	−0.3	0.7
Total	−0.7	−1.6	−0.3
Public debt charges	0.0	−1.0	−1.4
Net impact of economic developments	**−0.1**	**6.2**	**8.7**
Less: Net impact of policy changes			
Affecting revenues		0.3	4.6
Affecting programme spending		5.9	3.1
Net impact		6.2	7.7
Net change since 1999 Budget	**−0.1**	**0.0**	**1.0**
2000 Budget underlying surplus	**2.9**	**3.0**	**4.0**
Less: Prudence			
Contingency Reserve		3.0	3.0
Economic prudence			1.0
Net impact		3.0	4.0
2000 Budget budgetary planning balance		**0.0**	**0.0**

Note: Numbers may not add due to rounding.
Source: Department of Finance, Canada.

contingency reserve. Estimates for 1999-2000 presented in the February 2000 Budget suggest that, given much stronger-than-projected economic growth, tax revenues were significantly higher than expected. For the same reason, Employment Insurance benefit payments were lower. In addition, lower-than-projected interest rates resulted in reduced public debt charges. The net impact of these developments was expected to improve the budgetary balance by more than C$ 6 billion (over ½ per cent of GDP). This net revenue windfall has been largely used for new spending initiatives, mainly in the priority areas mentioned above, so that the underlying budget surplus for 1999-2000 would remain unchanged at C$ 3 billion. However, given the strength of tax revenues, it now seems likely that the final outcome for 1999-2000 will be better than thought at the time of the Budget. The additional surplus will be applied to reducing the federal debt.

The five-year fiscal projections in the November 1999 *Economic and Fiscal Update* suggested that the scope for new budget initiatives would be C$ 5.5 billion in 2000-01 and C$ 8.5 billion in 2001-02, reaching C$ 23 billion in 2004-05. Subsequent unexpectedly favourable economic developments have indicated, however, that these estimates were on the low side. The February 2000 Budget allocated nearly C$ 8 billion for new spending and tax initiatives in 2000-01 (as compared with the initial 1999 Budget plan for that year).

What distinguishes the latest Budget from its predecessors is that more of the net revenue windfall in the current fiscal year is devoted to tax measures than to extra spending (although, as noted above, considerable funds for new spending initiatives were pre-booked to the 1999-2000 fiscal year). As discussed in more detail in the following chapter, the Budget announced a five-year tax reduction plan that makes the most important structural changes to the federal tax system in more than a decade. Measures that take effect this year include the restoration of full indexation of the personal income tax system (from January), a reduction of the middle personal income tax rate (from July), corporate tax relief for small businesses (from January), and a decrease in the capital gains tax (from end-February). A first modest cut in the corporate tax rate for larger businesses in the highest-taxed sectors follows at the beginning of 2001. The estimated revenue cost of these tax initiatives this fiscal year and next is ⅓ and ⅔ per cent of GDP, respectively.

Provincial governments

In terms of both revenue and spending, the Canadian provinces and territories are larger than the federal government. In recent years, fiscal discipline and a renewed increase in federal transfers have helped improve their budget position considerably (Table 10). Federal transfers consist mainly of equalisation payments, for which seven provinces qualify, and a block fund providing support for health care, post-secondary education, and social assistance and services. Including tax transfers, they now again amount to about 4 per cent of GDP, about

Table 10. **Provincial budgetary balances and debt**

Public accounts basis, fiscal years, percentage

	Ratio of deficit/surplus to provincial GDP				Ratio of net debt to provincial GDP			
	1990-91	1994-95	1998-99	1999-00	1990-91	1994-95	1998-99	1999-00
Newfoundland	−3.8	−1.2	0.0	−0.3	38.9	48.2	43.2	42.7
Prince Edward Island[1]	−0.9	−0.1	0.2	0.1	10.3	39.4	34.5	32.6
Nova Scotia[2]	−1.5	−1.3	−1.9	−3.6	27.8	45.7	48.0	49.9
New Brunswick[3]	−1.4	−0.4	−1.0	−0.1	24.4	36.8	34.3	38.6
Québec[4]	−1.9	−3.4	0.1	0.0	24.4	33.9	45.8	43.6
Ontario	−1.1	−3.3	−0.5	0.2	15.1	29.4	30.9	28.1
Manitoba	−1.2	−0.8	0.1	0.0	21.7	28.5	22.6	21.1
Saskatchewan	−1.7	0.5	0.1	0.2	17.3	31.3	24.8	24.1
Alberta[5]	−2.5	1.1	1.0	1.7	7.7	14.5	4.6	2.6
British Columbia	−1.0	−0.4	−0.4	−1.1	8.0	11.9	11.7	12.6
Total[6]	−1.5	−2.1	−0.2	0.1	16.6	27.1	28.4	26.9
Memorandum item:								
Federal government	−4.7	−4.9	0.3	0.0[7]	57.6	71.1	64.0	60.2

1. Accounting changes implemented in1993-94 increased net debt.
2. Accounting changes implemented in1992-93 increased the net debt.
3. Accounting changes implemented in1992-93 increased net debt.
4. Reflects accounting reform implemented in1997-98 that substantially increased net debt.
5. Accounting changes implemented in1992-93 increased the net debt.
6. Total provincial-territorial budgetary balance and net debt as a share of national GDP.
7. Budgetary balance in1999-2000 would be a surplus of 0.3 per cent of GDP if the Contingency Reserve is not required.
Source: Department of Finance, Canada.

the level recorded before the swingeing cuts in the mid-1990s in the context of federal budget consolidation. While this has bolstered provincial finances, another factor has made for somewhat slower progress in eliminating deficits than registered at the federal government level. Provinces began cutting taxes earlier, with the first such measures implemented in 1996, before becoming widespread in subsequent years.

According to the latest estimates, the provinces and territories recorded an aggregate deficit of 0.2 per cent of GDP in 1998-99, a slight improvement from the preceding fiscal year. Six provinces and one territory achieved budget balance or a surplus, including Quebec, which had posted uninterrupted deficits for 40 years. Remaining deficits were still substantial (in relation to provincial GDP) only in two small jursidictions. The 1999 budgets emphasised key investments in social programmes, particularly health care, and announced additional tax cuts. As a result of strong own-source revenue growth – fuelled by a surging economy and high energy prices – the aggregate provincial/territorial budgetary balance is estimated to have moved into slight surplus in 1999-2000 (Table 10), the first surplus in 25 years. Most jurisdictions are on track to attain or surpass their fiscal objectives. Six provinces and one territory expect to have achieved a balanced budget or surplus for 1999-2000. Nonetheless, latest available estimates show a much more limited improvement in provincial finances in 1999-2000 than indicated by national accounts data reviewed earlier. To a considerable extent, this reflects a different treatment of recent increases in federal transfers in the provincial public accounts.[6] The latest provincial budgets generally continue last year's spending and tax initiatives. Given prudent planning assumptions, a majority of jurisdictions should at least achieve a balanced budget in 2000-01, the major exception being British Columbia, which has postponed the elimination of its deficit to 2004-05.

Debt developments

Progress in fiscal consolidation at all government levels has put Canada's public debt ratio on a clear downward track since 1996 (Figure 13). By end-2000, debt repayment and stronger growth in national income are estimated to have made for a fall in general government debt by about 15 percentage points relative to GDP. Nonetheless, so far this decline has only restored the situation prevailing in the early 1990s when the debt ratio was already high by historical standards. Moreover, both in gross and net terms, Canada's public debt-to-GDP ratio is still significantly above the average OECD level.[7] However, if prudent policies are maintained, economic developments may well allow the elimination of that gap in the coming few years.

While, as noted, the size of provincial-territorial governments in terms of spending and revenue exceeds that of the federal government, the federal debt burden is much higher. Nonetheless, the composition of public debt has changed substantially in recent years. With the federal budget moving into surplus earlier, the federal debt ratio has already declined much more than its provincial counterpart. As a result, since the early 1990s, the federal share of total public debt (in net terms) has fallen from three-quarters to two-thirds. Because of its higher debt load, the federal government's debt charges consume a much higher proportion of revenues than is the case with the provinces and territories. While this ratio has come down from more than one-third to about a quarter, it is still more than twice as high as the provincial-territorial share.

Over the last few years, the federal government has made some major decisions in managing its debt. In particular, it has increased the proportion of longer-term, fixed-rate debt from about one-half to two-thirds of the total. The government has maintained this target, although the Auditor General observed that it generally would imply higher costs while being less essential than in the mid-1990s, since declining debt had reduced the impact of unanticipated changes in interest rates on debt servicing costs. The Auditor General also noted the cost of rising foreign exchange reserves and of promoting the sale of retail debt (such

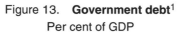

Figure 13. **Government debt**[1]
Per cent of GDP

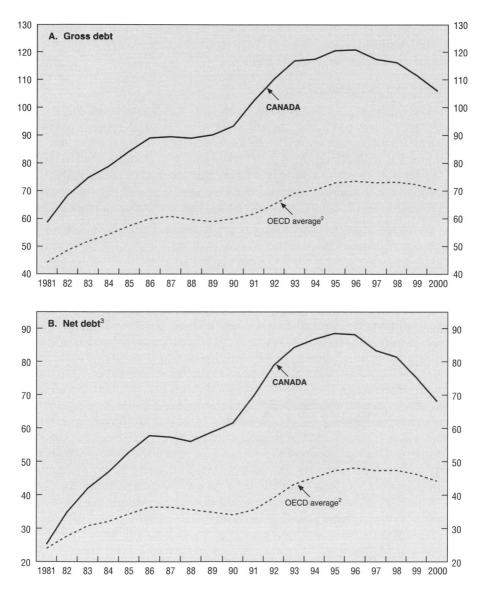

1. General government; National Accounts definitions. 2000 data are OECD projections.
2. Weighted average using 1991 GDP weights and exchange rates.
3. Liabilities less financial assets.
Source: Statistics Canada; OECD.

as savings bonds). Moreover, while recognising that the government has taken a number of measures to mitigate the impact of shrinking borrowing requirements, the Auditor General considered that there was room for more aggressive use of buybacks to enhance liquidity in government securities markets (which are less liquid than those in the United States where buybacks began in March). In this respect, the authorities have announced that they intend to operate a pilot bond buyback programme on an ongoing basis.

Assessment and challenges

Macroeconomic policies have been very successful over the past year. Monetary policy has been able to keep inflation low and interest rates below comparable US rates, thus contributing importantly to stronger economic growth. Fiscal policy has maintained the public debt ratio on a clear downward track. The challenge for policymakers now is to sustain this favourable performance. In this regard, they face a number of issues in the period ahead. Some of them are related to the current conjuncture, while others are more structural in nature.

A crucial issue for monetary policy at the moment is the considerable uncertainty as to where the economy stands relative to potential. When measures of the output gap are near zero, they cease to be very informative even about the direction of disinflation/inflation pressure, especially given the wide margin for measurement error. The fact that core inflation has so far been well contained could mean that the sustainable level of output is higher than conventional estimates suggest. On the other hand, as will be discussed in the following chapter, it is by no means clear to what extent technological advances and restructuring have enhanced efficiency, and hence productive potential. Nor is it clear to what extent any such changes, along with more global competition, have modified price- and wage-setting in product and labour markets. In these circumstances, the authorities have de-emphasised the output gap as a guide for monetary policy and are placing increasing weight on various indicators of future inflati on. This implies, however, a considerable degree of judgement. It is true that the Bank of Canada's success in maintaining low inflation has established the credibility of the targeting regime and provides the authorities with some room to explore the economy's productive limits. Nonetheless, given the time it takes for monetary policy to have its impact on activity, it would seem advisable to err on the side of caution now that economic slack has been at least largely eliminated if the strong momentum of the economy persists. The extent to which monetary policy responds should, however, take into account changes in the inflation process brought about by the achievement of a prolonged period of low inflation.

An ongoing challenge for monetary authorities is the improvement of their communications policy. While this is an issue for all central banks, it is arguably particularly important for countries that have adopted an inflation-targeting regime. To provide a firmer grounding for low inflation expectations and help markets and the public understand monetary policy actions better, the authorities have taken a number of measures to enhance transparency. Most recently, they have decided to give a detailed account of their expectations for the economy more frequently. At the same time, they have de-emphasised the MCI, considering that, while being a useful concept for small open economies, it has not proved successful as a communications device. Despite various articles and speeches explaining the role of the exchange rate in policy, the markets' search for simple rules of thumb has encouraged misinterpretation of the authorities' intentions. This was particularly evident in the context of the terms-of-trade shock associated with the Asian crisis. Arguably, however, the point that in such a situation exchange-rate movements do not necessarily warrant an offsetting interest-rate response could have been better explained to the markets, in the same way as the central bank has patiently, and it seems successfully, explained its inflation-targeting framework. The authorities' recent decision to leave it to the market to draw conclusions for the future path of monetary conditions on the basis of more frequent statements on the state of the economy may reduce the risk of misunderstandings and thus make monetary policy more effective. However, partly for technical reasons, even though they are issued at shorter intervals, such statements will inevitably be sometimes overtaken by events. Even with the number of key communication events having increased considerably and the creation of senior positions in major financial centres to facilitate communications with market participants, it may be necessary to do even more to keep the markets abreast of changing central-bank thinking.

Although the fiscal stance has become less restrictive since the mid-1990s, it has not complicated the task of the Bank of Canada. The decline in public debt has contributed to reducing the risk premia built into Canadian interest rates. However, while monetary policy is in a tightening mode, fiscal policies are now easing, a trend that may be reinforced by the fact that additional revenue beyond budgeted levels – which has been the rule, given prudent planning assumptions – is largely used for funding one-off spending initiatives. With the economy operating at, or above, full capacity, using any unexpected fiscal surpluses for debt reduction rather than funding new measures would be clearly preferable, so as to take some pressure off monetary policy. Accelerated debt reduction would also further reduce the vulnerability of public finances to interest-rate changes and reinforce the credibility of the government's overall macroeconomic strategy. Moreover, by lowering debt service charges, it would subsequently make room for more comprehensive (revenue-shrinking) adjustments to the tax system, where there is still considerable unfinished business despite the recent initiatives, as discussed in the following chapter.

The scope for tax reform would be further enhanced by tight control over spending and careful evaluation of new initiatives. It is true that, despite additional year-end spending in recent years, public expenditure has so far continued to decline relative to GDP. However, in contrast to the past, this now largely reflects decreasing debt service charges. Moreover, there is a question whether recent spending initiatives have always been helpful. More effort should be applied to measuring their economic benefits and to combining them with complementary structural reforms in the sectors concerned. For instance, as discussed in the next chapter, some extra spending in the areas of health care and education might be useful, but in general raising the quality rather quantity of public expenditure in these sectors would seem to be desirable. A dilemma for the federal government in this regard is that most of its spending in these areas is in the form of transfers to provinces so that it has no direct control over the alloca-tion. Nonetheless, it needs to continue to guard against a misallocation of funds that could result from an undue focus on the few areas where it has major direct spending responsibilities. The restoration of full indexation of the personal income tax system should have a positive side effect in encouraging spending discipline by limiting the fiscal dividend. But more direct efforts to control expenditure within a comprehensive medium-term framework could both allow faster debt and tax reduction and increase economic efficiency.

III. Structural issues and policies

As discussed in previous Surveys, since the mid-1980s Canada has embarked upon an impressive programme of microeconomic reform that has touched on all aspects of the economy. The regulatory landscape and the incentives facing businesses and individuals have all been substantially improved through a series of measures, including: wide-scale privatisation of public entities; free trade agreements signed with the United States and Mexico as well as the reduction and simplification of the tariff structure in line with multilateral commitments; the relaxation of inter-provincial trade barriers; financial-sector deregulation; tax reform; and a revamp of labour-market programmes to promote job attachment. These reforms are important factors underlying the sustained rise in output over the latter part of the 1990s and the fall in the unemployment rate to lows not seen in more than 20 years. The following sections review in more detail recent progress in structural reform, highlighting areas where further effort is required to improve the productive capacity of the economy. The chapter begins with an overview of supply-side performance before turning to developments in labour, product and financial markets, followed by a discussion of issues in the public sector.

Improved supply-side performance?

Economic fundamentals appear to have improved, but structural performance is still lagging

The recent improvement in Canada's economic performance (see Chapter I) came after an extended period of economic slack in the 1990s that saw stubbornly high unemployment rates and below-potential growth as the authorities sought to tackle the serious imbalances that had built up since the mid-1970s. The result of reforms, however, has been a gradual improvement in supply-side outcomes. Indeed, potential real GDP growth is estimated to have accelerated to just over 3 per cent (from about 2 per cent in the early 1990s) and the structural rate of unemployment to have dropped to about 7½ (from 9) per cent (Table 11, Panel A).

Table 11. **Indicators of structural performance**

Per cent

	Canada	United States	Japan	Germany	France	Italy	United Kingdom	OECD
Panel A: Output, employment and government								
Real GDP growth[1]								
1980-90	2.8	3.2	4.0	2.2	2.4	2.2	2.7	3.2
1990-99	2.4	3.1	1.3	2.6	1.6	1.4	2.0	2.5
1996-99	3.7	4.2	-0.2	1.7	2.7	1.6	2.6	3.0
Potential real GDP growth[1]								
1980-90	2.8	3.1	3.8	2.2	2.3	2.5	2.2	2.8
1990-99	2.5	3.1	2.0	3.1	1.8	1.8	2.3	1.8
1996-99	3.1	3.5	1.4	1.7	2.0	2.0	2.4	1.8
Employment, percentage of working-age population[2]								
1980-90	68.4	68.3	70.8	63.2	60.6	54.6	67.7	64.5
1990-99	68.9	72.6	74.4	65.7	59.4	52.0	69.3	65.4
1996-99	70.0	74.3	74.9	64.5	59.6	51.8	70.6	65.8
Employment growth[1]								
1980-90	1.7	1.8	1.2	0.5	0.3	0.1	0.7	1.6
1990-99	1.2	1.3	0.4	2.7	0.3	-0.3	0.2	1.7
1996-99	2.6	1.8	-0.1	-0.0	1.2	0.9	1.3	1.3
Structural unemployment rate[2]								
1980-90	9.2	6.6	2.4	7.0	8.2	8.1	9.3	..
1990-99	9.0	5.6	3.0	7.8	10.1	9.5	8.1	..
1996-99	8.4	5.4	3.6	8.1	10.4	10.1	7.4	..
Labour productivity growth[1]								
1980-90	1.3	1.5	2.9	2.2	2.6	1.9	2.5	2.1
1990-99	1.3	1.6	0.9	-0.1	1.6	1.6	1.6	1.7
1996-99	1.0	2.2	-0.1	1.8	1.5	0.9	1.3	1.7
Government deficit, percentage of GDP[2]								
1980-90	-4.9	-4.3	-0.8	-1.8	-2.4	-11.0	-2.1	-3.5
1990-99	-3.3	-2.7	-2.5	-2.6	-3.9	-6.7	-3.9	-3.0
1996-99	1.5	0.2	-5.1	-1.8	-2.5	-2.5	-0.2	-1.2

Table 11. **Indicators of structural performance** (*cont.*)

Per cent

	Canada	United States	Japan	Germany	France	Italy	United Kingdom	OECD
Panel A: Output, employment and government								
Government gross debt, percentage of GDP[2]								
1980-90	63.8	58.2	62.3	40.1	37.0	82.0	53.0	55.7
1990-99	92.6	72.2	77.1	54.5	56.5	118.3	53.6	70.1
1996-99	90.4	68.4	95.7	62.7	64.9	118.0	56.0	72.6
Panel B: Investment								
Investment in machinery and equipment, percentage of GDP[2]								
1980-90[3]	9.1	7.7	..	8.7	10.3	11.2	9.0	..
1990-99	8.5	8.3	..	..	10.1	10.1	8.3	..
1996-99	9.2	9.3	..	..	10.1	10.6	8.9	..
Investment in machinery and equipment, growth[1]								
1980-90	6.1	4.7	..	3.5	5.0	2.7	4.3	..
1990-99	6.5	9.9	..	..	2.4	2.3	4.1	..
1996-99	12.2	13.1	..	..	7.2	5.9	9.7	..
Panel C: ICT investment[4]								
Average annual rate of growth								
1985-90	17.2	19.6	23.6	18.8	16.2	20.8	25.5	..
1990-96	17.6	23.8	14.5	18.6	11.0	12.9	17.6	..
Share in nominal capital stock								
1985	4.3	6.2	1.2	2.9	2.4	1.3	3.6	..
1996	5.0	7.4	2.3	3.0	3.2	2.1	5.2	..
Contribution to output growth								
1985-1990	0.31	0.34	0.17	0.17	0.23	0.18	0.27	..
1990-1996	0.28	0.42	0.19	0.19	0.17	0.21	0.29	..

1. Compound annual growth rate. Per employed person, total economy.
2. Annual average.
3. For Canada, 1981-1990.
4. Business sector only.
Source: OECD.

Nevertheless, despite these promising signs, the expansion in potential output is still below that observed in the 1970s, and while recent economic performance compares favourably to that experienced by most G7 nations, it has not been as strong as in the United States, Canada's closest trading partner, in the 1990s. At the same time, the relative standard of living has yet to recover lost ground (Figure 1, Panel B in Chapter I). This has led to discussion of whether a new paradigm, led by the US example of rising labour productivity growth that allows economic activity to expand at a quicker pace without inflationary pressures, is yet present in Canada. The country's productivity performance to this point would suggest not. At the aggregate level, while broadly maintaining pace with its southern neighbour over the 1980s, and much of the 1990s, increasing at just over 1 per cent annually (and slightly more on an hourly basis than when calculated per worker), labour productivity growth began to diverge substantially in the second half of the decade when it picked up in the United States, opening up a growth-rate gap of more than a percentage point per year. While cyclical factors may be at work, there is burgeoning evidence to suggest that the trend rate has, in fact, risen in the United States (OECD, 2000a; Oliner and Sichel, 2000). Although data for Canada are volatile, they show no clear upturn.

Industrial structure plays a role in productivity performance differences...

A key contributor to aggregate productivity growth is the manufacturing sector, where there are important differences between the two countries. At the industry level, over most of the 1990s Canada's performance was at least as good, or better, than in the United States. Indeed, for many industries (12 of the 19 in Table 12), including wood, furniture, primary metals, transportation equipment, tobacco, food, textiles, petroleum, and rubber, labour productivity advanced at a more rapid pace. However, there were two notable exceptions: the industrial machinery and equipment, and electrical and electronic products industries, which encompass leading-edge technologies, such as computer and semiconductor manufacturing. Here, American performance vastly outpaced that in Canada over the period 1989-97 and accelerated between 1995-97, while falling off in Canada. Moreover, in the United States the share of these two industries in manufacturing output rose by about 16 percentage points, reaching 34.5 per cent in 1997, whereas in Canada this increase was a meagre 1.3 percentage points, and the share only 13.2 per cent. Taken together, the smaller absolute magnitude and lower growth implied relatively worse aggregate manufacturing and overall (economy-wide) productivity performance.

... as do differences in capital deepening and innovation

Labour productivity growth depends on the extent of capital deepening (capital per worker hour), and developments in this dimension at the economy-wide

Table 12. **Productivity and employment growth in manufacturing**

	Labour productivity¹						Employment growth		Share in output	
	Canada			Difference from USA						
	Annual percentage change			Percentage points			Annual percentage change		Percentage of manufacturing GDP	
	1981-89	1989-97	1995-97	1981-89	1989-97	1995-97	1981-89	1989-97	1989	1997
Total manufacturing industries	2.1	2.4	1.5	-1.3	-0.5	-1.4	0.2	-0.5	100	100
Lumber and wood products	3.9	-1.5	0.3	0.2	1.4	0.5	-0.1	1.9	5.3	4.7
Furniture and fixtures	0.3	6.0	13.6	-0.3	3.9	11.7	0.0	-2.6	2.1	2.3
Stone, clay and glass products	3.3	-0.7	9.4	0.0	-2.5	7.0	-2.5	-0.4	3.3	2.5
Primary metal industries	3.6	4.7	4.3	3.9	1.7	1.3	-1.4	-2.9	5.1	5.1
Fabricated metal products	2.6	1.2	2.6	-0.2	-0.8	1.4	-1.8	0.1	7.7	7.4
Industrial machinery and equipment	5.0	1.5	-1.5	-3.7	-6.4	-13.4	-5.8	0.8	5.2	5.5
Electronic and other electric equipment	4.5	4.0	-2.4	..	-9.9	-20.5	2.6	-0.3	6.7	7.7
Transportation equipment industries	2.8	2.5	-2.0	0.3	3.2	-0.5	3.4	1.3	14.9	17.6
Miscellaneous manufacturing industries	-0.1	0.5	-3.0	-5.9	0.2	-3.0	0.3	2.4	3.0	3.1
Food and kindred products	0.2	1.9	0.9	-2.6	2.0	9.1	-0.9	-0.3	14.0	13.6
Tobacco products	..	12.9	49.7	..	13.0	54.1	..	-13.4	1.2	0.9
Textile industries	3.0	6.4	9.6	-0.3	2.4	7.8	-2.7	-5.6	2.4	2.2
Apparel and other textile products	-0.8	1.8	3.1	-4.7	-2.0	-2.6	0.3	-2.2	3.0	2.4
Paper and allied products	0.1	4.4	5.8	-2.7	2.9	1.0	0.2	-2.7	5.7	5.4
Printing and publishing	-2.0	-2.5	0.3	-1.7	-0.7	1.1	3.8	0.2	8.3	5.7
Chemicals and allied products	3.4	3.5	4.0	-1.1	0.3	3.3	0.9	-1.1	8.1	8.3
Petroleum and coal products	0.6	6.5	-6.0	-8.0	4.9	-12.2	1.5	-4.8	0.9	0.9
Rubber and miscellaneous plastics products	1.7	5.2	4.3	-2.5	1.1	-1.3	2.6	0.1	3.5	4.6
Leather and leather products	2.8	-0.9	-7.9	-1.4	-5.0	-11.6	-5.5	-5.6	0.5	0.3
Manufacturing – Machinery and Electric industries	1.8	2.4	2.0	-1.1	2.2	4.4	0.3	-0.5	88.1	86.8

1. GDP per hour.
Source: Canadian Centre for the Study of Living Standards.

level have been quite similar between the two countries. There has been a marked
difference, however, in the manufacturing sector (Figure 14). There, the amount of
capital per worker hour began to plummet in Canada in the early 1990s, while
continuing to expand in the United States. This under-performance undoubtedly
contributed to the divergence in labour productivity growth. The reasons behind
this pattern are not clear. One underlying factor has probably been lower machinery
and equipment investment growth in Canada (Table 11, Panel B). The slow recovery,
its uncertain strength and duration, and the ensuing excess capacity would have
lowered the desire to invest, particularly in manufacturing, which was hardest hit in
the recession. Nevertheless, the more recent tailing-off is puzzling and not easily
explainable. Nor are its implications since the type of capital spending plays an
important role, discussed further below. In principle, this shortfall can be overcome
by a more efficient use of capital and labour inputs (improving total factor productivity or TFP). Canada's TFP record, however, has roughly followed a similar pattern
to labour productivity (Figure 1, Panel C). A recent study by Gu and Ho (2000) also
shows this has been the case at the sectoral level. Thus, the gap in labour productivity growth in manufacturing between the two countries has been reflected in TFP
and can be attributed almost entirely to the poorer performance in the machinery
and equipment and electronics industries.

Figure 14.   **Capital stock**[1]
1976 = 100

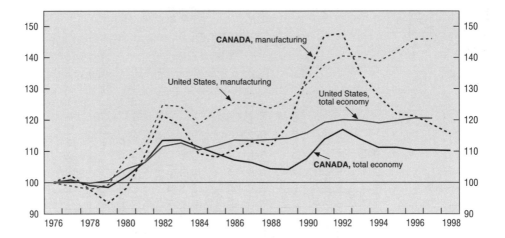

1. Per working hour.
Source: Centre for the Study of Living Standards, based on data from the US Bureau of Labor Statistics and Statistics
    Canada.

Where Canada typically increased labour productivity relative to the United States in the 1990s, it was largely through more extensive job cuts, for example in the tobacco, textiles and petroleum products industries, rather than by improving innovation in new products. This has led commentators to claim that Canada is a process, but not necessarily a product, innovator (Fortin, 1999). Indeed, Canada's comparative advantage remains in low- and medium-to-low technology industries, despite increasing investment in high technology. Moreover, compared with other OECD countries, the country lags in rates of technological innovation and adoption, and research and development. For example, Canada consistently devotes a relatively small share of GDP to R&D spending (about 1.6 per cent of GDP compared with an OECD average of 2.2 per cent; see OECD, 2000b) and the business-sector share is modest (Figure 15), despite very attractive incentives in the area (tax subsidies per dollar of R&D are second highest in the OECD, after Spain).[8] This suggests that a coherent supportive framework may be lacking. For instance, the current corporate tax environment may play an important role in discouraging and distorting investment decisions (in particular biasing investment away from knowledge-based activities in the service sector), as would inter-provincial barriers to trade, discussed further below. Furthermore, the high personal income tax burden and elevated marginal tax rates have probably been underlying factors in

Figure 15. **Expenditure on R&D**
Percentage of GDP

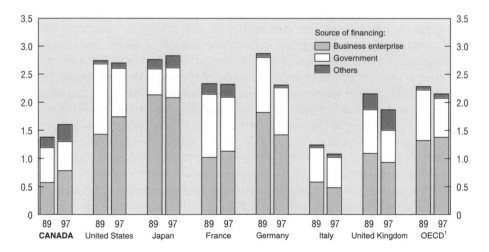

1.   OECD weighted average, which includes in 1997 Mexico, Korea, Czech Republic, Hungary and Poland.
Source: OECD, R&D database.

reducing work incentives and the impetus to upskill. They may also have encouraged a flight of top talent to south of the border – although the widely discussed "brain drain" is probably overstated (see below). In addition, labour-market reforms, although beginning in the early 1990s, became much more significant only in the middle of the decade, and these will have taken time to pay off in terms of increased mobility and improved productivity.

Another indicator of innovation, albeit imperfect,[9] is the number of registered patents, where Canada, once again lags well behind other G7 nations. Moreover, the composition of its patents is weighted towards so-called traditional sectors (for example, mechanical products and chemicals) and not relatively advanced industries such as computer hardware and software (Trajtenberg, 1999). Of course, Canada may still receive sizeable technology transfers in the absence of either high R&D spending or number of patents through its close economic links with the United States.

But the "new economy" debate has not been settled thus far

These trends have sparked a debate over whether Canada is getting left behind in the so-called "new economy", and the extent to which it has invested in the "wrong" industries (Wolff, 2000). It is becoming increasingly apparent that it is not just investment in physical capital that is important, but also the type of capital, and much focus has been on the role of the information and communication technology industries (ICT), which are part of the machinery and electrical equipment sectors, in which Canada's performance lags. Moreover, the implications may be quite serious if computers are part of a so-called new "general purpose technology" that leads to generalised productivity gains (Trajtenberg, 1999). The link to productivity performance, however, is not straightforward. On the one hand, when domestic production of ICT goods is relatively small, its overall contribution to aggregate productivity growth may be low, unless it is increasing at an extremely rapid rate. On the other hand, even if a small sector domestically, its importance in overall productivity developments could be large, to the extent that such goods are widely used as inputs to most industries (for example, imports of such goods by firms may also be large), thereby making a significant capital input in the production process. There would also be beneficial effects via capital deepening. In addition, when ICT leads to spillover effects that are widely diffused across industries (Schreyer, 2000), this should show up in total factor productivity, although the measurement of such externalities is notoriously difficult. Part of the problem lies in assessing and measuring ICT-based impacts since the relevant businesses and markets (electronic commerce, for example; see below) are still at an early stage of development.

The evidence is not clear-cut since, unlike the United States, there were only tentative signs by the end of the decade of a pickup in either labour productivity or TFP. This comes against the backdrop of relatively strong growth in ICT in the early to mid-1990s (Table 11, Panel C). Indeed, ICT contributed a relatively larger share of the business sector capital stock than in most other OECD countries, with annual growth in investment of roughly 17 per cent. This added about 0.3 percentage point to output growth and amounted to half of the contribution of fixed capital formation, faring second only to the United States. However, while American investment in ICT equipment accelerated fairly sharply, it remained relatively constant in Canada. The way prices are measured in the high-technology sectors has been suggested as an underlying factor explaining diverging productivity growth. The United States uses hedonic pricing techniques for high-technology sectors, but Canada does not do so for the semi-conductor industry. Initial evidence that corrects for these differences suggests that this is only a minor factor and cannot explain the full extent of the divergence (Elridge and Sherwood, 2000).[10] Nevertheless, since the United States now includes software outlays in investment and capital stock figures, while Canada does not, this may account for some of the difference.[11]

Promising signs exist, but further progress on structural weaknesses is necessary

Whether the slowdown in labour productivity persists has important consequences for Canada's future living standards. The upsurge in machinery and equipment investment, and in particular the strong spending on computer-related equipment (see Chapter I), together with better growth prospects and improved profitability, portend a promising pick-up in productive potential. The initial impact of the introduction of new technology may have been to reduce productivity growth as old capital was scrapped, while its absorption and full exploitation may have taken time, for example requiring the introduction of product- and labour-market reforms to reap the full benefits. As from now, Canada would therefore appear to be well placed to benefit given the reforms already undertaken, as well as through its high level of economic integration with the United States. Moreover, large productivity gains in the United States came late in the business cycle when labour became relatively scarce and the same may yet hold true for Canada. Nevertheless, progress towards convergence with that country will not occur without further action to address remaining structural weaknesses. As highlighted in previous Surveys, Canada needs to implement additional reforms in a number of areas, including: further adapting labour-market and social programmes to improve work incentives; bolstering factor mobility; and rolling back and restructuring taxes. These and other important areas, including developments in product and financial markets as well as the public sector, are discussed further below.

The labour market

Strong performance at the end of the 1990s, although concerns remain

Employment growth ended the 1990s on a strong note, and prospects at the beginning of the new millennium appear bright. The unemployment rates for all groups, except youths, had fallen to the previous cyclical lows of 1989 (Figure 16), although the incidence of long-term unemployment remained about 4 percentage points above its pre-recession level (Figure 17). Moreover, the employment/ population ratio for women was significantly higher than at the last cyclical peak, while that for older workers began to rebound in the latter half of the decade and approached the level seen in 1989. At the same time, the wage gap between men and women narrowed, as did the difference in their levels of educational attainment. Overall, the amount of human capital embodied in the workforce increased substantially, which should favour productivity gains over the medium term and lead to further declines in the structural rate of unemployment.

While in the long term productivity gains are probably the most important component in raising living standards, their stagnation over the 1990s was largely due to poor employment performance. Indeed, aggregate employment/ population ratios and labour force participation rates had still not reached levels recorded in 1989, principally because of a sharp drop for youths (Figure 16). Moreover, self-employment advanced more quickly than dependent employment by a wide margin, mainly via a large rise in own-account workers, which contributed to sluggish overall employee gains (Picot and Heisz, 2000a).[12] Relatively slow output growth played an important role in these developments, and in the wake of its recent acceleration, has allowed some of them to unwind (see Chapter I). For example, employment rates for youths[13] and older workers picked up, the share of self-employed began to fall,[14] and job creation for both men and women started to converge, reflecting the rebound in manufacturing. Regional unemployment differences also narrowed but remained large, probably related to some features of the Employment Insurance system (discussed below).

The potential for GDP to grow at an even faster pace will depend to some extent on the ability of workers to supply more hours and for participation rates to pick-up. Various measures of labour market slack published by Statistics Canada suggest large potential additions (Table 13). For example, including involuntary part-time workers (indicator R7) would see it increase by about 3½ percentage points for women and 5½ points for youths. The "brain drain" of highly skilled workers to the United States has also been touted as a potentially relevant factor, reducing labour supply. While an important policy issue, its impact appears over-stated (see Box 1).

Employment insurance

Concerns over work disincentives generated by the unemployment insurance programme led to a series of reforms in the 1980s and 1990s, largely in line with OECD *Jobs Study* recommendations. The most significant change occurred in 1996 when it was renamed Employment Insurance (EI), shifted to an hours basis to allow better coverage for part-time workers and re-oriented towards insurance

Figure 16. **Employment trends**

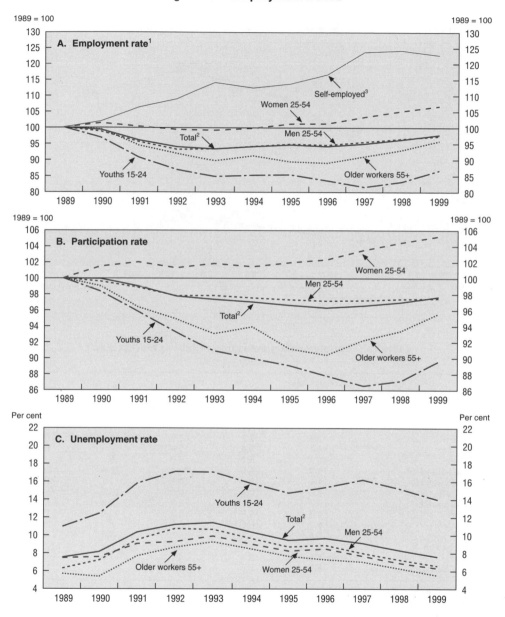

1. Employment/working-age population.
2. Age 15 and over.
3. Self-employed/total employment.
Source: Statistics Canada.

Figure 17. **Long-term unemployment**
Per cent

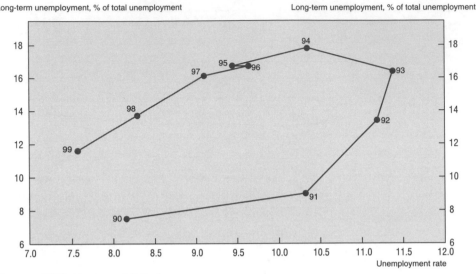

Source: OECD, *Employment Outlook.*

Table 13. **Supplementary measures of labour market slack**
1999

	Unemployment rate	R5[1]	R6[2]	R7[3]	R8[4]
Canada[5]	7.6	8.0	8.2	10.1	10.9
Men	7.8	8.2	8.5	9.2	10.4
Women	7.3	7.7	7.9	10.9	11.4
15 to 24	14.0	14.4	15.0	19.5	19.1
25 plus	6.3	6.7	6.9	8.6	9.3
Newfoundland	16.9	21.2	20.3	21.6	27.6
Prince Edward Island	14.4	14.9	16.1	17.7	19.2
Nova Scotia	9.6	10.3	10.8	13.2	14.6
New Brunswick	10.2	11.0	12.4	13.4	15.7
Quebec	9.3	9.9	10.3	12.0	13.2
Ontario	6.3	6.5	6.7	8.2	8.9
Manitoba	5.6	5.8	6.1	7.8	8.3
Saskatchewan	6.1	6.3	6.6	8.8	9.2
Alberta	5.7	5.9	6.1	7.6	8.1
British Columbia	8.3	8.6	8.8	11.7	12.0

1. Official rate plus discouraged workers.
2. Official rate plus those waiting for recall, waiting for replies and those with start dates in the future.
3. Official rate plus the underemployed (involuntary part-time workers) expressed in full-time equivalents and the underutilised portion of involuntary part-time workers.
4. Official rate plus discouraged workers; those waiting for recall, replies and future starts; and the underutilised portion of involuntary part-time workers.
5. Data refer to the age group 15 and over.
Source: Statistics Canada.

Box 1.   The brain drain

The brain drain, and its implications, are hotly debated topics in Canada, arising from claims that the country is losing its most skilled workers to the United States, with potentially negative implications for productivity and living standards.[1] It is difficult to get adequate data on which to have an informed debate, but those that have been used suggest the problem is not large. Helliwell (1999), using census statistics, finds that the proportion of university-educated Canadian citizens residing south of the border was greater in 1990 than in 1996 (6.7 vs. 6.5 per cent, respectively), although their absolute number did rise. In addition, a study by HRDC and Statistics Canada (Frank and Belair, 2000) notes that only 1½ per cent of all 1995 university graduates had moved to the United States two years later, although the figures were slightly higher for those with graduate degrees. More recent research suggests that Canada experienced a rising net outflow of skilled workers (particularly the young and highly-educated) to the United States over the 1990s in some knowledge-based occupations, including physicians, nurses, scientists and engineers (Zhao, Drew and Murray, 2000). Nevertheless, the magnitude was relatively small (less than 1 per cent of any given occupation), and these numbers also have to be placed in the context of overall net immigration. Here, Canada receives four university-educated immigrants for each person it loses.[2] In addition, the stock of university-educated individuals in Canada continues to rise sharply.

A number of factors have likely encouraged migration south of the border, particularly in some occupations. Job prospects were better in the United States over much of the 1990s; the returns to advanced education were higher (see Picot and Heisz, 2000b); and mobility probably increased as a result of NAFTA (via temporary visas, whose number is on the rise; see Nadeau et al., 1999). More robust economic prospects in Canada may therefore help to stem some of the flow. Attempting to shift policies to target potential migrants, however, may be impractical; rather the government should focus on the more general issue of ensuring that policies are consistent with raising living standards, helping to attract well-qualified immigrants, while encouraging prospective emigrants to remain in Canada.

---

1. See Nadeau et al. (1999), Frank and Belair (2000), Helliwell (1999), Schwanen (2000) and Zhao, Drew and Murray (2000) for more information.
2. Nevertheless, these immigrants may still face barriers to smooth entry into the labour market due to problems in foreign credential recognition, language difficulties and so on.

principles through: tightening eligibility requirements by making access to benefits more difficult for both new entrants and re-entrants; penalising repeat users with a partial experience-rating programme; and reducing benefit duration. Financial assistance for low-income families, however, is somewhat higher because of the family supplement (FS), which is designed to replace 80 per cent of earnings (up from 65 per cent in 1997). These individuals are also exempt from experience-rating. In addition, Canada has maintained the regional differentiation rule that eases entrance requirements and boosts benefit rates for eligible individuals in high-unemployment-rate areas (such as the Atlantic provinces). Nevertheless, taken together, these changes are estimated to have led to a marked reduction in the EI programme's disincentives (Figure 18). Furthermore, the tightening is expected to continue, since some changes would not be fully implemented until 2001, although recent policy moves, discussed below, will counteract this trend somewhat.

The federal government is obliged to monitor the impact of the reforms on recipients annually. Following their implementation, the number of EI claimants plummeted, particularly women and youths, and currently about 40 per cent of the unemployed receive benefits (Figure 18). This drop is attributed equally to

Figure 18. **Unemployment insurance indicators**

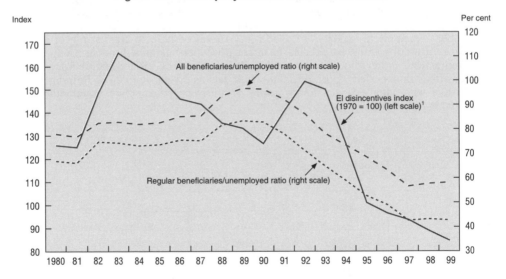

1. Taken from Sargent (1995). The index summarises the key parameters of the EI system (such as the duration of benefit receipt and replacement rate) for each region, which are then aggregated using population weights.
Source: Department of Finance, Canada; Statistics Canada.

programme changes and a different mix of unemployed (HRDC, 1998). However, of those for whom EI was intended (people who have lost or quit their job with just cause), about 80 per cent were eligible for benefits. The most recent monitoring report, which covers the period March 1998-99, portrays a mixed picture of the impact of reforms, partly because of the inherent difficulty in disentangling the role of EI changes from a number of other factors that would serve to reduce benefit receipt, including the business cycle and changing demographics. Nevertheless, three years after the reforms, the following trends have become apparent (Table 14):

- After dropping in the two years following reform, the number of new EI claims (all benefits) levelled off, as those for special benefits (sickness, maternity) rose, offsetting a small decline in regular benefits. A similar pattern was present for government outlays on EI benefits.

- The intensity rule has begun to take effect, reducing the number of frequent claims by almost 17 per cent since 1995/96, but the impact has been small.[15] Frequent claimants still received about a third of all benefit payments, almost unchanged from 1997/98, while the reduction in benefits was small, averaging about C$ 8 per week. Moreover, their average weekly payment in 1998/99 exceeded that for regular claimants by 8 per cent. This was largely due to workers in the fisheries sector where there has been little change in total benefits paid and a rise in the number of new claims since EI reforms were implemented (see Chapter IV). This reflects programme changes that made it easier to file multiple claims (for summer and winter benefits), along with the slightly longer duration of benefit receipt.

- In the area of special benefits, the most striking development has been the large increase in claims for sickness benefits, rising over 6 per cent since the introduction of reforms. They are potentially being used to extend overall benefit durations, since they are not included in the intensity rule and can be combined with regular benefits.

These findings suggest that behaviour may not have been altered substantially for frequent claimants, particularly those in the fisheries industry. Indeed, the combination of the hours-based system, the income top-up via the family supplement and the exemption from the experience-rating rule all serve to inhibit migration out of high-unemployment-rate areas.[16] Although the goal is to ensure that families with children do not face further hardship when unemployment strikes, this combination reduces the incentive to find new work outside the local area.[17] Even when the intensity rule is applied, the relatively small reduction in benefit rates may not be discouraging frequent use of the programme, particularly where few job opportunities are available (Fortin and Van Audenrode, 2000).[18]

Table 14. **Employment insurance benefit claims and payments**

	New claims[1]	Change from[2]		Amount paid	Change from[2]		Average weekly benefit	Change from[2]		Duration of benefit		
	1998/99	1997/98	1995/96	1998/99	1997/98	1995/96	1998/99	1997/98	1995/96	1998/99	1997/98	1995/96
	Millions	Per cent		C$ millions	Per cent		C$	Per cent		Weeks		
All benefits	1 835	0.1	-13.8	10 160	1.5	-14.4	283	1.9	1.8	..	..	..
Regular	1 488	-0.6	-18.4	7 754	0.5	-18.4	282	1.9	2.3	..	22	23
Fishing	26	-3.2	5.0	218	1.4	-0.4	353	-0.8	-10.3	23	23	22
Special[3]	389	4.8	2.2	1 683	4.5	3.5	..	..	..	..	..	..
Maternity	174	0.4	0.8	712	1.9	-1.2	277	0.9	-3.6	15	14	14
Parental[4]	167	1.6	-0.4	456	1.8	-0.2	286	0.9	-2.0	9	9	9
Sickness	220	8.5	6.6	508	11.0	14.9	258	2.3	1.5	9	9	9
Memorandum items:												
Frequent claimants[5]	604	-5.7	-18.4	3 419	-0.3	-16.0	305	1.2	-1.6	..	..	..
Affected by intensity rule[6]	533	67.3	..	..	..	..	289	2.0	..	..	..	..
Family supplement[7]	208	3.5	..	..	..	..	249	4.6	34.6	..	..	..

1. The number of new claims for benefits registered in the monitoring year (March 1998 to March 1999). This is not equal to the sum of the individual categories because an individual claim might include access to a number of different types of benefits (such as regular and sickness).
2. Change in the 1998/99 monitoring year compared with 1997/98, and with 1995/96 (the year prior to the reforms).
3. Special benefits include maternity, parental leave (biological and adoptive, the latter not being shown) and sickness.
4. Benefits paid to natural parents. Those paid to adoptive parents are not included.
5. Frequent claimants are individuals who have made three or more claims for regular or fishing benefits in the previous 5 years.
6. The number of frequent claimants who have had their benefit lowered because of the intensity (also referred to as the experience rating) rule.
7. The family supplement is paid to low-income households.
Source: Various monitoring reports from Human Resources Development Canada.

Against this background, the government has proposed in its latest budget an easing of the insurance principles, working against the 1996 reforms. Potentially the most troublesome change, given recent developments, is the plan to lower the number of hours of work needed to claim sickness benefits by 100 to 600. At the end of this year, the current maternity/parental-leave benefits will also be doubled to 50 weeks[19] and the qualification period reduced to the same as for sickness benefits. To encourage work attachment over this extended leave period, parents will be able to earn the greater of C$ 50 or 25 per cent of their weekly benefit rate without any penalty (currently, any additional income is deducted dollar-for-dollar from benefits). These changes are part of the government's overall plan to assist families (which is expected to benefit about 150 000 families at an annual cost of C$ 900 million), and to help parents qualify for EI parental leave benefits.

As highlighted in previous Surveys, a further tightening of some eligibility criteria appears necessary, in particular, reducing the variation in the regional differentiation rule since incentives for workers in high unemployment rate areas appear to have changed the least. Moreover, the government should avoid loosening the insurance principles enacted in 1996, which could create incentives for marginal labour force attachment, counteracting past efforts, and possibly re-instating a cycle of dependence. Where additional support is needed, it should be provided by helping workers to gain new skills and become more mobile. In this context, the work behaviour of individuals in seasonal industries and how it relates to the EI programme clearly needs further examination, which should include the reasons underlying the sharp rise in sickness benefits. Finally, the time appears ripe to introduce employer experience-rating since overall programme costs are falling and firm profitability is rising. Such a change would increase economic efficiency by encouraging employers to become more selective in how they organise their workforces, by directing their attention more closely to the effectiveness of the programme and associated active labour market (ALMPs), as well by diminishing the cross-subsidisation of industries and firms.

Active labour market programmes

Active labour market programmes were also revamped under EI reform as the authorities sought to combat structural unemployment, improve employment outcomes and emphasise accountability. At that time, they were re-organised under the broad umbrella of *Employment Benefits and Support Measures*, and funding for them was increased. Since then, the federal government has decided to further decentralise programmes to fulfil provincial commitments, and it has signed *Labour Market Development Agreements* (LMDAs) with most of the provinces and territories (except Ontario). These either transfer full authority to run programmes or involve co-management of these responsibilities. Both imply much greater provincial control over ALMPs and greater involvement of a range of actors in both formulating and carrying out policy. This should encourage more experimentation that could allow the most successful programmes to be copied throughout the country, while allowing a better tailoring of programmes to local labour market needs, although perhaps partly at the expense of increased administrative complexity.

Federal authorities spend well below the OECD average on ALMPs (Figure 19), at about 0.5 per cent of GDP.[20] The amount of resources devoted to them relative to all labour-market programme spending reached over 45 per cent in 1997-98, a record high resulting from a decision to target more resources to active programming, rather than to passive assistance, as well as more favourable labour-market conditions. The package of programmes offered to jobseekers has remained largely unchanged since EI reform, although the federal government withdrew from training activity in June 1999 as agreed with the provinces. In principle, this should allow training to be more responsive to the needs of local labour markets and jobseekers.

As labour-market conditions have improved, the Canadian authorities appropriately have begun to shift emphasis gradually from long-term adjustment measures to those of a short-term nature. Thus, in 1998/99, about 43 per cent of

Figure 19. **Active labour market programme expenditures**
1998 or nearest year available

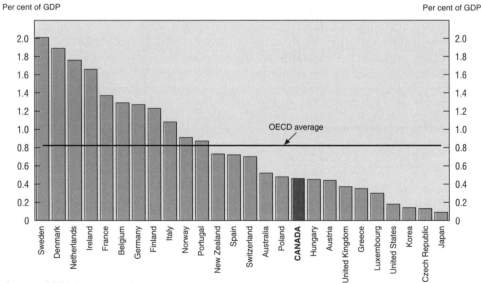

Source: OECD Database on labour market programmes.

clients received training, wage subsidies, self-employment assistance or participated in a job-creation programme compared with roughly 46 per cent in the previous year (Table 15). Training was by far the favourite long-term programme to
which jobseekers were channelled, but its persistently widespread use in a period
when labour-market conditions were improving is questionable. Indeed, with the
labour market remaining robust in 2000, much greater use of short-term interventions should be made, with public employment service staff encouraging jobseekers to take advantage of Canada's technologically advanced jobsearch tools:
jobseekers are able to search on the internet for jobs across the country as well as
accessing many information sources on jobsearch techniques. For those requiring
intensive assistance, wage subsidies should be even more widely employed since
participants can benefit from on-the-job training. The use of job-creation
programmes (about 4½ per cent of long-term interventions) should be reduced,
since international evidence (OECD, 1996a) suggests that they have a negligible
impact on raising earnings or employment prospects. This would free up additional funds (since wage subsidies are, on average, less costly) for more intensive
counselling of the most disadvantaged, such as high-school drop-outs, where
training can still be used as an option.

In the area of evaluation, Canada is to be commended for its efforts as
compared with other OECD countries. Impact evaluations[21] have been conducted
for many of the large programmes, while potential changes are usually piloted in a
number of regions before being introduced nationally. The authorities have now
turned to evaluation of the Labour Market Development Agreements, beginning
with an assessment of how they are working. Results from the first set of

Table 15.   **Active labour market programme participants[1]**

	1997/98	Per cent of total	1998/99	Per cent of total
Long-term interventions				
Wage subsidies	15 181	3.2	30 629	4.9
Self-employment	15 105	3.2	16 908	2.7
Job creation	21 468	4.5	28 990	4.7
Training	166 095	34.9	189 563	30.5
Total long-term	217 849	45.8	266 090	42.8
Short-term interventions				
Employment assistance	72 913	15.3	194 314	31.3
Counselling and other	184 819	38.9	160 708	25.9
Total short-term	257 732	54.2	355 022	57.2
Total interventions	475 581	100	621 112	100

1. Federal government programmes only.
Source: Various monitoring reports from Human Resources Development Canada.

© OECD 2000

provinces[22] suggest that, overall, they are meeting the goal of providing decentra-lised services effectively with high degree of client satisfaction (HRDC, 1999). Nevertheless, some important problems were identified, for example: lack of con-sistency of programme interventions across local areas; some overlap and duplica-tion of procedures, creating unnecessary costs; and deficiencies in data collection, stemming from confusion over responsibilities, inadequate computer systems and other factors. While some of these reflect growing pains and should diminish over time, the issue of data collection needs to be urgently addressed to ensure that monitoring results can be interpreted with full confidence, and so that resources can be adjusted accordingly. A number of performance targets are tracked, which also suggest that programmes are focussed on their targeted groups, although there are indications of "creaming" (assisting the easiest to place).[23] As targets are not binding, resources are not tied to meeting them, although in principle an LMDA could be renegotiated at some point. Linking funding to targets should be considered to improve programme functioning and data collection. In addition, moving forward quickly on an LMDA impact evaluation, as well as systematic eval-uation of all ALMPs, is essential to help tailor programmes to the evolving state of the labour market.

The need for several complementary evaluation instruments is high-lighted by the recent controversy surrounding the now-defunct Transitional Jobs Fund. An initial evaluation report of the programme was mostly positive (HRDC, 1998), indicating that a large share of jobs created were incremental (that is, new). But a more recent random audit of projects casts doubt on its overall effective-ness. In particular, it found many lapses, including inadequate supervision and poor financial monitoring of many projects. The Ministry has implemented staff training programmes to deal with these issues, but these problems highlight the difficulties in monitoring decentralised projects carried out with external partners (see below).

Social assistance and benefits targeted at families with children

Social assistance benefits have been cut in many provinces, as they sought to improve work incentives and link assistance to conditions in the labour market, while respecting a cap on payments imposed by the general situation of public finances (OECD, 1999a). This policy context, along with improved job prospects, led to a substantial decline in caseloads (Figure 20), although there has been a notable rise in disability claimants, suggesting that at least some of the caseload has been shifted to this benefit to avoid the more stringent welfare measures. In addition, there was also a large increase in the number of children living in poverty[24] over the 1990s, leading to new policy initiatives, particularly the National Child Benefit, discussed below.

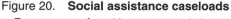

Figure 20. **Social assistance caseloads**
Percentage of working-age population

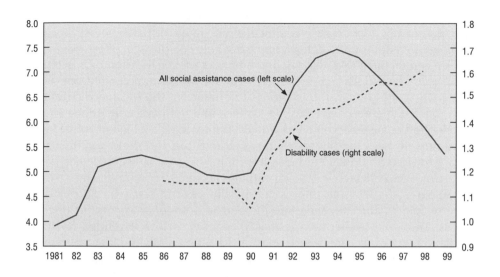

Source: Human Resources Development Canada; Statistics Canada.

The main tax expenditure programme for families with children (and incomes up to C$ 66 721 in the first half of 2000) is the federal Canada Child Tax Benefit (CCTB), which was enriched again in the recent budget (see below). In addition, the National Child Benefit (NCB) supplement was designed in co-operation with the provinces and implemented in 1998 (replacing the Working Income Supplement). Supplementing the CCTB, it is specifically targeted at low-income families with children, that is, those with incomes below C$ 27 750 in 1999 (to be raised to C$ 30 004 in July 2000), and its goal is to alleviate poverty and increase labour force attachment of families. In the first half of 2000, the combination of these benefits amounted to C$ 3 410 for a family with two children (rising to C$ 3 956 in July 2000). An underlying intention of the NCB initiative is that provinces could reduce assistance levels to families with children by the value of the NCB supplement received (thus keeping benefit levels unchanged) and re-invest the surplus funds in additional services and benefits for low-income families with children. Provinces have taken different approaches on how to use the surplus funds within the range of acceptable NCB reinvestments. New Brunswick, for instance allowed social assistance recipients to receive higher benefits. Provinces are also using them (plus additional funds) to create or enhance other income supplements, or invest in services such as day care and supplementary health-care benefits. Ontario, for example, offers a Child Care Supplement on top of the NCB for low-income working families with children under seven years.

One danger with this complex and cascading set of benefits is that they can create potentially high marginal effective tax rates (METRs), even if carefully co-ordinated (in addition to being administratively complex). In effect, once income reaches a certain threshold, the amount of benefit paid is reduced by some fraction for each additional dollar earned. This creates a well-known conundrum: benefits need to be taxed back in the low-to-middle range of the income distribution to remain tightly targeted on low-income families and not have deleterious effects on the work effort of higher-income individuals, but in doing so, high marginal tax rates and barriers to seek additional earnings above the threshold can be created. Canada's concerted efforts to reduce rates for low-income households has left them equal or lower in 2000 than in 1996 for earnings up to C$ 21 500 and higher thereafter up to about C$ 35 000. But, they still typically peak at just over 80 per cent for welfare recipients and may therefore discourage additional work effort (Figure 21, Panel A). The loss of other non-pecuniary benefits such as extended health care, subsidised rent or day care, where relevant, also raises METRs. In many provinces, these supplemental benefits have been extended to all low-income workers to ensure that, in addition to equity considerations, they do not create the incentive for people already in work to go onto welfare.

Recent budget developments should see METRs ease with the reduction of tax rates and with the re-indexing of the tax system and benefits (Figure 21, Panel B). Plans to increase the threshold at which the CCTB and NCB are taxed back will also help in this regard: the CCTB will begin its phase-out, and the NCB clawback will be completed, by the second tax-bracket threshold. Given all of these changes, it is important that the authorities carefully assess (either as part of the NCB evaluation underway, or separately):[25] *first*, the coherence of social assistance benefits, including the interaction between federal and provincial programmes to ensure that METRs do not rise, and, in fact, are lowered where possible, given their high level; *second*, the impact of the withdrawal of both financial and non-financial assistance on work behaviour around threshold points; and *third*, whether it is possible to simplify or streamline the large number of income-based tax programmes targeted at low-income individuals. *Finally*, more research needs to be conducted to ensure that the rising disability caseload is not a result of attempting to avoid more stringent welfare measures. This raises the more general issue of coherence between labour-market and social policies to ensure that changes in one area do not have unintended consequences in another.

Labour force skills and competences

Canada's record in educating its youth stands out among OECD countries. In 1996, for example, 48 per cent of its population had a post-secondary

Figure 21. **Marginal effective tax rates**

Ontario. One earner couple with two children receiving social assistance
Per cent

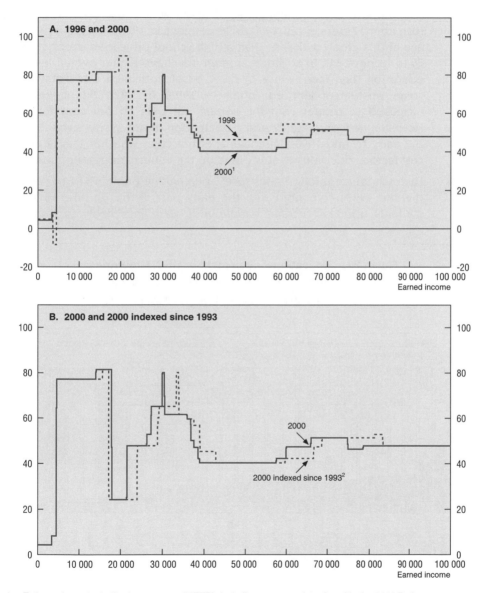

1. Estimated marginal effective tax rates (METR), including measures introduced in the 2000 Budget.
2. This shows how METRs would have evolved had the tax system been fully indexed to inflation since 1993.
Source: Department of Finance, Canada.

education, more than double the OECD average of 23 per cent, and 14 percentage points higher than the United States (Figure 22). A new set of pan-Canadian Indicators developed by federal and provincial authorities, released in early 2000, takes stock of outcomes from the education system, revealing:

- The proportion of Canadians aged 25-29 with a university education rose from 17 per cent in 1990 to 26 per cent in 1998, while the percentage of this group with less than a high school education dropped from 20 to 13 per cent. In addition, women now have higher overall levels of education than men: while 44 per cent of both men and women had some post-secondary education in 1990, in 1998 this figure had increased to 61 per cent for women but only 55 per cent for men. However, new enrolments and participation in university levelled off in the early to mid-1990s, although it is not clear whether this is due to cost factors, decisions to study outside the country or other reasons.

- High school completion rates rose 2 percentage points to 81 per cent in the late 1990s compared with the early part of the decade. However, students from low-income backgrounds were less likely to complete

Figure 22.   **Educational attainment in OECD countries**

Percentage of the population 25 to 64 years of age

that has attained a specific highest level of education (1996)[1]

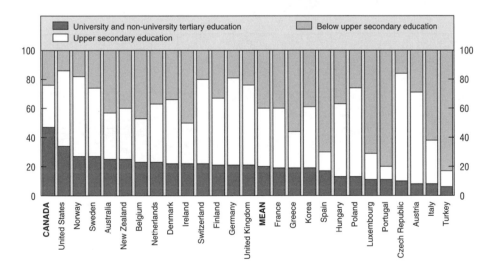

1.   Countries are ranked by proportion of the population attaining educational levels of university and non-university tertiary education.
Source: OECD, *Education at a Glance*, 1998.

secondary education (34 per cent dropout rate) and also had the lowest increase in university participation. Men, in general, were not only less likely to complete advanced education, but their dropout rates from secondary school were also higher.

- About two-thirds of 1995 post-secondary graduates were employed full-time in 1997, compared with three-quarters of those a similar period following graduation in 1986. Moreover, earnings of 1995 graduates were 4 to 6 per cent lower (in constant 1997 dollars). In addition, the financial burden on students increased, partly as a result of rising tuition fees which have almost doubled on average. This has led to rising student debt loads and might be one reason why youths from low-income families have been less likely to participate in tertiary education.

- Adult participation in formal education dropped slightly in the 1990s, with about 27 per cent of adults participating in job-related adult education and training in 1997, down from 29 per cent in 1991. It is unclear whether this reflects more informal training channels such as computer-based learning.

On the one hand, developments over the 1990s were positive as a whole, with educational attainment continuing to rise. On the other, they raise the possibility of a group of individuals who do not complete secondary school, or who do not advance to tertiary education, that are at risk of being unable to meet the demands of current and future labour-market needs. More research is therefore required to determine: the reasons underlying the still high dropout rates from secondary school (more individuals have not completed secondary school than the United States, for example); the impact of rising educational expenses on access to tertiary education and how government assistance (such as Canada Millennium Scholarships) is addressing this need, particularly for students from low-income families; the extent of informal training in the workforce and how it links to strategies to promote lifelong learning; and finally, the reasons underlying the relative decline in the performance of male youths. Any evaluation should consider the impact of educational reforms introduced over the past decade, such as the increased emphasis on "back to basics". In general, the relatively high level of spending (Figure 23) suggests that the authorities should first examine existing expenditures, with a view to improving their quality, before embarking on any increases.

Product markets

International and internal trade

Further trade liberalisation, both domestic and international, has been an important element of the Canadian agenda to secure and improve market access

Figure 23. **Educational expenditures**[1]
1997, percentage of GDP

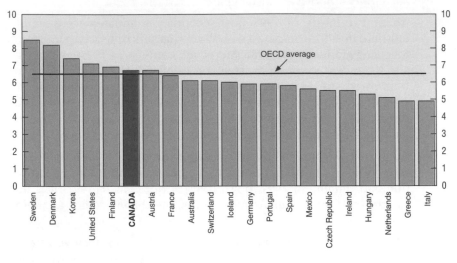

1. Public and private.
Source: OECD, *Education at a Glance*, 2000.

and to enhance competitiveness of Canadian goods and services. On the international front, this led to the signing of free trade deals with the United States (Free Trade Agreement), later extended to Mexico under NAFTA, and subsequent agreements with Chile and Israel. In spring 1998, Canada joined 33 other countries in beginning negotiations of a *Free Trade Area of the Americas*. In late 1998, Canada then launched negotiations to complete a Free Trade Agreement with EFTA countries (Norway, Switzerland, Iceland and Liechtenstein) by mid-2000. In addition, Canada has begun discussions on the possibility of a bilateral free trade agreement with Costa Rica and Singapore.

Several important WTO panel decisions and agreements came to the forefront in 1999 and early 2000. Although the large number (14 over the April 1999-March 2000 period) may give the appearance of increased trade tensions, they rather reflect the resolution, or subsequent panel decisions, of several outstanding issues, most following years of consultation and consideration, consistent with Canada's commitment to the multilateral process. One on-going trade issue involving Canada and Brazil has centred around the use of export subsidies on regional aircraft. A WTO panel ruled that Brazil's Proex programme provided illegal financial assistance to foreign buyers of aircraft and ordered its cessation, which that country has yet to agree to,[26] raising the prospect of retaliatory sanctions.

Indeed, Canada has asked for WTO approval to implement almost C$ 5 billion in trade sanctions over a seven-year period. The panel also ruled that incentives offered via Canada's Technology Partnerships Programme (TPC) for regional aircraft, and the Export Development Corporation's Canada Account debt financing programme, amounted to financial assistance that was not consistent with its trade obligations. The WTO has since found that Canada has adjusted the TPC to render the programme WTO-consistent. Canada is also finalising changes to the Canada Account to ensure it is in accordance with WTO recommendations. In the area of patent protection, both the United States and the EU had launched separate complaints regarding Canada's practices, with the United States focussing on the term of protection, arguing that the 17-year protection provided to patents issued prior to 1989 should be extended to the standard 20-year term. A WTO panel agreed with the American claim, a decision which Canada has appealed. The EU has also argued that Canada does not meet the minimum WTO standards for patent protection related to pharmaceuticals, by allowing manufacturers to begin the process of seeking regulatory approval for competing (generic) versions of the patented product prior to the expiration of the patent term, and then stockpiling the drugs to allow them to come on the market quickly. The WTO panel ruled in Canada's favour on the first question, but against it on the second (Canada is currently deciding whether to appeal).

Potentially, one of the most important decisions concerns the Canada-USA Auto Pact, which a WTO panel ruled in early 2000 to be inconsistent with Canada's trade obligations, arguing that the 6.1 per cent duty exemption for certain automobile manufacturers that meet minimum commitments on local production and value-added content was a violation of the most-favoured-nation and national treatment obligations.[27] Canada appealed this ruling in March 2000 and on 31 May, the WTO Appellate Body confirmed that the Auto Pact measures were inconsistent with its WTO obligations under GATT and the Agreement on Subsidies and Countervailing Measures. Canada has agreed to implement this decision, which it should do by removing tariffs on all imports of automobiles and parts although the issue before the WTO was the exemption rather than the tariff applied. The automotive sector is an integral part of the Canadian economy (accounting for about 13 per cent of manufacturing GDP and 160 000 jobs in 1999, or roughly 1 per cent of employment), raising fears that liberalisation could damage the industry substantially. This is highly unlikely. Sizeable capital outlays have contributed to productivity gains, helping Canada to gain market share. It takes fewer hours for the three main manufacturers to produce vehicles in Canada, and fewer persons per vehicle compared with both the United States and Mexico (Stanford, 2000). Relative unit labour costs are lower, driven partly by favourable exchange-rate movements and smaller health-care premiums, each of which has contributed to the investment boom (Stanford, 2000). There may, of course, be compositional affects, as some foreign manufacturers make inroads into the market, particularly for smaller cars. The macroeconomic consequences are more speculative (Brean *et al.*, 1999), but consumer welfare would be raised if the duty were abolished. The magnitude of the impact would depend to some extent on how much competition would be increased and on how tastes might evolve, among other things. The authorities have indicated that, while being committed to further tariff reductions, they have decided against unilateral action.

On the domestic front, progress in fulfilling provisions under the *Agreement on Internal Trade* (AIT) (see Annex I for a complete listing) is extremely slow (for example as compared with Free Trade Agreement/NAFTA; see OECD, 1998), with little change in the last two years in most areas. As regards labour mobility, however, and under the *Social Union Framework Agreement* (SUFA), mutual recognition agreements (MRAs) are in the process of being negotiated for occupations to remove barriers to mobility. Over 20 professions have developed draft MRAs (such as nurses, teachers and engineers); all professions are supposed to have completed them by 1 July 2001. Much swifter progress will be necessary if all 60 professional bodies are to meet this deadline. It is difficult to overstate the importance of not only completing but moving beyond the AIT/SUFA targets to liberalise internal trade. This would allow the country to reap the additional gains arising from further competition and improved factor mobility, complementing moves on the international front.

Agriculture

Over the last decade, Canada has improved the market orientation of policies in the agricultural sector and reduced the level of financial support. Nevertheless, the steep decline in some commodity prices (namely of cereals and oilseeds) led to the introduction of the *Agricultural Income Disaster Assistance Programme* (AIDA) in December 1998, a two-year income stabilisation programme for adversely affected farmers, along with extra funding for crop insurance. These are underlying reasons behind the almost 50 per cent increase in programme spending for agriculture (to C$ 950 million) between April 1999 and March 2000. The total amount of support provided to the sector therefore increased 10 per cent in 1998 and a further 2 per cent in 1999 (to 0.8 per cent of GDP), arresting a decade-long decline. As a percentage of the value of production, assistance amounted to about 20 per cent in 1999, down from the 34 per cent recorded in 1986-88 but up substantially from the 14 per cent provided in 1997. This is about half the OECD average and below the 24 per cent provided in the United States, but its provision may adversely affect production decisions, since it could lead farmers to expect that they will receive additional assistance whenever income falls. The dairy sector is the most heavily subsidised (accounting for 40 per cent of support), and no fundamental changes have been made to its supply-management system. Substantially more reform is necessary in increasing the market orientation of this sector. Some changes will be required as a result of a recent WTO panel ruling, which found that the practice of providing milk at lower prices to processors contingent on their use in exports effectively constituted an export subsidy. Canada is currently developing a new dairy export pricing system.

Electricity

Significant changes are underway to create a fully competitive electricity sector in Ontario, to be in place by November 2000. This should boost productivity and set an example for other provinces to follow. In April 1999, Ontario Hydro was split into two new companies: Ontario Power Generation (OPG) and the Ontario Hydro Services Company (OHSC).[28] The former owns and operates the generation facilities and sells electricity to industries and municipal utilities, while OHSC runs the transmission, distribution and retail business. In addition, two not-for-profit corporations have been established: an Independent Electricity Market Operator, which monitors the wholesale electricity market and ensures fair access to the transmission system; and an Electrical Safety Authority to install and inspect electrical equipment. A fifth body, the reconstituted Ontario Energy Board, is responsible for approving all rates for transmission and distribution and ensuring a level playing field with private operators once competition begins. A recent review of energy policies in Canada by the International Energy Agency (OECD, 2000c) suggests further scope for action in the electricity sector, including: addressing the overlapping roles of multiple regulators in an increasingly integrated North American market; promoting interprovincial (and international) sales of electricity; and encouraging further market-related reforms (in most other provinces little action has been taken).

Air and rail travel

Significant consolidation took place in the airline industry in early 2000 when Air Canada acquired Canadian Airlines Corporation. The resulting boost in concentration led the government to introduce new legislation to protect consumers. The Canadian Transportation Agency was given additional powers to limit price gouging behaviour, which if proven, could see Air Canada officials face a five-year jail term, a C$ 10 million fine or both. As required by the government, Air Canada has disposed of some airport slots and facilities (such as loading bridges and gates), will endeavour to sell its share in Canadian Regional Airlines Limited and will refrain from establishing its own discount airline until September 2001, allowing other companies to enter, or expand, operations on both the international and domestic fronts. One troubling aspect of the merger process concerns the government's decision to exempt it from the usual application of the Competition Act. The Act allows mergers to take place even when they lower competition if offsetting efficiency gains result, which would appear to have been the case. While concern over protecting the public interests was a factor underlying the exception, overriding the Act can undermine private-sector confidence that mergers will be assessed on clearly identified grounds.

In the area of rail freight service, in December 1999 Canadian National Railways (CN) announced plans to merge with Burlington Northern Sante Fe Rail (BNSF), linking together 50 000 route miles of freight track. American regulators, however, put a 15-month moratorium on rail mergers, citing the need to rewrite legislation in the area in the face of prospective consolidation, which could delay it until early 2002. CN-BNSF has appealed this decision, on the grounds that it is against their statutory right to a prompt and fair hearing, and that it is not in the public interest.[29] As regards rail passenger service, the government announced that it would inject close to C$ 400 million dollars over the next five years into VIA Rail for fleet renewal. The authorities have been of two minds on whether to privatise this crown corporation, something that should still be considered after the rolling stock is upgraded.

Telecoms, internet and e-commerce

Canada would appear to be favourably positioned to take advantage of internet applications such as electronic commerce (e-commerce). Household penetration of PCs and secure webservers for electronic commerce are among the highest in the world, while internet access costs are among the lowest. The government also recently launched its first internet spectrum auction to allocate 260 licenses to 12 companies in the 24 and 38 GHz frequency bands. This will increase broadband communication services in all areas of the country, ensuring access to high-speed internet and electronic commerce applications. Latest estimates place the value of business-to-business (B2B) e-commerce at C$ 4.5 billion in 1998, growing almost 200 per cent from the previous year, while business-to-consumer (B2C) purchases amounted to about C$ 688 million, or about 0.3 per cent of total retail spending (Retail Council of Canada, 1999). E-commerce spending is expected to more than quadruple by 2003. But these amounts pale in comparison with spending in the United States. Moreover, only about 10 per cent of internet users made on-line purchases in Canada, while the comparable figure in the United States was about 40 per cent, despite Canada's higher penetration of internet use.

The extent to which e-commerce will deliver efficiency gains remains unclear, given the rapid pace at which the underlying technology is changing and the uncertain nature of responses by both consumers and businesses. Nevertheless, barriers that could limit its expansion should be relaxed. A recent panel report that studied this issue highlights a number of obstacles (Boston Consulting Group, 2000). In particular the small size of the domestic market, an apparent limited desire by business to seize opportunities in the area, bottlenecks in the initial public offering (IPO) process and tax issues are all projected to see Canada lag behind the United States, particularly in B2B commerce. Clearly, some of these may dissipate over time, but the panel argues for changes to rules governing IPOs, reductions in capital gains taxes and deferrals of the liability stemming from the roll-over of funds into other investments, changes to escrow rules and to the treatment of the tax liability arising from exercising employee stock options to boost investment in the sector.

The latest Budget addresses two of these demands: tax liabilities arising from stock options will be deferred if less than C$ 100 000 annually, as will capital gains on investments of up to C$ 500 000 rolled over into new small firms. This, combined with a reduction in the capital gains inclusion rate (see below) should provide small firms with easier access to start-up capital. In addition, provincial regulators plan to change escrow rules, shortening the period when initial investors can cash in stocks after an IPO, that should boost access to start-up capital (the period will vary with firm size). Currently, the wait can be as long as six years, compared with only six months in the United States, and that may have persuaded some owners to take their companies public in that country. Another important source of early start-up funds is the venture capital market. While growing at a relatively rapid pace, it remains proportionally smaller than the United States and is dominated by labour-sponsored or government funds, which are not permitted to take large ownership stakes (which fund managers usually require to compensate them for their risk).

E-commerce has raised a host of emerging taxation issues. Primary among them are how to tax the online transmission of digital products and services to minimise market distortions as trade expands, and how to minimise the erosion of the income tax base. Canada is addressing these challenges through the OECD-led process based on the foundation of the 1998 Ottawa Taxation Framework Conditions. Currently, over 60 per cent of Canadian on-line purchases are from companies in the United States (Retail Council of Canada, 1999), but this may change as Canadian retailers take up this challenge. Nevertheless, Canada should ensure that it continues to tax e-commerce sales so that a level playing field exists among all retailers, avoiding the risk of tax-driven distortions in competition. An advisory committee on electronic commerce and tax administration has offered the federal government a detailed set of over 200 recommendations on how to deal with e-commerce tax issues (Ministry of National Revenue, 1998). It acknowledged that neither more onerous reporting requirements nor additional taxes would be conducive to helping the sector develop and could place Canadian firms at a disadvantage. Indeed, it notes that encouraging greater e-commerce within Canada's borders is the best way to ensure a vibrant tax base. The government is consulting with business on how to improve compliance and has set up four technical advisory groups on electronic commerce to provide expert advice on how to implement the Committee's recommendations. These groups should act quickly (in co-ordination with the OECD process), given the prospective development of the sector and the need to ensure a level playing field among all types of business.

New initiatives to boost productive capacity and innovation

The federal government also announced in its 2000-01 budget a series of spending measures to bolster productive capacity and innovation. The larger outlays included an additional C$ 900 million for the Canada Foundation for Innovation[30] to create 2 000 Canada Research Chairs in degree-granting institutions; a C$ 160 million grant to create five research centres for genomic science to ensure that Canada is well equipped in the field of biotechnology; C$ 160 million to get the government "on-line" with the hopes of stimulating electronic commerce; and expenditures of C$ 300 million in 2000 to improve infrastructure throughout the country.[31] Some measures may lead to positive externalities, while spending may be required in others that had suffered during the period of fiscal retrenchment (such as infrastructure). The links between many of the initiatives and their potential to boost productive capacity, however, are not clear. Given that the benefits of such discretionary spending measures are not always apparent, the government should ensure that both their implementation and impacts (including cost-benefit analysis where relevant), are carefully monitored in order to develop a list of "what works", so as to target future expenditures more efficiently. Along these lines, the Auditor General has recently recommended more rigorous evaluation of Canada's generous R&D tax-incentive programme (see above), in addition to noting that clearer rules on what constitutes an eligible project are necessary, as well as quicker resolution of claims. By generating investor uncertainty, problems in these areas may help, albeit probably only to a small extent, to explain why the take-up of the incentives is low by international standards.

Financial markets

Financial markets are another area undergoing extensive change, following several major reforms over the last two decades, as successive governments have sought to foster greater competition, while ensuring the safety and soundness of the financial system. Against this background, the current government initiated a review of the regulatory and supervisory framework, and based on the resulting MacKay Task Force report (with some 124 recommendations for reform; see OECD, 1999b), it tabled a proposed new policy framework package in June 1999. New legislation has been put before Parliament that would see sweeping changes to promote efficiency and competition, protect and empower consumers and improve the regulatory and supervisory framework. The main thrust of these proposals is to increase the flexibility of banking and financial services institutions to adapt to changing market trends, while expanding the scope for competition, and, at the same time, strengthening consumer protection.

The new framework

Annex II.A outlines the proposed framework in detail, but four areas in particular are noteworthy in the drive towards enhanced competition. First, the package includes a revamped size-based bank structure with revised "widely-held" rules to facilitate strategic alliances and joint ventures. Currently, banks are registered as either widely held, with an individual ownership limit of 10 per cent of any class of shares, or closely held, owned by eligible Canadian or foreign financial institutions. The proposals would see banks divided into three categories, depending on their equity base: large banks with equity in excess of C$ 5 billion that should be widely held with no single investor holding more than 20 per cent of voting shares (and 30 per cent of non-voting shares); medium-sized banks between C$ 1 and C$ 5 billion, which could be closely held (but are subject to a 35 per cent public float requirement of voting shares); and small banks (less than C$ 1 billion in equity) that would have no ownership restrictions (other than the standard "fit and proper" test). This new framework, together with a lowering in the capital requirement from C$ 10 to C$ 5 million, are designed to facilitate entry. Second, there would be a new holding company regime to provide greater structural flexibility, permitting banks to organise under a regulated, non-operating holding company whose affiliates may include other financial institutions and financial service companies. This option would enable a bank to achieve economies of scale and scope without having to merge or enter into a parent-subsidiary relationship with a specific institution. The bank would remain tightly regulated, but other structures would face a "light-handed" approach with capital adequacy imposed at the consolidated level. Third, the reform would attempt to create a strong second tier in retail banking. Structural fragmentation of the credit union system has been identified as a potential barrier to the expansion of local credit unions. The credit union movement has proposed an initiative to restructure their system and overcome these obstacles. The government will accommodate these suggestions with legislation to allow them to take on a national presence, should they wish. Finally, there are plans to open up the Canadian Payments Association, which provides federally and provincially regulated deposit-taking institutions with exclusive access to various payments systems. This will be broadened to include life insurance companies, securities dealers and money market mutual funds.

The Task Force acknowledges that strong competition, though a vital element in ensuring that consumers are well served, is not sufficient to create a balanced market place for consumers. The government, therefore, also proposes to strengthen their rights (with the help of a new federal agency, the Financial Consumer Agency of Canada), and to improve transparency and disclosure requirements, thus the functioning of the market place via consumers who are more informed and vigilant. Financing small and medium-sized enterprises

(SMEs) draws special attention. To provide more comprehensive information on the financing needs of SMEs and the supply of financing available to them, the government will give Statistics Canada the mandate to collect and publish data on the supply of debt and equity financing to SMEs, building upon the existing banking data of the Canadian Bankers Association to include all types and suppliers of SME financing.

In the meantime, some reforms have already taken place. *First*, the demutualisation process of life insurance companies began in March 1999. The resulting conversion to stock ownership provides these firms with access to capital markets to expand their investment scope, while also imposing market discipline upon their operations through better understood corporate governance, which can lead to greater competition and efficiency gains. Five companies[32] have already demutualised, leaving only a few small firms that intend to retain their mutual status for the time being. *Second*, legislation was passed in June 1999 allowing foreign banks to offer a full range of services via branches rather than as separate, fully regulated banking subsidiaries.[33] Not only does this new legislation finally put Canada on a par with many other OECD countries, it should also help promote competition in the sector and increase the variety of financial services and products offered to consumers, in addition to tapping new sources of capital. Indeed, two major foreign banks – Chase Manhattan and J.P. Morgan – have received regulatory approval to commence business as branches, and 10 more have applied to expand their corporate loan business in Canada. *Third*, Canadian exchanges recently underwent a major realignment of their responsibilities. The Toronto Stock Exchange is now the sole senior equity market in Canada, and the Montreal Exchange has assumed responsibility for all derivatives trading, while maintaining the listing of some small Quebec-based firms. The Canadian Venture Exchange (CDNX), created through a merger of the Vancouver and Alberta stock exchanges, is now Canada's main junior equity market. Both the Canadian Dealing Network, a dealer-driven over-the-counter market geared towards small firms, and the Winnipeg Stock Exchange have agreed to consolidate with the CDNX. Another recent development has been the announcement of Nasdaq's establishment in Canada. This consolidation will increase the critical mass and liquidity of each market, enhancing the ability of firms to access capital at favourable rates. *Finally*, despite addressing some areas highlighted by the Technical Committee on Business Taxation, one where there is unfinished business is capital taxes imposed on large (but not other) banks, which distorts the playing field in the sector. Further reductions, and ultimately their elimination, would be appropriate.

Supervision and regulation

In August 1999, the government introduced a new supervisory framework for federally regulated financial institutions[34] to address increasingly complex activities, enhanced structural flexibility, innovative products and globalisation. This framework provides the main supervisory body in the field, the Office of the Superintendent of Financial Institutions (OSFI), with a model whose focal point is to evaluate, and rate, the net risk for each significant activity of the institution based on the aggregate level of inherent risk stemming from their operations offset by the overall quality of risk management (see Annex II.B). Key components of this model are its flexibility and forward-looking elements, which are thought to be sufficient to balance safety and soundness against further competition and innovation.

Financial institutions must deal with a number of regulators. In addition to OSFI, the insurer of deposits of federally chartered banks, the Canada Deposit Insurance Corporation (CDIC), plays an important supervisory role by compelling banks to complete an annual self-assessment of their compliance to its *Standards of Sound Business and Financial Practices* (see Annex II.B). Full responsibility rests with the senior officers and the board of directors of each CDIC member institution, and the CDIC is currently consulting with its members on a proposal to update and streamline these Standards. Provincial authorities are also involved, supervising securities markets, deposit-taking institutions and insurance companies that operate within their borders. Thus, federally regulated institutions that operate in each area on a national basis may well face over 30 regulatory bodies and the reporting requirements that go along with them.[35] This has a number of associated drawbacks, such as elevating compliance costs, hindering the quick and timely sharing of information that is increasingly necessary for adequate supervision, and creating situations where similar products are regulated in different ways, thus confusing consumers and potentially raising costs to them. Against this background, the Canadian Securities Administrators (CSA)[36] have put forward a proposal to harmonise and realign regulatory responsibilities, reflecting the fact that stock exchanges, formerly confined within the boundaries of a single province, are now operating nationally. The CSA would like to create a web of formal and informal agreements between themselves to serve as a co-ordinated structure for the supervision of market activities across the country, in essence creating a national securities system. However, the effect of this structure may not be the same as having a unified market regulator.

Outlook

The goals underlying the new framework are commendable and should lead to deeper and more liquid financial markets, which will benefit all participants. It is imperative, therefore, that the authorities move quickly to pass the requisite legislation so that investment decisions can be made in a more certain environment. Nevertheless, the scope for increased competition seems limited in the retail market, given the dominance of the large banks, although potential exists for new players to make inroads in niche and corporate markets. Some challenges for regulators will undoubtedly arise: for example, the proposed holding-company structure would see stronger links between traditional banking and commercial activities, and with a light-handed regulatory approach planned for non-bank affiliates, cross-lending among companies would have to be carefully monitored since financial troubles of one entity could have spillover effects on the banking sector. In addition, the potential for self-dealing is also raised, requiring vigilant supervision.[37] Corporate governance rules would, of course, play a central role. The pending legislation proposes increased oversight of related party trans-actions, but a competitive marketplace, along with appropriate disclosure require-ments, will also play a complementary role in strengthening internal control.

The prospect of further competition raises the likelihood of bank failures. The new framework offers additional and enhanced powers to OSFI to maintain safety and soundness in an environment of more vigorous competition. While flexibility is necessary, transparent rules could promote stability in the event of any closure. Meanwhile, a sensitive issue continues to be the approval process for large bank mergers. Under the proposed framework, large banks will be required to produce a *Public Interest Impact Assessment* to outline all the costs and benefits associated with a merger, which would then be examined by the Minister of Finance in conjunction with rulings by the Competition Bureau and OSFI (which would examine competition and prudential implications, respectively). Finally, the move to create harmonised supervisory standards is welcome, and efforts should be continued to reduce duplication and complexity and to regulate com-parable products and services in a similar manner. Nevertheless, it is important that OSFI, and other regulatory bodies, continue to be adequately staffed and resourced, commensurate with the new challenges that they are likely to face.

Public sector

Tax policy

Emerging budget surpluses have led to renewed pressure for increased public spending, as well as to calls to further reduce taxes and lower the public debt. Previous Surveys have suggested a priority list for the use of the "fiscal dividend", recommending cuts in Canada's debt load (see Chapter II), followed by tax relief, particularly in the areas of personal and corporate income taxes, and re-indexation of the tax system, before any spending initiatives are taken. The 1999-2000 Budget had introduced small reductions in personal income taxes (see OECD, 1999b). The 2000-01 Budget further augmented these cuts and announced for the first time a five-year tax reduction plan that sets targets through to the year 2004-05 and envisages relief reaching about C$ 22 billion in the final year (including Employment Insurance reductions) (see Table 16 and Chapter II).

Table 16. **Main features of the federal five-year tax reduction plan**

Tax measure	Introduced in 2000	Introduced by 2004	Amount of annual tax relief in 2004-05 (C$ millions)
Indexation of tax system	Effective 1 January.		6 215
Middle tax rate and tax thresholds	Reduced from 26 to 24 per cent, as from 1 July.	Reduce to 23 per cent.	3 600
		Increase the level of income at which the middle tax rate applies from C$ 29 590 to at least C$ 35 000.	2 940
		Increase tax-free income exemption to C$ 8 000 from the current C$ 7 131.	2 760
		Increase the income at which the top tax rate begins to be applied from C$ 59 180 to at least C$ 70 000.	730
Five per cent surcharge.	As of 1 July, applies to incomes above C$ 85 000 (previously, C$ 65 000).	On 1 July 2001 lower to 4 per cent on incomes above C$ 85 000 and eliminate by 2004.	865
Canada Child Tax Benefit	Increase C$ 70 per child on 1 July. Increase the maximum tax benefit from C$ 1 805 to C$ 2 056. National Child Benefit is fully phased out by second tax bracket.	1 July 2001 increase by C$ 200 per child with a goal to raising it to C$ 2 400 for the first child by 2004.	2 525
Corporate tax relief		1 January 2001 reduce basic rate from 28 to 27 per cent for firms not already receiving special treatment. Reduce to 21 per cent by 2004.	2 995
Small business tax relief	As of 27 February allow tax-free rollover of capital gains on qualified investments from one small business to another.	As of 1 January 2001, for business with revenues between C$ 200 000 and C$ 300 000, reduce basic tax rate from 28 to 21 per cent.	75

Table 16.   **Main features of the federal five-year tax reduction plan** (*cont.*)

Tax measure	Introduced in 2000	Introduced by 2004	Amount of annual tax relief in 2004-5 (C$ millions)
Capital gains tax	As of 27 February reduce gains inclusion from ¾ to ⅔.		295
Stock options	As of 27 February postpone the taxation of gains on shares acquired under stock options to when shares are disposed subject to C$ 100 000 per year limit.		75

Source: Department of Finance, Canada.

Previous OECD Surveys have highlighted a number of undesirable features of Canada's tax environment, including the relatively high tax burden and heavy reliance on personal and corporate taxes as sources of revenue (Figure 24), partly the result of high statutory ("all-in") marginal tax rates on both corporations and individuals.[38] Each has important negative consequences: high marginal tax rates on income distort labour supply and saving decisions, while encouraging skilled labour to migrate to lower-tax jurisdictions; those on corporations bias firms' location decisions away from Canada, while encouraging profit-shifting abroad. These are particularly important problems given the proximity of the United States.[39] In addition, the differential tax rates levied on corporations depending on their industry and location (manufacturing and processing, and the resource sector receiving a preferential 21 per cent rate – see Chapter IV), distorts the allocation of investment away from the service sector where many potential "new economy" jobs reside.

The latest budget offers both *general* and *targeted* tax relief based on the principles that: reductions should be fair, thus offering larger cuts to lower-income earners and families; they must be prudent and should not increase government indebtedness; and they should be broad-based and focused first on personal

Figure 24. **"All-in" statutory tax rates in OECD countries**
1998

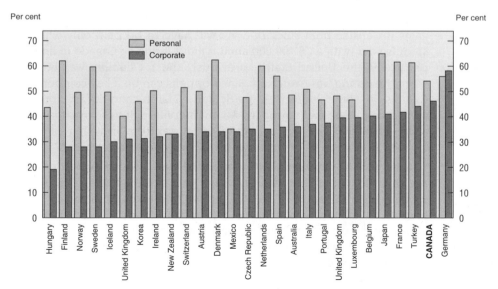

Source: OECD, *Revenue Statistics.*

© OECD 2000

income taxes where the burden is greatest and most out of line with other countries. Some of the more important measures introduced are:

- Re-indexing the tax system. The costliest but most welcome move sees the tax system fully indexed as of 1 January 2000, ending "bracket creep", while safeguarding the value of tax credits and expenditures (such as the Canada Child Tax Benefit), both of which reinforce the government's social objective of targeting extra tax relief on low-income workers, in addition to the obvious economic benefits that will accrue via a less distortionary system. It will also constrain the government's revenue intake, helping to enforce prudence in expenditure decisions.

- Reducing the statutory middle-income tax rate. The budget reduces the middle rate to 24 per cent in July 2000 with a further 1 percentage point reduction planned. This will restore symmetry to the rate brackets: currently, the rate jumps unevenly from 17 to 26, and then only to 29 per cent. In addition, the government plans to increase the thresholds at which the rates apply, raise the amount of tax-free income to C$ 8 000 and enrich the Canada Child Tax Benefit to assist low-income earners (although the timing of these moves has not been specifically set). These changes should help improve labour supply and savings incentives among low- and middle-income taxpayers.

- Removing the surtax for high incomes. This is applied to incomes up to C$ 85 000 on 1 July 2000, with a 1 percentage point per year reduction planned on those above this level starting in 2001, marginally improving work incentives for the highly skilled.

- Postponing the taxation of stock options. Beginning in February 2000, capital gains tax arising from stock options will have to be paid only when the stock is sold (with a C$ 100 000 annual limit), bringing Canada in line with practice in the United States; previously the tax liability was imposed when the option was exercised. Since options can be a key component of salaries in some industries, particularly high-technology sectors, this should help level the playing field with the United States. In addition, the share of income subject to capital gains tax (the inclusion rate) was lowered from 75 to 66 per cent (which will also benefit business).

- Lowering the basic corporate tax rate. The initial step lowers this by 1 percentage point to 27 per cent in 2001, with a goal of reducing it to the special 21 per cent rate by 2004 for all sectors. This takes appropriate action towards levelling the playing field for corporations in the service and non-service sectors, helping to improve the allocation of investment towards its most productive use. Small firms (those with annual revenues between C$ 200 000 and 300 000 in all sectors) will, however, continue to receive preferential treatment, becoming eligible for the 21 per cent rate at the beginning of 2001.

These announced measures are an important and appropriate step, reducing to some extent distortions on savings and investment and labour supply decisions. But a much larger stride forward will be needed in future budgets to implement the proposed reductions. Indeed, marginal tax rates on individuals remain high, while corporate tax relief still leaves rates for knowledge-based sectors well above those in the United States and go only a small way to addressing the recommendations of the Technical Committee on Business Taxation (see OECD, 1998). Moreover, these changes are unlikely to affect firms' investment and research decisions fundamentally. The government would maximise the impact of its corporate tax reduction plan in these areas if it accelerated rate reductions over the next few years and considered further reductions, especially since other countries also envisage tax cuts over the medium term.

The government's indication that, should additional funds become available, tax relief will be brought forward and expanded is welcome, but it has not outlined its priority for subsequent measures. Moreover, competing claims on budget surpluses will most likely not recede and could well see more money allocated to new spending over tax relief and debt reduction. Nor is it clear whether the current five-year plan will be extended on a rolling basis. To help pin down expectations, which could have immediate beneficial effects on behaviour, the authorities should therefore: *first*, establish clearer guidelines with respect to how future priorities will be set, including how the five-year tax reduction plan might be amended, and how additional tax relief will be weighed against debt reduction and new spending initiatives; *second*, as noted above, indicate how spending initiatives will boost the productive capacity of the economy, including a framework for their evaluation; and *third*, engage the provinces in tax reform discussions, since they are also in the process of revamping their tax systems, to ensure that moves at each level of government are consistent with lowering the overall tax burden on firms and workers in a cost-effective manner.

One area that is conspicuously absent from the government's agenda is payroll tax reform, and in particular reform of those taxes that are used to fund Employment Insurance. The need to raise payroll levies to put the Canada Pension Fund on a more sustainable footing will imply sharply rising rates that are not offset by EI premium reductions[40] (see OECD, 1999b). EI contributions flow into the general government coffers, and the substantial revenues generated from this source are an important reason why tax relief is possible. As discussed in previous Surveys, however, this is troublesome because not only are there already sufficient resources to cover any projected shortfall of EI (as mandated in its implementing legislation), but the combination of this tax, and rising rates for other payroll taxes, could have an adverse job creation impact: even though low by international standards, the sharp ncrease in the early 1990s was found to have contributed to rising unemployment – see OECD (1996b). Thus, as income tax rates are lowered, the authorities should decide whether there is scope to increase the use of indirect taxes, notably consumption taxes, as suggested in previous Surveys. Here, there has unfortunately been no additional progress on trying to harmonise provincial and federal sales taxes since 1998, despite the obvious benefits that would result in the form of reduced compliance costs and a boost in competitiveness through fewer distortions.

The pension system

Concerns over the financial sustainability of the Canada Pension Plan (CPP)[41] led to the passage of new legislation in 1998 to put the system on a firmer footing (see OECD, 1998 for more details). In this context, funding is gradually being moved from a pay-as-you-go to a steady-state basis, which has seen the contribution rate rise from 6.4 per cent in 1998 to 7.8 per cent in 2000, before rising to 9.9 per cent in 2003, after which it will be capped. The other main reform has been to change the portfolio mix from one of investments solely in provincial government bonds to a bond/equity mix, the goal being to raise the fund's rate of return. In this regard, a new CPP Investment Board began functioning in late 1998, adopting an interim investment policy that all new cash flow into the fund (CPP contributions and maturing bonds,[42] in excess of payment needs) be invested passively in equities that broadly replicated the composition of three market indices.[43] This was subsequently amended in late 1999 to allow up to 50 per cent of the assets to be invested actively in domestic equities. At that time, the Investment Board held C$ 1.7 billion in equities (about 4 per cent of assets), but this share is likely to rise to between 20 and 35 per cent of total assets, which it is assumed will raise the real long-term fund return to 3.8 per cent per annum (from 2.5 per cent) and the reserve to about five years of payments from the current two (or to about 20 per cent funding). By mid-2000, the Board is to decide on its longer-term investment policy and the optimal bond/equity split of the fund.

The latest audit of the fund, carried out every three years and submitted to the government in late 1998, (the 17th Actuarial Report of 31 December 1997) was both clear and comprehensive, outlining fund projections to the year 2100 along with the assumptions behind key driving variables[44] as well as sensitivity tests that evaluated both low- and high-cost alternatives to the best estimate of the contribution rate. On this basis, it found that the steady-state financing rate of 9.9 per cent would be sufficient to achieve the goals set out by government for fund sustainability. A subsequent review by outside auditors was in accordance with the main findings, but it raised a number of suggestions to improve the triennial report, which the government has agreed to. In particular, it suggested the use of stochastic simulations to better determine the probability distribution of results derived from the long-term projections as well as more consistency on how sensitivity tests are performed.

The review was conducted before the Investment Board began operation and had decided upon its investment strategy. A number of additional factors will therefore have to be re-assessed in the next review, including the rate of return on the fund, any additional risk that might arise to earnings from the investment strategy and under what circumstances this should lead to a revision in the contribution rate. For example, the authorities will have to decide whether any sustained increase (or shortfall) in returns (or *vice versa*) is passed along in increased (decreased) benefit levels, thus affecting retirees, or lower (higher) contribution rates, thereby affecting workers. In addition, the analysis of the indexing mechanism will have to be updated once the new long-term inflation target is set by the authorities and consideration will need to be given as to whether some formula that adjusts benefits to both wages and prices is appropriate (adjusting solely to prices would imply falling benefits relative to wage s over time). Finally, as noted in previous Surveys, further effort is necessary to reduce incentives for early retirement (and to improve those for later retirement) and to relax clawback mechanisms that discourage further work effort, even though re-indexation is a positive step in this regard.

Health care

Nowhere is the demand for increased spending more apparent than in the area of health care, which is highly prominent in public discourse in Canada, arising from claims of overcrowded emergency rooms, and concerns over the availability and access to health-care professionals (including specialists), diagnostic and treatment services. Although there are ongoing discussions among public authorities about the need to provide stable and adequate funding for health care, underlying many concerns is the need to both manage health-care resources and deliver health-care services better. The health-care system in Canada was last discussed in detail in the 1993 Survey, and is outlined in Box 2. Many of the current problems were also apparent at that time, including: an increasing demand for more expensive health care services and rising input costs; limited competition; and moral hazard problems leading to excess demand for services.

According to the most recent internationally comparable figures (for 1997), Canada ranks fifth highest in spending as a share of GDP across OECD countries (behind the United States, Germany, Switzerland and France), allocating 9.3 per cent, predominantly from the public purse (Table 17). This comes against the background of large cutbacks in health-care funding as part of the fiscal consolidation process, which saw the amount of resources devoted to health care fall by 0.9 per cent of GDP between 1992 and 1997. Recent budgets have restored some funds to the system, but provisional estimates for 1998 place expenditures only slightly higher at 9.4 per cent of GDP. Nevertheless, there is generally a strong positive relationship between health-care expenditures and per capita GDP (that is, wealthier countries tend to spend more on health care), and in this regard Canada's expenditures are close to what would be expected (Figure 25, Panel A). As regards other health-care indicators, Canadians have nearly the highest life

---

Box 2.   The public health care system in Canada

Canada's health care system, known as Medicare, provides universal, comprehensive coverage for medically necessary hospital, in-patient and out-patient physician services. Each province manages and delivers its own system, respecting national principles set out at the federal level in the Canada Health Act.[1] The system revolves around primary care doctors (or general practitioners), most of whom are in the private sector, and who are paid on a fee-for-service basis.[2] Over 95 per cent of hospitals are non-profit entities run by the community or voluntary sector, or municipalities. For-profit hospitals do exist but are mainly long-term care facilities or offer specialised services. In addition to insured hospital and physician services, provinces and territories also provide public coverage for other health services that remain outside the health insurance framework (for example, prescription drugs, dental care, vision care, assistive equipment and appliances) to certain population groups, including seniors, children and welfare recipients. Most supplementary benefits are, however, privately financed such as those offered by firms to their employees. Provinces operate a single-payer approach whereby hospitals' expenses are reimbursed based on their negotiated budget with either the provincial Ministry of Health or regional authority. About 70 per cent of Canada's health care expenditures are publicly funded.[3]

---

1. The Canada Health Act has five criteria that make up the principles of the national healthcare system: *public administration*: the province's insurance system must be operated on a non-profit basis and be accountable to the provincial government; *comprehensiveness*: all medically necessary hospital and physician services must be covered; *universality*: 100 per cent of the insured population must be covered; *accessibility*: access must be provided without barriers, including no supplementary charges and no discrimination; and finally *portability*: residents of Canada are entitled to services no matter where they move or travel.
2. GPs do not play a gate keeper function to control access to specialists, although the latter could decide to accept only referrals from them.
3. The split in health-care expenditures among levels of government is difficult to calculate. The federal government provides financial support via the Canada Health and Social Transfer, which is a block grant to provinces (introduced in 1996) who can use it to finance health care, post-secondary education and social assistance/services as they see fit. It is composed of a cash element and tax transfer, the latter where the federal government lowers its personal and corporate income taxes, allowing the provinces to raise their rates by a similar amount. Prior to the introduction of the block grant, the federal share of health-care spending was about 33 per cent.

---

expectancy in the OECD (Table 17), and, in general, the number of physicians and people employed (per 1 000 persons) in the health sector is similar to those in other countries. But one area where Canada appears to compare less favourably is in access to high-technology diagnostic equipment, as exemplified by the number of MRI scanners.[45]

Table 17. **Health-care indicators**

1997 or nearest year

	In-patient care beds	Health sector employment	Hospital employment	Practising specialists	General practitioners	Magnetic resonance imaging units	Life expectancy			Expenditures
							Total at birth	Males At age 40	Females At age 40	
	Per 1 000 persons					Per million persons		Years		Per cent of GDP
Australia	8.5	26.3	16.9	0.9	1.4	..	..	37.8	42.5	8.4
Austria	9.1	..	15.4	1.6	1.3	8.4	77.5	36.2	41.7	8.3
Canada	**4.2**	**25.0**	**12.1**	**0.9**	**0.9**	**1.7**	**78.6**	**37.7**	**42.6**	**9.3**
Czech Republic	9.0	21.7	12.4	2.2	0.7	1.1	..	32.6	38.7	7.2
Denmark	4.6	21.1	15.9	0.1	0.6	..	..	34.8	39.2	8.0
Finland	9.2	42.0	..	1.4	1.6	..	77.1	35.4	41.6	7.4
France	8.5	26.3	18.5	1.5	1.5	2.5	..	36.4	43.3	9.6
Germany	9.4	42.3	11.6	2.2	1.0	6.2	77.3	35.9	41.4	10.7
Hungary	8.3	16.1	6.8	2.8	0.7	..	69.8	29.0	36.8	6.5
Iceland	15.9	33.6	..	..	0.6	7.4	..	38.0	42.2	7.9
Ireland	3.7	18.5	4.7	0.3	0.4	..	..	35.0	39.8	6.3
Italy	6.5	18.0	11.4	0.5	0.9	4.1	..	36.6	42.0	7.6
Japan	16.4	20.4	12.4	..	..	..	..	38.6	44.8	7.2
Korea	4.8	..	..	..	..	5.1	73.5	32.4	39.2	6.0
Luxembourg	8.1	18.1	..	1.6	0.8	2.4	..	35.0	40.8	7.0
Mexico	1.1	6.1	..	0.7	0.6	..	73.6	35.5	40.1	4.7
Netherlands	11.5	23.8	9.0	1.0	0.5	..	..	36.2	41.2	8.5
New Zealand	6.1	17.2	..	0.7	0.8	2.7	77.6	37.4	41.6	7.6
Norway	14.7	71.4	16.1	1.9	0.8	..	77.7	37.2	42.0	7.5
Poland	5.4	..	..	1.8	..	0.4	70.9	30.8	38.3	5.2
Portugal	4.1	12.9	10.1	2.1	0.6	2.8	75.0	34.7	40.3	7.9
Sweden	5.2	39.0	24.4	2.2	0.6	..	..	38.1	42.7	8.6
United Kingdom	4.3	20.3	16.6	..	0.6	..	76.8	36.1	40.6	6.9
United States	4.0	32.6	16.1	1.5	0.8	..	76.5	35.9	40.7	13.9

Source: OECD *Health Data* 99.

Figure 25. **Health-care expenditures**

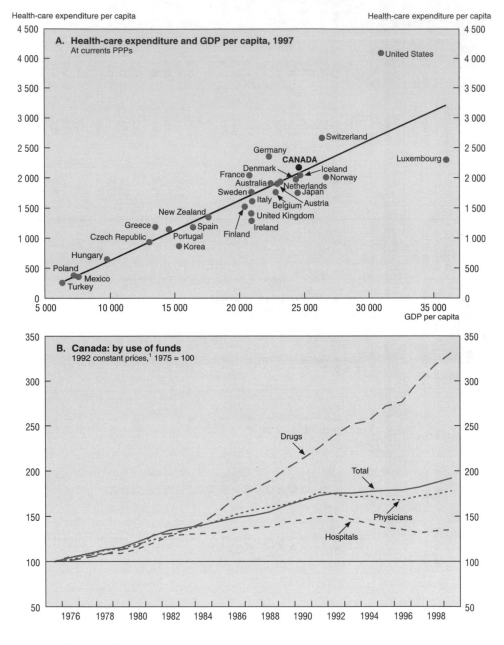

1. Deflated by the health-care price index.
Source: OECD *Health Data* 99.

Over the 1990s, various measures were implemented to tackle rising costs in the context of fiscal restraint. In the area of physician remuneration, most agreements with doctors included some form of payment cap to the fee-for-service model, but the perception that this was not always sufficient to contain costs persists, for example through scheduling of apparently unnecessary follow-up visits (Naylor, 1999).[46] Drug costs have been easily the most rapidly rising component of health-care expenditures (Figure 25, Panel B), reflecting, among other things, the rapid introduction of new medicines and population ageing (the elderly are the largest consumers of drugs). To cap them, provincial governments' drug plans have limited the types of medicine for which reimbursement occurs, set reimbursement ceilings, introduced reference-based pricing, limited pharmacy dispensing fees, restricted the eligible payments and introduced co-payments (Health Canada, 1997). The federal government has suggested the possibility of a national "pharmacare" programme to allow Canadians better access to medically necessary drugs, while reining in expenditures, but little progress has been made, partly because the provinces are worried about the potential fiscal costs (Naylor, 1999).

The lack of continuity in an individual's health care is considered by many experts to be a crucial problem in the current system, leading to unnecessary testing and elevated costs, while restraining the quality of service. To address these concerns, the main threads of reform have focused on regionalising health care (reducing the number of actors in the system)[47] and moving towards home and community care when it is the most appropriate form of care to reduce unnecessary hospital stays where costs are higher (Naylor, 1999). Most recently, Ontario, supported through the Health Transition Fund (a federal government initiative), has introduced primary-care delivery pilots, setting up networks where patients are guaranteed 24-hour service by either their personal doctor or other doctors and nurses who participate in the network. This approach, referred to as "rostering", would allow patients to receive continuous oversight and, it is hoped, reduce pressures on emergency wards and minimise unnecessary interventions. A component of this project is the introduction of a capitation system where doctors are paid on a per-patient basis (in addition to some fee-for-service consultations), with payments varying by age and other characteristics (many countries have already introduced a mixed fee-for-service and capitation remuneration system).[48] Alberta is experimenting with a range of primary health care and integrated service delivery projects that bring together not only health-care practitioners but other relevant specialists such as social workers to deal with the multiple needs of client groups.

Probably the most controversial of recent legislative changes is Alberta's plan to pay private, for-profit clinics to deliver certain services to the public, funded out of the government purse.[49] This has led to important questions about the role of the private sector in the system. In particular, it has raised fears that a "two-tier" system would result, whereby patients who attend private clinics would receive better care than those who are patients in not-for-profit hospitals. Opponents argue also that it would encourage so-called "queue jumping" for those who are able to pay supplements. In addition, there are concerns that the public sector would be left with the most expensive interventions, or more complicated cases that would require costly care, while private clinics would expand their services, and attract increased funding and more (and better) physicians ("cream skimming"). Nonetheless, allowing individuals the choice between these two types of establishments may foster greater competition among them and perhaps reduce overall costs, at the same time as increasing quality. Indeed, should quality not be sufficient, or services not provided under agreed-upon terms, the government could refuse to contract with for-profit establishments.

Finally, the Health Transition Fund is supporting a pilot project in Western Canada, involving a consortium of medical associations, regional health authorities, health research centres and ministries of health to develop valid, reliable and clinically transparent tools to assist in the management of waiting lists. Currently, Ontario is the only province that operates a comprehensive waiting-list management system. The provinces have also initiated a major study to detail costs in the health-care system, the results of which are expected to be reported in mid-2000. Late in 1999, a Senate Committee on Social Affairs, Science and Technology was also set up to examine, over the following two years, the state of the health-care system in Canada.

The current situation suggests the need for a comprehensive action plan that should set out the priorities for health care. In this context, better information on waiting lists and costs would help to improve public debate over how much existing expenditures could be reallocated, before embarking on additional spending. Experimenting with different forms of physician remuneration, primary-care reforms, and more integrated delivery all hold some promise for containing costs and boosting the quality of service. A greater role for the private sector, while controversial, should be studied, but with a close eye kept on quality and cost, allowing an evaluation of whether the increased competition leads to declines in overall expenditures. It is essential, however, that the client have free choice over which type of institution should deliver the medical service to avoid any possible self-dealing by physicians, and that the authorities carefully manage the contractual arrangements with private-sector institutions.

Public sector programme expenditures and delivery

The government has taken steps over the past few years to improve control and accountability in spending, as noted in the previous Survey, with each Ministry now expected to produce a Performance Report that outlines departmental objectives, expected results and indicators on which to assess them. However, the Auditor General notes that in most cases these objectives are vague, the results are either not clearly stated or difficult to measure, and the focus is on outputs instead of outcomes. Nevertheless, the introduction of these reports is a positive step in ensuring that funds are used wisely. To foster their improvement, the Auditor General suggests that they be used to allocate resources. But better information on costs will also be necessary: the government's plans to finalise the overhaul of its financial reporting system will help in this regard. In particular, the introduction of full accrual-based accounting methods should assist in the planning of longer-term projects. Nevertheless, the sometimes *ad hoc* nature of spending, particularly at budget year-end, that is not explicitly linked to depart-mental objectives diminishes the incentive to adhere to previously-set plans (see above and Chapter II).

The federal government has begun to more actively involve external partners in the planning, design and delivery of its programmes, or so-called Alternative Service Delivery (ASD) by forming collaborative agreements with some partners where it maintains a substantial role and delegating authority to others. ASD arrangements have a number of objectives: reducing costs and increasing efficiency; spurring innovative practices; better linking services to local needs; improving client satisfaction and so on. A recent government audit found a total of 77 new governance arrangements put in place over the 1990s, which in fiscal year 1999-2000 were responsible for over C$ 5 billion in spending. The Auditor General has raised some concerns over these practices. *First*, there is no adequate framework in place to evaluate whether the ASDs are achieving federal objectives and whether any lessons can be learned to improve the process; and, *second*, in some cases the agencies undertaking the work are not accountable to Ministers or Parliament. Indeed, in many cases, government departments were unsure of how many ASDs were in place. The Auditor General therefore recommends that several key elements be addressed when using ASDs, particularly since their use is likely to grow over time. These include: credible reporting, effective accountability mechanisms, adequate transparency and protection of the public interest.

Concluding remarks

The pace of microeconomic reform has slowed, reflecting the already considerable progress made in many areas to promote economic efficiency and growth. Nevertheless, the still sluggish productivity performance leaves no room for complacency. While the low inflation environment and fiscal consolidation have set the stage for continued growth, the authorities are urged to push forward with a comprehensive agenda to boost the productive capacity of the economy (summarised in Table 18) by:

  – *Bolstering work incentives with further changes to social and labour market programmes*. The government should strive towards adhering to all *Jobs Study* recommendations, including: elimination of the variation in

Table 18. **Structural surveillance assessment and recommendations**

Issue/1999 recommendation	Action taken	Assessment	New or follow-up recommendation
A. Labour market and social programmes			
I. *Reform unemployment benefits and related benefit systems*			
Reducing variation in regional Employment Insurance (EI) generosity.	None.	The large differences in region-based eligibility requirements contribute to raise disparities in regional unemployment rates and hamper labour mobility.	Implement.
Further strengthening experience-rating.	None.	This would help to reduce dependence on the EI system. If introduced on employers, it would increase economic efficiency.	Gradually introduce employer-based experience rating.
Rising use of sickness benefits under EI.	New issue.	The rising use of sickness benefits may indicate an attempt to increase benefit duration to offset tighter provisions.	Examine the reasons behind the rise in the use of sickness benefits to ensure that they are being given for their intended purpose.
Loosening of the insurance principles enacted in 1996.	Proposals in latest Budget to relax eligibility criteria for parental leave.	This could increase reliance on EI, moving away from the insurance principles re-enforced in 1996.	Do not loosen eligibility criteria beyond plans already announced.
Coherence of social assistance benefits offered at all levels of government.	Evaluation of the National Child Benefit programme is underway.	The multiple programmes offered at the federal and provincial levels of government create a complex web of assistance that may elevate administrative costs and perhaps lead to unintended consequences on work incentives.	Determine whether the various tax incentive programmes offered to social assistance clients could be simplified.
The impact of withdrawal of financial and non-financial welfare benefits around threshold points.	New issue.	Marginal effective tax rates remain in the 80 per cent range for lower income levels. In addition, the withdrawal of non-financial assistance would raise them, further distorting work incentives.	Examine the impact of the withdrawal of financial and non-financial assistance on work behaviour. Ensure that changes by federal and provincial authorities are consistent with improving work incentives.
Rising disability cases under social assistance.	New issue.	Alongside falling social assistance caseloads has been a rising number of disability claimants, which could imply an attempt to avoid tighter welfare provisions.	Ensure that disability benefits are being used for their intended purpose and not to avoid tighter welfare provisions.
II. *Wage formation system*			
Grade minimum wages by age.	None.	This would reduce the harmful impact of the minimum wage on youth employment.	Implement.

Table 18. Structural surveillance assessment and recommendations (cont.)

Issue/1999 recommendation	Action taken	Assessment	New or follow-up recommendation
III. Active labour market programmes (ALMPs)			
Adopting a more rigorous system of evaluation.	Preliminary evaluation of Labour Market Development Agreements (LMDAs) is underway.	These evaluations have assessed how the LMDAs are working in some provinces and indicate that, while achieving objectives overall, there have been data collection problems that could hamper monitoring and evaluation of ALMPs.	Address data collection problems quickly. Begin full LMDA evaluations to determine their impact on increasing earnings and employment, while ensuring that all ALMPs are regularly and systematically assessed.
Shifting the focus of ALMPs towards those of a shorter-term nature.	There has been a small shift towards short-term adjustment measures.	Job creation and particularly training, remain too widely used.	With robust labour-market conditions, there should be a continued shift towards shorter term and less costly ALMPs. Job-creation schemes should be used minimally with much greater emphasis on job search.
IV. Labour force skills and competences			
Developing pan Canadian Indicators on the education system.	First set of pan Canadian education indicators (PCI) published.	Comprehensive overview of outcomes from the education system.	Continue tracking the indicators, and gear the development of any additional ones to areas outlined below.
Impact of rising education expenses on access to tertiary education.	New issue.	Participation in university education levelled off in the 1990s, while lower-income students were less likely to participate at that level.	Assess how rising education expenses are affecting participation in tertiary education, and how well government financial assistance is meeting needs.
The extent of informal workforce training.	New issue.	Adult participation in formal and informal education showed little change over the 1990s.	Research the significance of informal training channels in the workplace and determine whether lifelong-learning strategies are consistent with them. In general, ensure that the strategy in place is improving incentives to upskill over the lifecycle.
Elevated secondary school drop out rates.	New issue.	The PCI show that while drop-out rates fell slightly into the 1990s, they remain high, particularly for students from low-income households.	Continue research on the reasons behind Canada's elevated drop-out rates.
Evaluation of educational reforms.	New issue.	The impact of educational reforms is unknown.	Ensure comprehensive evaluation of education reforms, particularly those implemented at the primary and secondary levels.
Reducing barriers to mobility.	Some progress is being made on developing mutual recognition agreements (MRAs) for occupations.	While 20 draft agreements are in place, much swifter progress will be necessary to meet the 1 July 2001 deadline for all 60 occupations.	Swiftly conclude MRAs for all occupations.

Table 18. **Structural surveillance assessment and recommendations** (*cont.*)

Issue/1999 recommendation	Action taken	Assessment	New or follow-up recommendation
B. Product markets			
Further progress on the Agreement on Internal Trade (AIT).	Progress has stalled.	Further impetus is needed to not only meet targets, but to move beyond them in order to reap the benefits that would accrue from more liberal internal trade.	Move more swiftly to complete the AIT and set up new targets, perhaps under the Social Union Framework Agreement.
Evaluating discretionary public spending.	New issue.	Canada has targeted new spending on areas that will enhance the productive capacity of the economy, but careful evaluation of new initiatives is necessary.	Set up a comprehensive framework to evaluate discretionary spending measures to determine whether they are achieving their objectives and to develop a list of "what works" to target future expenditures effectively.
Barriers to expansion of electronic commerce (e-commerce) and tax issues.	Advisory groups have provided recommendations to reduce barriers and address emerging tax issues.	The government has taken a welcome step by creating technical advisory groups to implement tax recommendations.	Address recommendations stemming from the advisory group on e-commerce while taking quick action on tax issues to ensure a level playing field among businesses.
Trade policy	Canada continues to push forward on opening up international trade.	Nevertheless, in some areas, WTO panel decisions should be implemented without resistance. Canada has agreed to implement the recent panel decision on the Auto Pact.	When implementing the WTO panel decision on the Auto Pact, do so by eliminating tariffs on all imports of automobiles and parts.
Agriculture	Over the last decade Canada has improved the market orientation of its policies in this sector.	More progress is necessary in areas where supply management systems exist particularly in the dairy sector.	Continue to improve market incentives where supply management systems exist.
C. Financial sector			
The proposed financial services sector framework.	New issue.	The new framework holds promise to boost competition and deepen capital markets and legislation has been tabled in Parliament.	Quickly pass legislation to implement the new framework.
Harmonised supervisory standards.	New issue.	Some efforts are being made to harmonise standards to reduce the regulatory burden on financial institutions, particularly banks, but more progress is necessary.	Continue efforts to harmonise regulatory standards and, where possible, to reduce the number of bodies involved.

Table 18. **Structural surveillance assessment and recommendations** (*cont.*)

Issue/1999 recommendation	Action taken	Assessment	New or follow-up recommendation
D. Public sector			
I. *Tax policy*			
A framework and timetable to prioritise tax relief measures on an annual basis.	Five-year federal tax reform plan outlined in 2000-01 Budget.	The five-year tax plan is a welcome step, but it does not prioritise tax relief over the remainder of the plan. Moreover, it does not allow a transparent assessment of the potential benefits arising out of debt reduction or tax relief *vs.* additional spending.	Establish clearer guidelines on how the tax plan will be amended. Give priority to corporate tax relief and personal tax reductions. As noted above, in conjunction with the evaluation of spending measures, consider ways to determine the relative benefits arising from additional tax relief and debt reduction.
Engaging the provinces in tax reform.	New issue.	Provinces are also implementing corporate and personal tax changes.	Ensure that combined tax changes are consistent with lowering the tax burden on Canadians.
The scope to increase the use of indirect taxes.	Some progress made in 1998 in harmonising the Goods and Services Tax with provincial sales taxes.	Since that point, progress has stalled. In addition, EI payroll taxes more than cover any potential shortfall in the funding of the programme that might occur in the event of a downturn. More fundamental tax reform would allow them to be lowered further.	Examine the extent to which greater use could be made of indirect taxes, allowing lower EI payroll taxes.
II. *Pensions*			
The impact of the Canada Pension Plan (CPP) Investment Board's actions on contribution rates.	New issue.	The Investment Board has begun operation and has started to invest surplus CPP funds in equities. This may increase the rate of return on the fund, but also the risk associated with more volatile income streams.	Under the triennial review, due in 2001, assess the impact of the new investment strategy on contribution rates.

Table 18. **Structural surveillance assessment and recommendations** (*cont.*)

Issue/1999 recommendation	Action taken	Assessment	New or follow-up recommendation
III. *Health care*			
Pilot projects on primary care.	New issue.	Several provinces are experimenting with new forms of primary care that could both help to contain costs and boost the quality of service.	Continue pilots and assess their impact as soon as feasible.
Different forms of physician remuneration.	New issue.	Many countries have put in place a mixed fee-for-service capitation system to help reduce costs.	Introduce a capitation/fee-for-service payment system.
Information on waiting lists and costs of health care.	New issue.	Better information would help improve public discourse as well as help to target expenditures more effectively.	Create a database to track key data, such as waiting lists.

Source: OECD.

regional EI generosity, moving the programme towards employer experience-rating, and re-focusing of active labour market programmes on those that improve on-the-job skills. In addition, further moves to relax eligibility for EI benefits should be resisted and action taken to ensure that abuse of sickness and disability benefits is avoided. Evaluations of labour-market and social programmes should be systematic, and those underway completed quickly to ensure that programmes are enhancing work incentives and reducing dependency. Education reforms should also be assessed in a similar light.

– *Continuing with product market reforms.* To reap the benefits that greater factor mobility would bring, the provisions of the Agreement on Internal Trade and the Social Union Framework Agreement, should be swiftly completed, and indeed, the authorities should consider moving beyond the targets already set. On the international trade front, Canada's noteworthy efforts to further liberalise trade should be continued, while the authorities should accept WTO panel decisions that would clearly benefit consumers. In this regard, Canada has agreed to abide by the recent ruling on the Auto Pact, and it should implement the decision by eliminating tariffs on all automobiles and parts. Other areas where attention is required include: continuing to address tax issues arising from electronic commerce, as well as examining the regulatory framework, to ensure unfettered expansion of this emerging sector; and moving more towards market-based mechanisms in the dairy sector.

– *Quickly implementing financial sector reforms.* The legislation before Parliament should be quickly implemented to reduce uncertainty, assisting market participants in their decision-making and planning. Indeed, the proposals contain a number of welcome initiatives that have the potential to boost competition and enhance liquidity, benefiting both companies and individuals. The recently introduced supervisory framework appears flexible enough to deal with the new challenges, but steps towards reducing regulatory burdens as well as harmonising rules should continue. Supervisory bodies must also continue to be provided with sufficient resources to carry out their evolving duties.

– *Pushing forward on further tax relief.* The latest budget contains very welcome initiatives to reduce the tax burden on Canadians, but additional steps are essential to reduce remaining distortions. Further personal tax relief is necessary to improve labour-supply incentives and support Employment Insurance and social assistance reforms, while corporate tax relief needs to be accelerated to level the playing field among enterprises, removing the bias against knowledge-based activities and reducing investment distortions. This would also complement other measures that may help to boost innovation, such as R&D expenditures.

- *Focusing public expenditures on areas that boost productive capacity.* Governments at all levels are under considerable pressure to share the fiscal dividend, and claims on it are most evident in the area of health care. With the competing claims on funds likely to escalate, the authorities are urged to set out priorities for new expenditures, as well as to ensure their careful evaluation, with an underlying goal to target new spending on areas that will increase the productive capacity of the economy, as weighed against the potential benefits of additional debt reduction and further tax relief.

IV. Making growth more environmentally sustainable

Introduction

Canada accounts for a relatively large share of the planet's natural resources (for example, around 10 per cent of both the world's forests and renewable fresh water supply). The economy still relies considerably on resource-based activities, whose development has been encouraged by government policies. Although, apart from the Atlantic groundfish sector, the limits to the availability of resources have generally not been reached, the sustainability of such policies is an issue in the long run. Resource-based production is generally pollution-intensive and may cause serious problems, notwithstanding the Canadian environment's substantial assimilative capacity in most regions compared with other OECD countries.

In the Canadian context, policies to address these issues face a number of specific constraints: the proximity and extensive economic integration with the United States; the enormous inter-provincial differences in environmental conditions and resource availability; the shared jurisdiction between the federal and provincial governments in this area; and the need to honour commitments to Aboriginal management of resources.

In an effort to strengthen the federal government's performance in protecting the environment and bring consistency to its policies, legislation was enacted in 1995 that requires departments to table sustainable development strategies in 1997 and subsequently every three years – comprising objectives and action plans to achieve them – under the auspices of a *Guide to Green Government*. This guideline document directs that environmental interests be included with social and economic concerns for more balanced decision-making in all sectors. Recently, the government has committed itself to place greater emphasis on sustainable development in policy decisions.

Rather than looking at sustainable development in its broadest definition – including the environment, economic and social pillars – this chapter examines how to make growth more environmentally sustainable, and places less emphasis on social aspects. After a presentation of the institutional and policy setting, a limited number of important natural resource and environmental issues are reviewed,[50] looking at how they are being tackled, and in particular at how well natural resource, environmental and sectoral/economic policies are integrated so as to take account of spillovers between them. Some of the apparent policy problems are then outlined, including the integration of policies, the choice of instruments and institutional aspects of policy implementation.

The institutional and historical context[51]

Shared responsibilities

Canada is a federal state in which each of the ten provinces and three territories has considerable jurisdictional power, much more than states in the United States, for example. As the environment is not explicitly addressed in the Constitution, the division of powers regarding environmental policy between the various levels of government flows to a great extent from jurisdiction over resources. Natural resources fall largely within the provincial domain, and they have the authority to legislate with respect to both publicly and privately owned resources within their territory. However, the federal government also has responsibility over some resources transcending provincial boundaries, in particular fish, as well as through its sectoral power over agriculture and navigation, and through more general constitutional provisions (see Annex III). In addition, the federal government is in charge of the environmental assessment of projects for which it has decision-making authority, for example as a proponent, land manager, source of funding or regulator.

Hence, for many resource and environmental areas and issues, responsibility is shared between the federal and provincial governments, implying that the two levels of government have to co-operate to act effectively. Co-operation between the federal government and the provinces is necessary when negotiating, and signing international agreements over natural resources or the environment. Foreign affairs are the exclusive responsibility of the federal government, but treaty obligations within areas of provincial competence require implementation by the provinces. Environmental issues where responsibility is shared include climate change, transborder (vis-à-vis the United States) environmental problems (such as acid rain, an issue in the eastern provinces), biodiversity,[52] toxic substances (due to the health dimension), pollution of navigable waters and fresh-water fisheries.

The shared nature of environmental jurisdiction is at the root of the "stakeholder" approach often used in the country. The Canadian Council of Ministers of the Environment (CCME), composed of the environment ministers of the ten provinces, the three territories and the federal government, is the main forum through which federal/provincial co-ordination on environmental matters, both national and international, is negotiated and formalised. In addition, various types of bilateral agreements for environmental management have been signed between the federal government and individual provinces (see Annex III). Federal-provincial-territorial ministerial councils have also been established for natural resource issues, such as forests, agriculture, wildlife, minerals and metals, fisheries and aquaculture, and a joint body for energy and the environment. The stakeholder approach also implies broader consultation with the private sector, individuals and environmental and other interest groups which are affected by decisions.

Environment departments have responsibility for environmental protection at both levels of government, but substantial powers have been left in the hands of other departments, responsible for agriculture, energy (and more widely natural resources) and transport, but also fisheries and health. As in other OECD countries, this division of responsibilities also reflects the fact that other goals may sometimes override environmental objectives.

One interesting institutional feature, unique in the OECD, is the existence of a Commissioner of the Environment and Sustainable Development, created in 1995 to audit federal policies for sustainable development and implementation of other environmental commitments by the federal government. The yearly reports of the Commissioner play an important role in providing and disseminating information, raising public awareness and providing recommendations for policy reform to the departments concerned.

Emerging policy features

Initially, provinces focused on encouraging resource development, as royalties were (and still are in some cases) an important source of revenues. For the past several decades, they have also progressively worked towards achieving long-term resource conservation, creating the regulations and institutions for that purpose. The federal government has also played some role in resource development and conservation, through its spending power, as well as with more direct policy intervention (see Annex III).

The main mechanisms to regulate pollution were established in the early 1970s, when a number of incidents both within Canada and abroad heightened public concern about environmental problems and brought them onto the policy agenda. Environmental policy activity subsequently slowed but revived in the late 1980s when public concern about environmental issues re-emerged. Important environmental laws were introduced in this period, including the Canadian Environmental Protection Act. In 1990, the federal government also launched the Green Plan, a policy framework and action plan for sustainable development, in which it committed itself to C$ 3 billion in additional spending on the environment over the following five years. In 1995, it proclaimed the

Canadian Environmental Assessment Act. As a result of fiscal consolidation efforts at both levels of government, however, the 1990s were marked by important cuts in the federal and provincial budgets for the environment.

Initially based mainly on regulatory standards, environmental policy has increasingly looked to voluntary agreements over the 1990s. The use of economic instruments has been rare at all levels of government, and, even though the issue has raised interest in the past decade, it is not increasing significantly. Litigation has also played a relatively small role, in contrast to the US experience. Cost-benefit analysis has been relatively rarely used as a basis for policy decisions. However, it is becoming more common in policy discussions. For example, at the federal level, Environment Canada has developed models to estimate the environmental benefits of reducing air pollution, and these models are being diffused to provincial and territorial governments, thereby enhancing their capacity to use cost-benefit analysis.

Incentives for resource-based activities: the conflict with sustainability

Various direct and indirect subsidies to resource-based activities or consumption, initially provided to encourage the exploitation of the generous endowment of natural resources, remain in place. This can result in over-exploitation, over-harvesting or over-use. Harmful environmental consequences can also be serious in some cases.

Taxation favours resource-based activities

Historically, resource-based sectors have benefited from preferential tax treatment from the federal and provincial governments.[53] This has encouraged the development of resource extraction activities, contributed to depressing costs and to some extent (depending on the degree of market competition) prices. The incentives are particularly important in the non-renewable resource sectors, which face especially low effective tax rates on marginal investment; in the oil and gas sector, for example, the rates are a third of those in the manufacturing sector and a quarter of those in most services activities (Figure 26).[54] Tax incentives provided to investment in the forestry sector are lower than for non-renewable resource sectors, close to the range of those granted to manufacturing when both large and small firms are considered. Grouped with agriculture, the fisheries benefit from the same kind of tax treatment as non-renewables. As far as energy investments are concerned, the federal income tax treatment given to renewable and non-renewable energy is relatively similar (Report of the Commissionner of the Environment and Sustainable Development, 2000).[55] Tax incentives to investment are provided mainly through the corporate income tax regime, with taxes affecting the cost of capital, as well as through resource levies such as royalties.

Figure 26. **Effective marginal tax rates on investment**[1]
1997

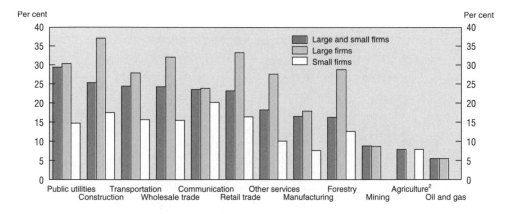

1. The effective tax rate on marginal investment measures the amount of tax paid on income earned by investing in a marginal project. The marginal project earns profits that, after the payment of taxes, will just be sufficient to attract funds from investors. The effective tax rate on marginal investment is therefore an indicator of how taxes affect the incentive to invest. In these calculations, resource levies such as provincial royalties and mining taxes are treated as a cost.
2. Including fishing and trapping.
Source: Report of the Technical Committee on Business Taxation (1997).

By and large – with the exception of Quebec – provincial corporate income tax regimes mirror the federal system. Both levels of government provide preferential tax treatment to mining and oil and gas, through generous write-offs for exploration, development and capital expenses borne by firms in those sectors.[56] In addition, exploration and development expenses can be associated with a flow-through share issue, a unique provision of the Canadian tax system, which allows a company that has insufficient taxable income to utilise the deductions to transfer them to investors.[57] Prior to the tax measures announced in the 2000-01 federal budget (see Chapter III), no substantial step had been taken to level the playing field for business investment.[58]

The special treatment is meant to recognise exploration risk and other specific risks unique to the non-renewables sector, and to be comparable with the kind of treatment granted to the same sectors in other countries (Government of Canada, 1996). However, the necessity to mitigate investors' risk by lowering effective tax rates on marginal investment appears questionable. In fact, taxation in itself is a factor attenuating such risk, as losses can be deducted from taxable income, and flow-through share provisions provide a guarantee that the investor will be able to profit from the deductibility of losses.[59] As for the competitiveness

Figure 27. **Average effective tax rates for base-metal operations**[1]
10 per cent internal rate of return
1997

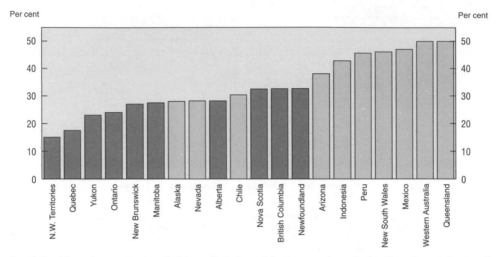

1. Ratio of the net present value of all taxes (including mining taxes and royalties) to the net present value of
    accounting income, for a project with a 10% pre-tax internal rate of return, using a 7.5% discount rate.
Source: Technical Committee on Business Taxation, based on data provided by Natural Resources Canada.

issue, recent calculations by Natural Resources Canada for the mining sector show that average effective tax rates, including corporate income taxes and royalties, are generally below those of other countries or states (Figure 27) (Brewer, 1996).

Resource levies, such as royalties or stumpage fees can also affect investment decisions. In theory, they are meant to tax the rent associated with the exploitation of the resource owned by provincial governments, that is the profit earned in excess of the level required to induce a firm to undertake the investment, and should therefore not affect firms' incentive to invest. In practice, however, it is very difficult to estimate the rent and design a tax system that does not distort production decisions. Resource levies are generally based on output or income and are therefore not neutral. They vary substantially across Canadian provinces, which also earn revenue from the auction of sub-surface exploration rights.[60] In the oil and gas sector, they have tended to diminish as development shifts from conventional reserves to more costly offshore production or oil sands mining. In the forestry sector, the level of stumpage fees is at the centre of a long-standing trade conflict opposing Canadian provinces, in particular British Columbia, Quebec, Ontario and Alberta, and the United States, the latter accusing the former of subsidising lumber exports through low stumpage fees. This subject is highly controversial and has given rise to many disputes and agreements, with no clear final resolution. While assessing the extent to which provinces subsidise production by not taxing all the economic rent is a complex task, there is at least one example of resource for which it seems that the economic rent is not at all extracted by governments, namely water.

Water supply: managing a common good

Fresh water is generally an extraordinarily abundant natural resource in Canada.[61] That abundance and the ensuing policies have resulted in relatively heavy water use – water abstraction (withdrawal)[62] per capita is the second highest in the OECD, although, overall, the intensity of water use remains very low compared with most OECD countries (Figure 28).[63] Jurisdiction over water resources is shared among the three levels of government. In general, Canadians view water as a special resource requiring particular protection. The exploitation of water is partly inhibited by a reluctance to consider it as a commodity as any other and to allow it to be traded. This reluctance exacerbates water shortages in some areas,[64] while potential export opportunities may be lost in part for fear that international trading rules would impose economically rational allocation domestically. Canadian governments have prohibited water export also because of concerns that bulk removals of water may have significant ecological effects which at present are uncertain.

The need for water trading or pricing

The regulatory framework for water withdrawals is based on "use permits" or licenses tied to a specific site and use for an indefinite period of time.[65] Some provinces require that a fee be paid for these permits, but in most of them, including Alberta and Ontario, licenses are simply granted without charge.[66] The systems differ when dealing with shortages: in Alberta, the seniority of a license defines its priority to draw all of its maximum allowable volume, while in Ontario, the allocation of water withdrawal is left to a large extent to the discretion of the administrators of the permit system.

These systems do not allow an efficient allocation of water, even in periods of plenty, and their shortcomings become obvious during shortages. First, the rights are not allocated according to the relative net benefits of the proposed water use – opportunity costs are ignored. Second, since rights cannot be traded after being issued, their allocation cannot easily be changed if the relative value of alternative uses change (Renzetti and Dupont, 1999). This is particularly problematic when the water rights in a water basin have been fully allocated, because a new user or a user of "higher" value cannot get access to the resource. This problem is most striking in southern Alberta, where it is envisaged to make water rights transferable (see Box 3). Making rights transferable is the only way to achieve allocative efficiency when availability is limited. If transactions were to take place, they would also provide market prices for water and allow the estimation of the rent associated with its use.

Figure 28.   **Water resources in Canada: an international comparison**
1997

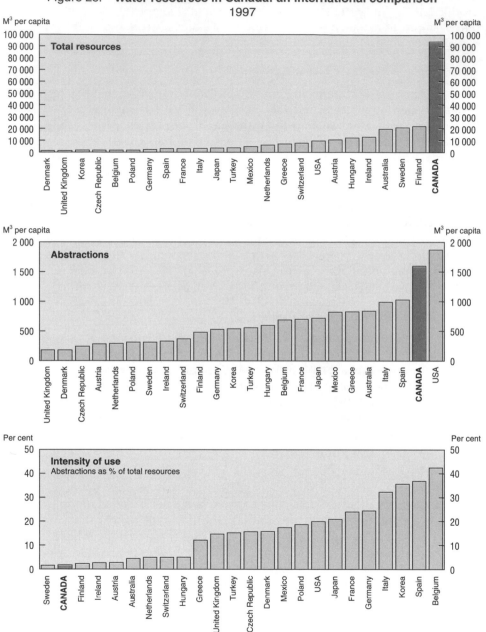

Source: OECD Environmental Data Compendium, 1999.

Box 3.   Improving water allocation through water markets in Alberta?

Alberta is probably the region where the highest potential gains could be expected from having water markets – the Alberta authorities prefer to refer to water transferability. Perhaps reflecting this fact, the province's water legislation was changed in 1996 to allow the transferability of water rights, but to this point in time, this has not yet occurred. Water rights are fully allocated in many river basins of southern Alberta, and licenses are tied to the land and use for which they were issued. As about 90 per cent of water use in southern Alberta goes to irrigation of agricultural crops during summer months (Horbulyk and Lo, 1998), this crowds out non-agricultural but possibly more valuable use.

The aim of the reform of the Alberta's Water Act is to bring some flexibility into the system, while avoiding the use of direct pricing mechanisms. In fact, the pricing provisions contained in the initial draft of the Water Act were removed during the five-year long public consultation process. Hence, the new Act does not allow the taxation of the rent associated with water use, but it will nevertheless increase the allocative efficiency of water consumption.

Water transfers envisaged by the government of Alberta would have the following characteristics: *i*) they would mainly concern surface water; *ii*) they could be temporary or permanent; *iii*) they would be allowed across location and use (agriculture, industry and residential); and *iv*) they would be restricted at the river basin level, and possibly even at the stream level. According to Horbulyk and Lo (1998), this last restriction is not very constraining, as transfers at the river basin level would already allow society to reap 90 per cent of the potential welfare gains from water reallocation.

Transfers would be strictly regulated, as government approval would be required for every transaction for a number of reasons:

- To control for the possible impact of the transfer on the priority system. Water rights are operated with a seniority priority; shifting the location of a right and its attached priority could have significant impact on third parties (as in some cases one person's return flow is the next person's water right).
- To control for the impact that the change in use and location may have on the water body and the aquatic environment.
- To allow for public consultation.

Restrictions of this type are also common in places where such markets have been developed, in particular in Australia. The government would also have the possibility to hold back up to 10 per cent of the water being transferred to be left in the water source for conservation purposes. Uncertainty remains, though, on the type of public consultation mechanisms envisaged, and their possible impact on the decision to allow the transfer. While effective conflict resolution mechanisms have been found to be important (OECD, 1999c), it would be important to specify clear rules.

Uncertainty also remains regarding the timing for implementing the transferability of water rights. The legislation was proclaimed four years ago and came into force on January 1999, but the reform has not yet taken effect. Implementation is conditional on the development of water management plans, which are not expected to be completed prior to end-2001. Alternatively, before water management plans are established, transfers could be authorised by cabinet order, which has not been done.

Ideally, water pricing should cover both the (fixed and variable) cost of supplying water, the environmental costs of its extraction, and the associated rent.[67] In Canada, however, water pricing is underutilised as an instrument. In fact, despite some moves in that direction over the recent period, the pricing structure for water supplies is far from an "economic" approach with full-cost recovery and charges based on consumption. The federal government endorses such principles, but municipalities are in charge of water pricing. That water prices are low in Canada compared with other OECD countries is not surprising, as water is plentiful (Figure 29). However, they are far from covering even infrastructure costs.[68] Such subsidisation is working against water conservation and also increases long-term capital and operating and maintenance costs. In the case of Ontario, for example, Renzetti (1999) finds that the gap between marginal cost and prices for municipal water supply has led to consumption exceeding efficient levels by an average of 50 per cent.

As in other OECD countries, subsidies are particularly important for agricultural uses. In the mid-1990s, the average water price for agricultural uses represented less than 3 per cent of even the modest average price paid by households (OECD, 1999b).[69] Even when taking into account all the necessary caveats in comparing prices – the quality as well as the transport costs of water used by

Figure 29. **Water prices and residential water use**
Mid-1990s

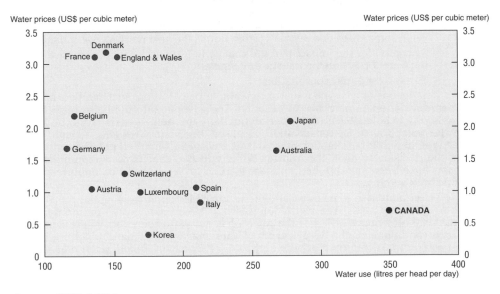

Source: OECD (1999d).

farmers are lower than for households – the gap remains huge. Estimates indicate that subsidies for irrigation amount to about 90 per cent of supply costs.[70] In recent years, many provincial water agencies have increased the use and levels of agricultural water charges, their aim being to cover about 60 per cent of operating and maintenance costs in 2000.

Rate structures are moving only slowly towards volumetric pricing for households and industries. The clear trend observed in most OECD countries away from flat-fee pricing for households consumption is much less pronounced in Canada. In fact, only 56 per cent of the households were metered in 1996;[71] there would therefore appear to be some distance to go before metering turns out to be too costly at the margin compared with the benefits it provides. In any case, having the rate structure decrease with the quantity consumed – valid for 14 per cent of households in 1996 – should be immediately suppressed. Flat-rate tariffs are also widespread for industries, a rare feature in the OECD; metering would probably be cost-effective in all such cases.

The rent associated with water use is also obviously not directly taxed. That deficiency is most questionable for the agricultural sector, as a much smaller share of the water used for irrigation is returned than for most other uses. The question is also topical for electricity production. Hydropower plants are generally charged a misnamed "water rental" based on the kilowatt-hours of electricity produced (between 0 and 0.50 cents per kWh).[72] As hydropower resources have been developed by provincially owned monopolies with a mandate to supply power at cost, provinces charge far less than the economic rent. The rent issue is becoming much more topical, though, with the recent deregulation and privatisation of the sector in Ontario, and the government is actually consulting with the companies to adopt a new approach to setting water charges.

Water exports

Water exports have been high on the political agenda lately. The issue is not new, as a number of ambitious and controversial schemes for diverting Canadian rivers towards the United States have been put forward in the past. The recent debate, however, was spurred by an increasing number of proposals and applications in Newfoundland, Ontario and Quebec to ship water by marine tankers, mostly to Asia or the Middle East.[73] As Canada is well endowed with water resources and water is rare and therefore highly valued in other countries, exports of water could represent a potential economic opportunity for the country. For a number of reasons, however, the opposition to such bulk exports has been large and, in February 1999, the federal government announced a strategy to prohibit the bulk removal of water from Canada. Acting within its jurisdiction, the federal government introduced amendments to the International Boundary Waters Treaty Act which would prohibit bulk removal of water from Canadian boundary waters, principally the Great Lakes. This was based primarily on water quantity obligations under the 1909 Canada-US *Boundary Waters Treaty*, and secondarily on the need to preserve the integrity of water basin ecosystems. The federal government is also working on a federal-provincial accord that would prohibit the bulk removal of water, including for exports, from major drainage basins. In fact, all provinces have put into place, or are developing legislation and policies to prohibit bulk water removal.

The relevant public debate is sometimes rather emotional. There are three main underlying issues: opposition to the "commodification" of water; a fear of the potential social and environmental consequences of large scale "out-of-basin" water transfers; and fear that international trade rules may prevent restrictions on exports in times of water shortage.

Water is a common property resource, and environmental groups and other citizens' groups are campaigning for banning bulk water exports, arguing that they would gradually make water "a commodity as the others", which private companies would try to control in order to make a profit, and that ultimately water may only be available to those able to pay for it.[74]

Environmental concerns have played an important role in Canada's approach to protecting freshwater resources. Bulk removal of water may have varying impacts on the ecological integrity of a basin, ranging from negligible in some cases to significant in others. This depends on a number of factors such as the amount of water being removed in relation to the volume of water available, existing water demand and uses, and the seasonal, annual and long-term variability in water levels and flows. The prohibition of all bulk water removal is based on a precautionary approach, particularly in the face of the risk of more significant cumulative impacts of removals on the ecosystems and communities dependent on these watersheds, and potential effects of climate change on water availability and distribution.

A good example of the concerns about environmental consequences of bulk water removals is provided by the March 2000 report of the International Joint Commission (IJC), the body dealing with all Canada-US boundary water, including the Great Lakes – the main potential source of exports.[75] An average of less than 1 per cent of the waters of the Great Lakes is renewed each year by precipitation, surface water runoff and inflow from groundwater sources. In the face of uncertainty about the availability of Great Lakes water in the future, in particular as climate change may lower the Great Lakes levels and flows, as well as uncertainty about the environmental consequences of water removals,[76] the IJC advocated a precautionary approach and recommended very restrictive rules for bulk removals, which would make it virtually impossible to engage in large-scale, long distance bulk removal from this source.

The perception that international trade agreements may limit governments' ability to control water exports has also played a role in the debate. Water in its natural state is not covered by the WTO Agreement or the North American Free Trade

Agreement (NAFTA), but provisions regarding export restrictions may apply if water that has been extracted is turned into a tradeable good.[77] Although they prohibit quantitative restrictions, the GATT and NAFTA provide for exceptions, in case of threat to human, animal or plant life or health, or for the conservation of an exhaustible natural resource. In these cases, however, the non-discrimination principle would have to prevail, and exports may have to be restricted, for instance, by means of a proportionality requirement. In this case, the proportion of exports to total shipments would have to be maintained. This would imply that, if a precautionary approach dictates reduced water extraction, domestic consumers would have to suffer cuts together with those countries importing Canadian water.

A moratorium may be justified in the short run to clarify the implications of free-trade agreements and try to assess more precisely the economic and environmental costs and benefits of bulk water removals. In the longer run, it may be possible to design an export licensing regime that would take into account environmental concerns and provide for the possibility of interrupting trade flows in case of environmental problems, while giving Canada the opportunity to reap some benefits from water exports.[78] If permits are provided for that purpose, Canadian governments should ensure that they extract the associated rent. A "restrictive" licensing system,[79] if judged necessary by the authorities due to environmental costs, would in any case probably discourage potential buyers that need a guaranteed supply.[80] As for the distributional concerns, water exports, or the pricing of water in general, does not prevent governments from ensuring that every Canadian has continued access to plentiful clean water.

In sum, there is a paradox in Canadian attitudes to water management. On the one hand, prohibition of bulk water removal underlines the high value put on water; on the other hand, there is a strong reluctance to recognise this value by allowing proper pricing that would enhance water conservation and allocative efficiency, and cover the cost of infrastructure.[81]

The Atlantic groundfisheries: an example of conflicting policies

The Canadian fisheries, and in particular the Atlantic groundfishery,[82] provide an illustration of how well-intentioned policies may contribute to overexploitation of a common resource. Other factors played a role in the 1992 collapse, such as particularly unfavourable environmental conditions and overfishing by foreign fleets. Policy setting is complicated by the difficulty of disentangling regional and social issues from the protection and renewal of the resource. Some regional and social policies have the perverse effect of increasing incentives to remain in the fishing industry, while resource management policy is trying to reduce fishing capacity. This section analyses these issues focusing on:

- The origins of overfishing and the inability of policy in the 1970s and 1980s to address the "common pool" problem.

- The political response to the collapse, with programmes to support fishers and plantworkers and to reduce the number of fishing licences, as well as longer-term reforms of management practices with the introduction of property rights management and co-management.

- The inconsistency of the signals provided by social policies notably (un)employment insurance, and some management decisions taken in fisheries other than groundfish, with the stated objective of reducing overcapacity.

The origins of the problem

In 1992, the stocks of groundfish, the mainstay of the Atlantic fishery, were so depleted that it had to be closed to commercial fishing, with only partial re-openings since 1995. The consequences of this collapse have been severe, particularly in Newfoundland where fishing and fish processing have traditionally been the core economic activities and unemployment is chronically high. Environmental factors, such as changes in ocean temperature and salinity were at play in this crisis,[83] and overfishing from foreign fleets also had a role. There is nevertheless a widespread recognition that overfishing from Canadian fishers has played a part, and that past policies contributed to the collapse (see Box 4).

The response to the problem: a progressive recognition of the necessity to reduce the capacity

Since the closure, conservation measures aimed at rebuilding the stocks have underlied fisheries management policy. The main programmes implemented in response to the crisis were the Northern Cod Adjustment and Recovery Program (NCARP) in 1992 and the Atlantic Groundfish Strategy (TAGS) in 1994, the latter including a stated objective to reduce harvesting capacity by at least 50 per cent.[84] Measures used for this purpose included the buy-back of licenses, early retirement and training. Overall, about C$ 3.5 billion were spent through these programmes between 1990 and 1998, when TAGS ended, but income support and employment insurance have had the lion's share, accounting every year until 1996 for more than four-fifths of federal assistance to the sector (Figure 30).[85] As of end-1998, the sums spent on buy-backs had served to retire only 1300 groundfish licenses, that is slightly less than 10 per cent of the total outstanding in 1994. An international comparison shows that for 1996, the most recent year available, Canada's aggregate fisheries support remained one of the highest, in relation to landed value, among OECD countries, largely reflecting the substantial adjustment expenditure (Figure 31).

Recognising the necessity to reduce both capital and labour in the sector, the federal authorities have focused their latest programme, the Canadian Fisheries Adjustment and Restructuring (CFAR) scheme, announced in June 1998, on

Box 4.   **The collapse of the Atlantic groundfishery**

A number of factors led to catches exceeding sustainable yields and to the resulting collapse of groundfish stocks in Atlantic Canada.

Harvests have been regulated by the Department of Fisheries and Oceans for a long time in Atlantic Canada, but total allowable catches (TACs) were set systematically higher than required to conserve the resource (Report of the Auditor General of Canada, 1997). As early as 1986, scientists began to become aware that they had been greatly overestimating the size of stocks. This over-estimation reflected in part an incomplete understanding of the biology of fish stocks and data limitations. Prediction errors were compounded by a decision-making process that failed to take uncertainty into account, as decision-makers were allowed substantial flexibility *vis-à-vis* the scientific recommendations (see Annex IV). Canada, as other countries, at the time did not follow a precautionary approach to fisheries management.

Competition among fishers led to a "race for fish" and the over-investment "trap" observed in many parts of the world, which makes for more forceful resistance to TAC reduction and enforcement, not to say to shrinkage of the sector. Overfishing by foreign vessels in the area adjacent to the Canadian 200-mile limit has also contributed to the decline in fish stocks.

The large subsidies provided to Canada's fisheries have exacerbated the overfishing problem by increasing both employment and investment in the sector and creating pressures on resource management decision-making and implementation (see Annex IV). Some of the subsidies directly favoured the development of the sector. Until the mid-1980s, the federal and provincial governments provided loans and loan guarantees to build and purchase boats and to buy new gear to improve fishing technology. Fuel purchase was also exempt from the provincial fuel tax. Other subsidies were provided to compensate for declining profitability resulting from the "race for fish". In the mid-1970s, inshore fishers and fish-processing companies were supported by a temporary assistance programme, and at the start of the 1980s, the fish-processing firms were temporarily

Table 19.   **Unemployment insurance benefits**

	Per cent of fishing income		Per cent of total income	
	1981	1990	1981	1990
Self-employed fishing				
All Atlantic	43	81	21	34
Newfoundland	96	160	31	47
Fishing processing				
All Atlantic	21	33	30	63
Newfoundland	30	57	48	94

Source: Report of the Auditor General of Canada (1997).

Box 4.   **The collapse of the Atlantic groundfishery** (*cont.*)

nationalised to avoid bankruptcy. Finally, but not least importantly, the easy-eligibility conditions of the unemployment insurance for fishers also contributed to maintaining overcapacity. Table 19 shows the growing dependency of fishers and fish-processing workers on unemployment benefits.

It is no surprise in this context that regulations put in place in the 1980s to limit entry into the groundfish Atlantic fisheries failed to do so. In fact, the number of vessels increased over that decade, while in the inshore fisheries, fishers responded to limits on the number of vessels by increasing the use of unre-stricted inputs, improving their catching power. Input substitution in the fisheries concerned as well as spillover effects on other fisheries have shown the limits of this form of management based on "command and control" regulation.

Figure 30.   **Federal government assistance to the Atlantic fishery**
C$ millions

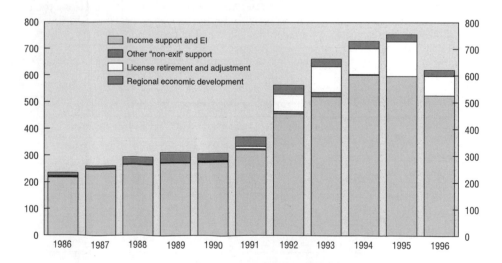

Source: OECD (2000), "The Impact on Fisheries Resource Sustainability of Government Financial Transfers: Case Studies", OECD Committee for Fisheries (free document), Paris (forthcoming).

Figure 31. **Government transfers to marine fisheries**[1]
Percentage of total landed value, 1996

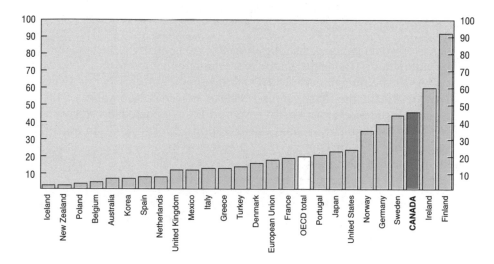

1. Financial transfers to marine capture fisheries, *i.e.* excluding inland fishing, aquaculture and fish processing.
Source: OECD, Transition to Responsible Fisheries, Paris (forthcoming).

measures aimed at achieving permanent exit from the fishery. An amount of C$ 730 million is to be spent by 2001 in the Atlantic and Pacific regions on licence retirement, early retirement, final cash payments, adjustment measures for labour and economic development measures (see Annex IV). Up to now this has allowed the retirement of 1 857 more licences and 1 800 older harvesting and processing workers. Overall, since 1993, the number of groundfish licenses has been reduced by 47 per cent.

To help address the common pool problem and past failures of regulations to limit capacity, the government has also been reforming management practices, extending in particular the use of individual quotas systems. As they provide the fishers with a right to a specified share of the annual total allowable catch, these systems encourage more orderly harvesting by stopping the "race for fish" and thus remove the incentive for over-investment. In addition, when they are transferable, they allow for an efficient self-rationalisation of the sector, as lower-cost operators can buy quotas from their higher-cost rivals and increase the overall profitability of the fisheries. In Canada, the first major quota system was introduced for the offshore groundfish fleet as early as 1982, but transferability was allowed only in the 1990s. Individual quota systems have been gradually introduced in other offshore and inshore fisheries, mainly for fleets of medium-

and large-size vessels, and in 1999, they covered about 50 per cent of the total landed value of fish. Scope may remain, though, for extending this share, which covers all major commercial species in some other OECD countries such as Iceland and New Zealand.[86] Inshore groundfisheries, in particular, have been left out of property-rights-based management.[87]

As for other types of fisheries management, to be effective, individual transferable quotas (ITQs) require a properly functioning monitoring and enforcement system. A problem specific to ITQ management systems is that fishers face incentives to discard the least valuable fish to maximise the value of the catch against quota, a practice which has been noted to have increased since the introduction of ITQs (Fisheries Resource Conservation Council, 1997). In his 1997 and 1999 reports, the Auditor General also pointed to weaknesses in controls over dockside monitoring and enforcement capacity. Controls at sea are indeed costly to implement when there is a large number of small vessels.

In part to remedy this type of problem, the federal government has also promoted the co-management of the fisheries, another longer-term reform of management practices. Co-management consists of providing harvesters with a greater decision-making role as well as more responsibility for the costs of resource conservation and management through charging, both in fisheries managed with individual quotas and others. In the longer-run, the objective is also, under the framework of the 1997 Canada Oceans Act, to integrate fisheries management with that of other activities based on the ocean resource (see Annex IV). While in principle co-management should enhance the cost-effectiveness of fisheries management, there seem to be some weaknesses in the current system. First, the accountability of cost-sharing arrangements appears limited and industry is not really involved in decision making (Report of the Auditor General of Canada, 1999). Second, the charging system lacks a clearly established basis, which prevents it from delivering all its potential beneficial efficiency effects. Third, the Department of Fisheries and Oceans is also limited in its legal authority to enter into real partnership with fishers under the current Fisheries Act.

There are two main theoretical reasons for establishing user charges in the fishing industry. One is to recover the costs associated with fishery management, such as administration, research, monitoring and enforcement, instead of paying it out of general taxation. Provided there is adequate opportunity for consultation with industry, recovery of costs should increase the efficiency of management services, as it creates a link between the primary beneficiaries of services and the costs of providing them. Appropriately structured charges can also make the industry operate at an economically optimal level of activity, discouraging fishing effort from becoming excessive. A second reason for introducing charges is to extract the resource rent associated with the property rights, or access rights, provided to fishers, through, for example, auctioning of quotas or license fees.

Theory suggests that this will not affect the market's allocative efficiency, but will have distributional consequences. Up to now, quotas have never been auctioned, but some of them bear a fee per tonne of quota.

A problem with the Canadian approach to charges is, however, that it does not clearly distinguish between user charges and rent taxation and is not consistent across fisheries, in contrast with Iceland and Australia, for example. The types of costs recovered from industry are quite varied (Report of the Auditor General of Canada, 1999).[88] According to the Canadian authorities, charges more systematically related to the costs of managing each fishery (at least the specific costs) would result in unwanted distributional effects, as high-cost low-rent fisheries would be charged more than their low-cost high-rent counterparts. Hence, the current charging system only achieves partial recovery of total management costs across all fisheries, as opposed to cost recovery on a fishery-by-fishery basis (Kaufmann and Geen, 1997), which is required to improve efficiency in the provision of management services.

The Department of Fisheries and Oceans is also developing – in collaboration with the fishing industry – a Canadian Code of Conduct for Responsible Fishing, within the FAO framework. The code will set general principles and guidelines for all commercial fishing operations in Canadian waters, allowing for more co-operative management of fisheries and greater involvement of the industry itself in achieving sustainable management of the resource.[89]

The challenge: integrating social and economic policies

The 1996 employment insurance reform had as one objective a reduction in the frequency of use of the system, by lowering benefits and tightening eligibility requirements, which might have been expected to encourage fishers to exit from the sector.[90] However, to date, the impact on this group seems to have been limited in practice (see Chapter III). Indeed, eligibility conditions appear to have been eased rather than tightened, through multiple claims provisions, while the regional differentiation of benefits continues to deter mobility. In fact, total benefits paid to fishers have not declined significantly since the 1996 reform.[91] While the latest adjustment programme (CFAR) has no income-support component, when the TAGS programme came to an end in August 1998, weeks of TAGS income support were counted as labour-force attachment to allow qualification for employment insurance. However, data show encouraging signs of changing behaviour, especially among younger fishers.[92]

According to an evaluation conducted in 1998, the TAGS labour adjustment measures – which were abandoned in 1996 when funds were switched towards income support – had little success in reducing dependency on unemployment benefits, and in increasing exit from the fisheries sector (see Annex IV). The labour adjustment measures included in the CFAR have not been evaluated yet. As for the regional economic development components, only since 1999 have the relevant programmes aimed at avoiding investment in fishing and processing of other species, thereby allowing real diversification away from the fisheries.

In fact, in the Newfoundland region in particular, harvesting capacity has increased dramatically in the shellfish fisheries, both in the form of new large vessels and upgrading of existing vessels. By and large, this growth is attributable to increased abundance of shellfish stocks since the 1980s due to changes in environmental conditions including water temperature and salinity. In some shellfish fisheries, however, the recent increase in harvesting capacity results partly from management decisions taken for unspecified social concerns (Report of the Auditor General of Canada, 1999) that conflict with conservation objectives. In some instances, the scientists' recommendations for TACs were not followed. In one case in Newfoundland, TACs were increased contrary to the scientists' recommendations, in order to issue new entrants with temporary quotas (of a size so small as to be incompatible with economic viability), mainly for small boats particularly affected by the closure of the groundfish fisheries.[93] These changes are damaging to individual quota programmes, as they undermine the security of property rights. They also provide the wrong signal, encouraging increased harvesting capacity despite uncertainty about how long the increase in stock will last.

In sum, despite the recognition of the necessity to reduce overcapacity in the Atlantic fisheries[94] as well as dependence on government transfers, notably employment insurance (cf. Department of Fisheries and Oceans, 1999) in order to make fisheries ecologically sustainable and economically viable, policies have tended to send conflicting signals and have hampered the achievement of these objectives. The federal nature of the Canadian political system has also played a part in slowing the response. Jurisdiction over fisheries is shared, the federal authorities being responsible for fish harvesting and the provinces for fish processing. One result, as demonstrated by Schrank (1996), is that even when the federal authorities have tried to take a firm stand to reduce some subsidies, for example, provinces have prevented the implementation of that policy. Moreover, the fact that unemployment insurance is paid by the federal government, and not from the provinces' budgets, may also contribute to the provinces' resistance to any change in the system that would result in increasing their own expenses in the area of social welfare.

The Atlantic Fisheries Policy Review, launched in May 1999, aims to address some of these issues by establishing a cohesive policy framework to guide fisheries management.[95] Developed by the Department of Fisheries and Oceans in consultation with stakeholders and provincial governments, the review seeks to consolidate current management policies, clarify direction where there are competing priorities and establish a set of principles. The recently announced Oceans Management Strategy, which adopts an integrated approach involving all government levels as well as all potential users with the creation in particular of protected marine areas and integrated management programmes (see Annex IV), may also have an effect on fisheries management. However, both initiatives are still in their development phase, and it is difficult to be sure at this stage what their impact will be on fisheries management. A further challenge for policy makers, however, is to integrate social and economic policies more generally, in order to avoid having conflicting incentives in place, thereby preventing the achievement of stated objectives.

Environmental policy challenges

Dealing with pollution

As noted, because of the size of the country, environmental pressures are low in Canada, compared with most OECD countries, but resource-based activities are generally pollution intensive and cause problems in some cases. Important progress has been achieved regarding air, soil and water pollution in some areas, such as the Great Lakes, the St. Lawrence River and the Fraser River. The recently developed Pilot Environmental Sustainability Index actually puts Canada in the top quintile of the world's nations, although difficulties in interpreting such indicators imply a need for caution.[96] However, problems remain in particular areas, both in terms of environmental and cost-effectiveness.

The polluter pays principle has been established for some time as one of the basic ways to promote a coherent approach to environmental problems.[97] In Canada, this principle is not systematically applied. Instead a variety of *ad hoc* approaches is employed, both in setting targets and standards and in their enforcement. Reductions in funding – which have for the most part occurred without corresponding reductions in the level of ambition of policy targets – have also reduced the authorities' enforcement capability. Increasingly frequent recourse to voluntary agreements, with the concomitant danger that they are used not only to reduce the cost of meeting targets but have the practical effect of weakening them, is partly a result of these reductions. Economic instruments are also rarely employed, partly because of a political reluctance or inability to impose new taxes, although some recent proposals, such as the "cap and trade" scheme for emissions of sulphur dioxide and nitrogen oxide in Ontario (see below), reflect a recognition of their effectiveness. This section presents examples of the variety of policies used to deal with a number of problems, showing that where either the polluter pays principle is not applied or economic instruments are not used, it is very difficult to achieve both environmental and cost-effectiveness.[98]

Toxic substances

Toxic substances released into the air, water and soil are a shared jurisdiction in Canada. They fall under the umbrella of three relevant pieces of federal legislation: the Canadian Environmental Protection Act (CEPA), the Pest Control Products Act (PCPA) and the Fisheries Act. The federal departments concerned must work with their provincial counterparts, who have jurisdiction over the industry sector and agricultural practices. Provinces also have their own laws covering toxic substances. However, in this area, the role of the federal government is more important than for other polluting substances, due to the health dimension. A number of recent reports, in particular the 1999 report of the Commissioner of the Environment and Sustainable Development, have identified important weaknesses in the federal management of toxic substances.

The first weakness concerns the evaluation of the risks associated with such substances (Report of the Auditor General of Canada, 1999). There seems to be a substantial divergence of views among the various federal departments about such risks, with schematically the "environment-friendly" departments on one side (environment, fisheries and health) and the "business-friendly" ones on the other (natural resources, industry and the pest regulatory authority). The ensuing lack of co-ordination of research among the various departments and their different interpretation of legislation have led in many cases to indecision and inaction, as well as to inefficient use of federal resources. This points to the lack of a mechanism for decision-making. The federal budget cuts have also made it difficult for the services concerned to meet growing demand. For example, the re-evaluation of pesticides, whose need has been recognised for more than 10 years, has not been conducted due in part to a lack of resources.

The 1999 Report of the Auditor General also questioned the effectiveness of some policy measures. For example, a number of toxic substances were identified for virtual elimination in 1989, but federal departments have not yet developed a plan for eventually meeting this objective. The consultation processes launched with a number of industries to recommend management tools for substances listed in the legislation as highest priority provide another example where concrete action has followed only slowly. In general, the federal government's policy in this domain has been based mainly on voluntary measures, and this approach seems to have failed to provide the proper incentives to achieve the established targets.

In fact, as in other OECD countries (see Box 5), voluntary measures have shown their limits in achieving cost-effective reduction in pollution, due not least to accountability and enforceability problems. The main voluntary agreement is the Accelerated Reduction/Elimination of Toxics accord (ARET), a government-industry agreement initiated in 1994, which involves firms producing about 40 per cent of Canadian industrial output. In addition, nine agreements have also been negotiated between the federal government and targeted industries. ARET participants have reported large reductions in their emissions of toxic substances, but these cuts are not subject to any independent verification. This is also the case for

---

Box 5. **Voluntary agreements: the international evidence**

The OECD has recently conducted an evaluation of voluntary approaches for environmental policy (OECD, 1999e). In general, the environmental effectiveness of voluntary approaches, and in particular negotiated agreements (involving commitments elaborated through bargaining between an industry and a public authority), is found to be modest.

First, the evidence points to the central role of the industry in the target-setting process, the scope for deficient participation of firms (free riding) and the uncertainty over regulatory threats, leading to generally rather unambitious goals. Second, at the implementation stage, negotiated agreements perform poorly due to non-enforceable commitments, poor monitoring and lack of transparency. In addition, as far as economic efficiency is concerned, it seems that the burden-sharing between firms is more driven by equity considerations than by cost-efficiency concerns, and that voluntary agreements do not rely on price mechanisms to induce pollution abatement. Finally, the usual claim that negotiated agreements tend to reduce administrative burdens is not confirmed either by empirical evidence or analytical arguments.

An evaluation conducted by Krarup (1999) on voluntary agreements in energy policy in some European countries (Denmark, Germany, France, the Netherlands and Sweden) also provides similar conclusions. While the agreements reviewed had clear targets, no business-as-usual estimation had been carried out before the schemes were implemented. In the end, targets were achieved, but they were found to correspond to outcomes that required no behavioural changes. Some of the agreements had achieved significant abatement but at a high cost, while others had low effects at low cost.

OECD (1999e) provides some policy recommendations. Voluntary approaches can play some beneficial role when used as complement to traditional command-and-control systems, as they allow for some flexibility in meeting targets. Although it has been rarely implemented up to now, voluntary agreements may also be mixed with economic instruments. However, the target itself should be set outside the negotiated agreement, as in some of the Dutch agreements, for example. Possible safeguards against the main drawbacks of voluntary approaches include: clearly established targets, characterisation of a business-as-usual scenario, credible regulatory threats, reliable monitoring, penalties for non-compliance and third-party participation in the process of setting objectives and performance monitoring.

---

all but one of the agreements with particular industries, which generally do not have measurable targets and cover only a small share of their sector. The Responsible Care Programme, initiated by the chemical industry, is an exception, as it is characterised by relatively ambitious targets, strict control procedures and a high level of participation. A shortfall common to all these agreements, however, is that they do not specify actions or sanctions to be taken in case of non-compliance with performance objectives.

The penalty threat in case of non-compliance with federal regulation also sometimes appears to lack credibility. Shortfalls in enforcement of federal regulations related to toxic substances were also identified by a parliamentary committee in 1998 (Standing Committee on Environment and Sustainable Development, 1998). First, enforcement capacity has been reduced following budget cuts.[99] At the same time, the workload has been increasing, due in part to the growing share of pollution coming from smaller and more diffuse sources (farms, households, sewage plants) and to more sophisticated regulations. This combination, in turn, partly explains the increasing reliance on voluntary approaches.

In a number of instances, enforcement problems have stemmed from jurisdictional conflicts between the pollution permits granted at the provincial/territorial level and the federal legislation, as provincial/local authorities may be more subject to regulatory capture by business interests.[100] When there is federal-provincial co-ordination, such as under the federal-provincial agreements that were negotiated to streamline administration and regulatory activities, enforcement was also found to be problematic in some cases.[101] Examples include the Canada-Quebec agreement on federal pulp and paper mill regulations, where the numerous discharges in excess of the regulated standards in 1996 were not prosecuted.

In general, monitoring of toxic releases and pesticides is also insufficient. The National Pollutant Release Inventory – which exists also in other OECD countries such as the United States and Japan – is a very good information source that every Canadian can consult, and which should encourage enterprises to strive for a "clean" image in the eyes of the public. In Canada, however, its scope and coverage are limited.[102] ARET also provides information, but data are inconsistent, incomplete and unverified. Finally, data on pesticide sales are missing (a regulation requiring registrants to submit sales data is anticipated by 2001). This makes it difficult to establish clear objectives and policy targets.

Recently, the federal government has acted to remedy these problems. First, the new Canadian Environmental Protection Act (proclaimed in April 2000) adopts a tougher stance on toxic substances. The 1999 budget provided C$ 42 million over three years for the examination of some 23 000 substances to determine their toxicity; the most dangerous will be eliminated, and deadlines have been adopted for taking action to manage effectively the others causing pollution. In addition, the powers of enforcement officers have been substantially expanded. Specific funding was also reserved for the implementation of the new CEPA (C$ 72 million over five years) and for enforcement (C$ 22 million over three years).[103] To some extent, the Canada-Wide Standards initiative may also be a step in the right direction, as it provides clear guidelines to the various governments, but it concerns only six toxic substances.[104]

Towards a NO_x-SO_2 trading scheme in Ontario

Acid rain and smog are largely transboundary environmental problems in Canada and concern mostly the eastern provinces.[105] Policy instruments used to date to reduce sulphur dioxide (SO_2) and nitrogen oxide (NO_x) emissions have been mostly command-and-control and voluntary measures.[106] Recently, however, the Ontario government has announced its intention to establish a trading scheme for SO_2 and NO_x emissions from the electricity sector, in the perspective of the opening-up of the electricity market at the end of this year. Such a scheme has already been in place for sulphur dioxide in the United States since 1995 (see OECD, 2000a). It has proved quite successful in reducing emissions in a cost-effective way, and one for nitrogen oxide emissions has also been recently established in some parts of the United States.

Declining caps on SO_2 and NO_x emissions from the electricity sector have been in place in Ontario since 1986. The proposed scheme would reduce the current cap by 10 per cent for sulphur dioxide and 5 per cent for nitrogen oxide for the year 2001, which is relatively little compared with the reductions envisaged by the Acidifying Emissions Task Group in 1997.[107] The scheme would allow the utilities concerned to engage in buying and selling emissions credits with other entities sharing the same airshed as Ontario, provided they meet certain criteria.[108] The value of distant emissions would probably be discounted to reflect their smaller environmental impact. The plan is to extend the scheme to cover the other major (non-electricity) emitters in Ontario in 2003. In addition to the cap-and-trade scheme, the Ontario government plans to introduce emissions standards per unit of electricity produced and imported equivalent to those in effect in the United States and has announced that it will modify its regulations accordingly when new US Environmental Protection Agency standards are implemented.

Setting up such a scheme would certainly enhance the cost-effectiveness of air pollution policy. Given the transboundary nature of the environmental problems, it would also be sensible to aim towards regional trading including other provinces concerned, in particular Quebec (where 50 per cent of the acid rain and 60 per cent of the smog come from Ontario and the United States).[109] This would eliminate the need for introducing emission standards on top of the cap, which are meant to ensure that electricity imported is produced with the same type of standards as in Ontario. Given the local nature of the environmental problem, this makes sense only for electricity imported from firms producing in the same airshed. If they were also participating in the cap-and-trade scheme, standards and the possibility of "over- determination" could be eliminated.

In any case, it is important that the coverage of the scheme be extended to industrial emitters other than electricity, as they make up more than two-thirds of SO_2 emissions and about a quarter of NO_x emissions in Canada (in contrast to the United States, where the electricity sector is the major point source emitter).

Another issue raised by this project is whether the objectives announced will be compatible with those that are currently negotiated nationally under the framework of the Canada-Wide Acid Rain Strategy and in that of the Canada-US agreement on ground-level ozone; both are expected to be completed late in 2000.

The scheme also raises interesting regulatory challenges. Up to now, there has been no regulatory agreement with the US authorities. Since 1995, a pilot trading scheme for NO_x and SO_2 emissions (PERT) has existed in Ontario, which allows transactions between Canadian and US companies. A transaction in which a US firm from Connecticut bought a NO_x credit from a Canadian firm has been accepted by the US state authority as a "penalty" payment. At this stage, it remains a case-by-case approach, whereby regulatory authorities can make their own decisions. It is expected that the criteria in footnote 108 above will be the basis for the trading scheme being developed. The current approach is probably a necessary first step before reaching a bilateral regulatory agreement that would allow a more efficient functioning of the market, with less official intervention. Ultimately, it seems reasonable to suggest that, as the airshed is largely transboundary in nature, the trading schemes should be integrated.

Climate change

The issue of climate change is gaining in importance on the environmental agenda in Canada. Canadian emission intensities of carbon dioxide are high by international standards, both per capita and per unit of GDP, especially when compared with western European countries (Figure 32). Under the terms of the as yet unratified Kyoto Protocol, Canada is committed to bringing its overall emissions of greenhouse gases (GHGs) – adjusted for possible permit trading – down to 6 per cent below their 1990 level on average between 2008 and 2012. This is a very challenging objective, since carbon dioxide emissions in 1997 were already 13 per cent higher than in 1990 and official projections published in December 1999 suggest that under current policies GHG emissions in 2010 would be some 27 per cent above their 1990 level.

If Canada was to meet the Kyoto target exclusively with domestic abatement measures, simulations from a number of models provide a cost estimate, in terms of GDP foregone in 2010, ranging from 1 to 2.3 per cent (Table 20). If an international market for emission permits is established and Canada purchases permits from the so-called Annex B countries[110] who have lower abatement costs, the estimated GDP loss in 2010 would be reduced, ranging between 0.2 and 0.7 per cent.[111] The costs could be cut even further if trade in greenhouse gas permits were to include developing countries, as strongly supported by the United States.[112]

Even with a substantial amount of emissions trading, meeting the Kyoto target will require a significant decline in fossil-fuel use. The carbon dioxide intensity of GDP has gradually declined since the start of the 1970s, but CO_2 emission

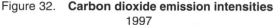

Figure 32. **Carbon dioxide emission intensities**
1997

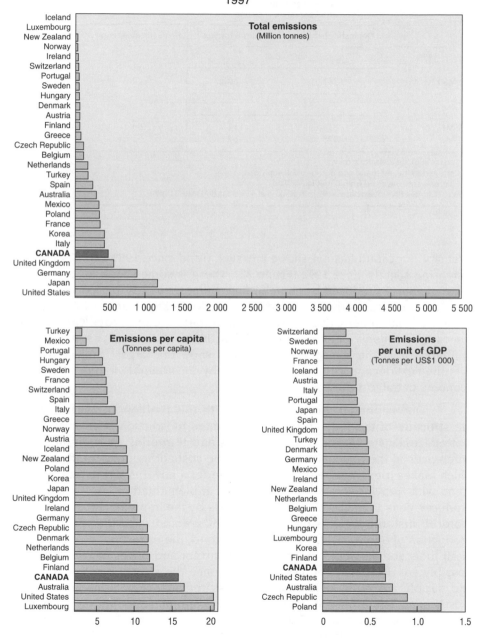

Source: OECD.

Table 20.   **Economic costs of implementing the Kyoto Protocol**

Model	Price of emission permit, US$ per tonne of carbon		GDP foregone in 2010 (per cent)	
	Domestic abatement	Annex B trading	Domestic abatement	Annex B trading
	1995 US$			
MS-MRT[1, 3]	347	69	2	0.7
	1992 US$			
GTEM1[1]	835	114	2.3	0.3
GTEM2[2]	378	87	1	0.2

1. Carbon dioxide emissions only.
2. Carbon dioxide, methane and nitrous oxide emisions.
3. Figures were converted from Canadian dollars.
Source: Charles River Associates (1999), Tulpulé *et al.* (1998) and ABARE (1999).

intensity per capita has not shown any such trend since 1983 and has even been increasing slightly since 1992 (Figure 33). There is some scope for extending the share of energy produced by non-emitting sources, but it is limited, as 75 per cent of electricity is currently generated from non-fossil-fuel sources (OECD, 2000e).[113] Compared with other OECD countries, an important part of total GHG emissions comes from energy-intensive industrial activities based on natural resources. Emissions from the transport sector, which show the largest projected increase over the next decade, could be curbed only by considerable improvements in fuel economy or traffic reductions.

One important aspect of dealing with this problem in Canada rests with the structure of the federation, which allocates jurisdiction over many activities that affect climate change to the provinces and territories. In addition, there are differences in the regional distribution of the costs of meeting the Kyoto targets, which makes it even more difficult for the federal government to reach an agreement with provinces on ratification and implementation. Being a fossil-fuel producer, Canada will be affected in two ways by the implementation of the Kyoto Protocol: first, reducing its emissions of GHGs would raise the cost of domestic production of energy-using output; and, second, the reduction in consumption of fossil fuels abroad would reduce the demand for and prices of Canadian oil and possibly gas. Resource endowments and hence the structure of energy demand and supply are quite differentiated across regions, with fossil-fuel production mostly concentrated in Alberta and of major importance to that province, nuclear production concentrated in Ontario, and hydro-electric production important in a number of provinces, in particular Quebec.[114] Fossil-fuel-producing provinces will thus bear a higher cost than the others.[115]

Figure 33. **Evolution of carbon dioxide emissions intensities**

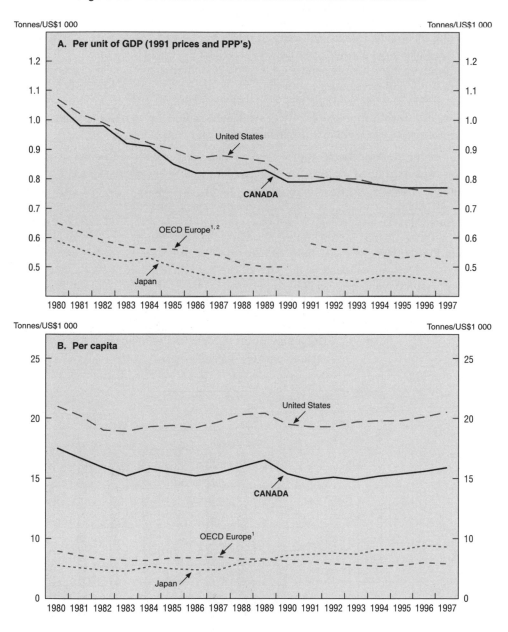

1. Excluding Czech Republic, Hungary and Poland.
2. Including West Germany until 1990 and total Germany afterwards.
Source: IEA.

The Canadian governments have not finalised their climate change strategy yet. The comprehensive but lengthy consultation process launched in 1998 with 16 "issues tables" looking at costs and benefits of mitigation options in various areas (including electricity, forests, tradable permits) is expected to lead to a final report to the joint ministers of energy and environment at the end of this year. Up to now, a number of measures have been taken in various domains, many of which are voluntary initiatives and government spending programmes.[116] Natural Resources Canada estimates that policies in place will lead to a reduction in GHG emissions of 8 per cent by 2010: with no measures, GHG emissions would be expected to be 37 per cent above their 1990 level in 2010, instead of 27 per cent.[117]

In the *transport sector*, fuel economy has been dealt with mainly through average consumption standards for new cars, set in a voluntary agreement with the automobile industry, equivalent to the US CAFE standards.[118] Other instruments include a federal excise tax on high energy-consuming motor vehicles and a graduated sales tax according to fuel consumption in Ontario. The effectiveness of these instruments has been limited, however, as essentially no improvement in average fuel efficiency of new light vehicles has occurred since 1982 (Figure 34). In part, this reflects an increase in the size of the average vehicle, with sales of mini-vans, sport utility vehicles and light trucks growing faster than those of automobiles.

Figure 34.   **Canadian motor vehicle fuel efficiency**
Litres per 100 kilometres

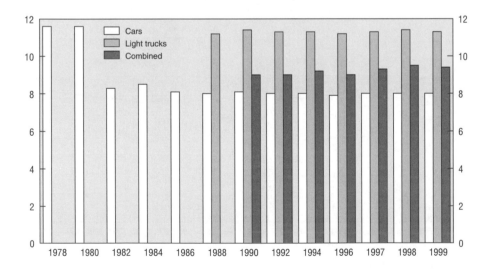

Source: Transport Canada, 1999.

If GHG emissions from the transport sector are to be contained, a substantial increase in fuel prices will be required.[119] Given the direct link between fuel use and such emissions, an increase in fuel prices is a perfectly targeted instrument, and such price signals would be needed to induce the necessary structural change (that is more rapid technological change favouring vehicles with better fuel economy and a shift towards transport modes producing fewer emissions). Voluntary agreements, regulations and subsidies favouring fuel efficiency may have some effect at the margin, but, as observed, they may also be offset by an increase in vehicle weight or in the number of passenger- or tonne-kilometres travelled.

The current low level of fuel prices provides little incentive to reduce fuel consumption. Taxes on fuel are higher than in the United States, but significantly lower than in most other OECD countries (Figure 35).[120] Although there is no recent quantitative study on cost recovery in the transport sector, it is generally recognised that the costs of externalities associated with road traffic exceed

Figure 35. **Petrol taxes in international comparison**

Total taxes levied in 1998, US$ per litre[1]

A. Unleaded premium (95 RON)

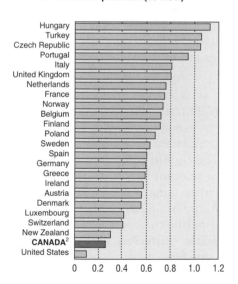

B. Diesel fuel (for non-commercial use)

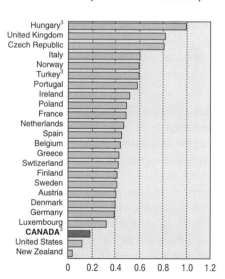

1. Using current purchasing power parities.
2. 98 RON.
3. For commercial use.
Source: IEA, Energy Prices and Taxes and OECD, *Main Economic Indicators.*

revenues from fuel taxes in Canada. A study sponsored by the Ontario Roundtable on the Environment and Sustainable Development estimated the total external costs (including those resulting from climate change) of car and truck use to be around C$ 12 billion in 1994, compared with C$ 2 billion for other transport modes (IBI Group and Boon, Jones and Associates Inc., 1994).[121] Correspondingly, the highest increase in user charges required in order to cover external costs was found to be for urban passenger cars. Since that date, price incentives have probably been twisted further towards road transport. With shrinking public-sector budgets, subsidies to urban public transit have been reduced over the 1990s, substantially increasing its price,[122] while road maintenance and construction have not faced the same decline in funding levels as have other transport modes (Resource Futures International, 1996).

As in the United States, the resistance to an increase in fuel price is intense, as illustrated by the fact that the preferred options retained by the issue table on transportation are mostly non-price measures.[123] There are fears that, given the proximity with the United States, a unilateral increase in fuel prices would both reduce the competitiveness of Canadian firms and be ineffective due to cross-border fuel purchases by Canadians. While it is true that increasing the fuel price will affect the competitiveness of firms relying heavily on road transportation, this is part of the structural change that the commitment to GHG emission reduction implies. Trying to reduce emissions without such a structural change and without using direct price signals would damage the overall competitiveness of the Canadian economy even more.[124] As for the cross-border "leakage" argument, it is difficult to estimate the scale of that possible leakage,[125] but in any case, retail fuel purchases in the United States would count towards US GHG emissions, not Canadian ones. The problem is more one of tax revenue losses for the federal government rather than ineffectiveness of the measure.[126]

The sharp increase in road traffic is also very much related to the phenomenon of urban sprawl. As in the United States, the car has made it possible for an increasing share of the population to live in low-density suburbs. Urban land development policies have encouraged this trend – with, for example, zoning restrictions limiting residential densities.[127] The current structures of property tax, based on market value assessment, and of development cost charges (that is the mechanisms for raising revenues to pay for new infrastructure) also play a role (Municipalities Table Options Paper, 1999). Automobile-dependent urban sprawl, in turn, is also self-sustaining, as traditional public transport systems are rarely cost-effective in these low-density and widely dispersed areas.[128] As in the United States, urban sprawl and low prices for fuels tend to be mutually reinforcing (OECD, 2000a). On the one hand, car-dependent residents resist proposals to increase the cost of driving, and on the other cheap fuel favours the continuing development of low-density housing. However, higher fuel prices may be more effective in reducing emissions from transport than subsidies for public transport.

In the *industrial sector*, most federal and provincial governments' initiatives taken up to now to mitigate greenhouse gas emissions rely on voluntary measures. The Voluntary Challenge and Registry (VCR), initiated in 1995, registers voluntary commitments to reduce GHG emissions. Despite very wide coverage, the effectiveness of this initiative has been widely questioned, as it provides few incentives and has low accountability and verifiability.[129] According to the OECD (2000c), it is difficult to determine whether a particular action would have taken place in its absence. At the provincial level, some initiatives seem to be successful in reducing emissions in a cost-effective way, such as Alberta's efforts to reduce those from oil and gas flaring.

Voluntary programmes fostering energy efficiency are also an important element of the current Canadian measures for climate change mitigation.[130] As in the case of VCR, though, the agreed rate of improvement does not appear to be a large step beyond autonomous energy efficiency improvement (IEA, 2000). More generally, there are some limits to cost-effective reduction of GHG emissions through energy efficiency programmes. First, as discussed above for the transport sector, energy-efficiency improvement cannot be expected to result in equivalent decreases in energy intensity, because if prices stay the same, relative cost effects will increase energy demand.[131] Second, energy intensity as such is not what matters in the case of climate change, and policies focused on energy use rather than GHG emissions *per se* run the risk of orienting incentives in a direction that is not cost-effective.

All this points to the importance of relying on market and price mechanisms to achieve a cost-effective reduction in GHGs. "Win-win" opportunities, that is measures reducing emissions without costs (or at least without significant costs) are probably scarce, therefore limiting the scope of mitigation achievable with voluntary initiatives. The possible contribution of forestry activities to Canadian climate change mitigation policy is also very uncertain, as depending on the outcome of ongoing international negotiation over the definitions of afforestation, reforestation and deforestation, Canadian forestry may be considered a substantial source of GHG emissions or a sink (a source of GHG absorption) (Sinks Table Option Paper, 1999).

The possibility of setting up a domestic market for GHG emission quotas is one of the options being considered in the consultation process. This option has also been studied by various stakeholders in the framework of the National Round Table on the Economy and the Environment, which concluded that it would be a cost-effective way of meeting the target (National Round Table on the Environment and the Economy, 1999). Disagreement remained, though, on the coverage of the scheme and the extent to which other regulatory and voluntary instruments should be used complementarily. In fact, some voluntary credit trading has already taken place in Canada, allowing firms to gain some experience in trading, which, compared with the usual regulatory/technical instruments, involves relatively new skills. Several emission reduction projects have been accepted for registration under the umbrella of the Greenhouse Gas Emission Reduction Trading Pilot (GERT), launched in June 1998.[132] In addition, two Canadian firms have been involved in the purchase of larger emission credits (or options) from American companies or organisations.[133]

Overall, Canadian greenhouse gas emissions are likely to exceed the Kyoto target for the period 2008-12 substantially, and Canada will thus have to use the Protocol's flexibility mechanisms. In this perspective, though, it would be important to get an agreement on a domestic permit scheme, which could be linked to international permit trading, with a coverage as broad as possible. Keeping some sectors out of the scheme, like transportation or any other energy-intensive industry, would end up increasing the overall cost of reducing emissions. Distributional effects, on the other hand, could initially be handled with the rules retained to allocate the permits. Grandfathering part of the emission quotas may be an option to make the scheme more acceptable to industry. Given that the costs of meeting the Kyoto target will be unequally distributed among provinces, some kind of regional compensatory scheme may also be required to get an agreement with the provinces.[134] It would be important, however, that it be completely independent of future emissions.

Concluding remarks

This chapter has focused on a selected number of key natural resource and environment issues, with particular attention to how these interact with the wider policy-setting framework. General features of Canada's policies dealing with natural resource and the environment stand out. The main recommendations that emerge from this analysis are set out in Box 6.

The rich endowment of natural resources has led to policies favouring their development and use. Support has been important for activities based on non-renewable resources, such as oil and gas, and metals and minerals, mostly in the form of preferential tax treatment distorting investment incentives. Given that non-renewable-resource-based activities are generally intensive producers of GHGs and polluting substances, the overexploitation of such resources also has direct environmental consequences. Recently announced tax measures that will contribute to levelling the playing field are therefore to be welcomed.

In the same way, the implicit subsidisation of water supply lowers its price and leads to overuse. While the federal government has been endorsing the principle of "economic" pricing of water for some time, local governments, which are responsible for water management, are moving only slowly in this direction. Water availability has started to be a problem in some regions, in particular those with large irrigated areas, and in these cases current systems of water rights end

Box 6.   **Summary of conclusions and recommendations**
for reform

Objective setting and implementation

All levels of government need to work further on clarifying the objectives of their policies. This is particularly the case for fisheries and environmental policies. Designing *mechanisms for decision-making* when there are conflicting views among various departments (at the federal level, at the provincial level, among provinces, and between provinces and the federal government) and increasing *transparency in decision-making* – for example by making greater use of cost-benefit analysis and making it more frequently available to the public – would also improve cost-effectiveness of policy.

To reduce the gap between objectives and achievements, a particular focus should be put on trying to find commitment devices for stakeholders. A number of specific changes would be useful in this regard:

- Increasing the quantity of environmental information made available to the public.

- Setting clear rules for actions (for example, to fix total allowable catches; to assess the reference level of emissions of firms participating in voluntary agreements and the actions to be taken in case of non-compliance with voluntary agreements or regulation).

- Making more extensive use of economic instruments. Compared to a fine, a tax or charge leaves much less room for discretion. Individual quotas formalise a commitment to a certain harvest level or emission target, and when transferable, those who own them all have an interest in effective enforcement as otherwise their value drops.

Energy, minerals and metals

The preferential tax treatment of conventional resource sectors, such as oil and gas and minerals and metals, should be eliminated. The federal government has started moving in that direction in its 2000-01 budget, but the process should be accelerated. This would also help to meet environmental objectives, in particular the Kyoto commitment.

Water use

To allow more efficient water use, provincial and territorial governments should:

- Speed their move towards "economic pricing", by shifting the burden from taxpayers onto users and charging according to volume consumed. This requires increased use of water metering, which is currently relatively scarce. The current subsidies to irrigation water result in higher levels of agricultural production and thus increased level of pollution.

- In areas where availability of water has become a problem, make water rights transferable (provided it does not harm the ecosystem) to increase allocative efficiency.

Box 6.   **Summary of conclusions and recommendations
for reform** (*cont.*)

Maintaining a moratorium on bulk water removal may be justified in the short run to assess more precisely the associated economic and environmental costs and benefits. But in the longer run an export-licensing regime may be designed that takes into account environmental concerns.

Atlantic fisheries

Progress has been made in managing the Atlantic fisheries. However, the sector is still overcapitalised and comprises too many fishers, and the incentives provided by economic and social policies conflict with the long-run sustainability of the sector:

– The share of fisheries managed through individual quotas has increased (to 50 per cent), but further extension should be considered. Increasing the transferability of quotas where none exists and removing restrictions on such transferability would be beneficial, as it would allow the reduction of excess capacity.

– A precautionary approach should be applied more strictly when setting total allowable catches for shellfish, as otherwise similar problems as for groundfish may arise. Rule-based management could be adopted for specific fisheries, in which scientific recommendations for total allowable catches have to be followed, as has been done for some fisheries in Iceland, for example.

– The current system for charging should be clarified. User charges should be consistently applied to the various individual fisheries, to allow for efficiency gains in the provision of services and reducing the incentives for oversize. To tax the high rents likely to result from transferable quotas, they should be auctioned or at least more systematically charged for.

– The effects of the reform of the employment insurance scheme seem to have been limited for the fishery sector. The regional differentiation of employment insurance inhibits mobility. In general, the support provided to fishers and fish-processing workers affected by the crisis should be designed so as not discourage seeking other employment possibilities.

– The federal government should consider increasing the generosity of the amounts proposed for license retirements as a measure to reduce the size of the sector.

Box 6.   **Summary of conclusions and recommendations
for reform** (*cont.*)

Pollution

Policies dealing with pollution should apply the polluter pays principle more systematically. In this regard:

- A mechanism for decision-making regarding the classification and evaluation of toxic substances should be created.
- There is scope for substantially increasing the use of economic instruments. Possible examples include: charges on toxic emissions, effluent or waste; water discharge permit trading; a tax on pesticides; and advance disposal fees for products containing toxic substances.
- The federal government should continue its efforts to provide provincial and territorial governments with information and tools (models, available cost-benefit analysis on similar subjects) to favour their use of economic instruments.
- The coverage of the National Pollution Release Inventory should be increased, as it provides a valuable information source both for the public and the authorities.
- Reliance on voluntary agreements has not been sufficient to achieve environmental objectives. When relied on, they should provide for accountability and verifiability and specify actions to be taken in case of non-compliance (that is they should be backed up by regulation or economic instruments).
- The project to set up a tradable scheme for NO_x and SO_2 emissions in the electricity sector in Ontario should be welcomed. However, for it to be cost-effective, it would be important to extend its coverage to emissions from other industries as well as to emissions from provinces sharing the same airshed. The aggregate cap put on emissions must be consistent with forthcoming objectives negotiated nationally under the framework of the Canada-Wide Acid Rain Strategy and in the framework of the Canada-US agreement on ground-level ozone.

Climate change

In the field of climate change, the Canadian government has taken a rather high profile in international fora, but GHG emissions are still increasing strongly and more actions should be taken. Even if Canada is able to buy GHG emission quotas on an international market, it will have to take steps to accelerate the reduction in fossil-fuel consumption per unit of GDP. To this aim, it should:

- Implement an economic instrument with an emission base as large as possible in order to reduce the overall costs of emissions abatement. Voluntary agreements to reduce GHG emissions and improve energy efficiency have shown their inefficiency. A "cap-and-trade" scheme is probably the most appropriate approach.
- In the absence of a cap-and-trade scheme covering fuel-based emissions, increase the tax on fuel, as it will be more effective and less costly than average consumption standards to reduce emissions from transport.

up excluding other potential users. To improve allocative efficiency, plans to introduce the transferability of water rights have been announced. Resistance to such
moves as well as to full cost pricing is high, in particular from those benefiting
most from the current subsidies, but the benefits of correcting this unsustainable
situation are substantial, and the authorities should therefore speed up their
move towards "economic" pricing. This would be consistent with the recent decision to ban bulk water removal, preventing therefore bulk exports, which reveals a
very high implicit valuation of water. In the longer-run, however, a carefully
designed export licensing system would allow Canada to reap some benefits from
its abundant water resource, while at the same time preventing harmful environmental effects.

What happened in the Atlantic groundfisheries provides an example of
how public support provided in different forms, including through employment
insurance and labour market policies, can contribute to the depletion and
collapse of fish stocks, as it reinforces the already existing incentives for overexploitation resulting from the common nature of the resource. Canada is not the
only country that has faced such problems, and natural factors may also have been
particularly unfavourable there, but the reaction to the reduction of the stock has
been slow, illustrating the difficulty in trading off the short-term adjustment costs
for fishing communities, with their distributional and regional implications, against
the long-term sustainability of the activity. Not directly addressing the current
distributional problems, however, will lead to more serious distributional
problems in the future. Measures to tackle them should be clearly separated from
those designed to improve resource management.

The support provided by governments for resource development may be
linked with the use of a rather "co-operative" approach in environmental policy, in
which standards are often closely negotiated with the industry, rather than being
based on a consistent cost-benefit approach, and their enforcement is not systematic and also subject to negotiation. This is particularly the case for the provinces,
as their role as promoters of natural resource development conflicts somewhat
with their ability to impose the costs of environmental protection and resource
conservation on the firms who are their agents. The political economy of environmental regulation, which imposes concentrated costs on the regulated sector in
order to provide diffuse benefits to the public, always makes it difficult to implement a regulation and apply the polluter pays principle. In the Canadian case,
though, this effect seems to be reinforced by governments' role in resource development, as well as by the constitutional ambiguity and overlapping jurisdictions
with respect to environmental matters.

The federal government has taken a rather high profile on some issues,
having announced important steps to be taken in the realm of toxic substances
management policy, and being, for example, a strong proponent of international

action on issues such as climate change and an active promoter of international agreements for fisheries management. Each federal department has developed strategies for sustainable development, and a unique and valuable function of Commissioner of the Environment and Sustainable Development has been created. Many consultation processes have been launched, such as, for example, the issue tables for climate change. However, as underlined by many observers and the Commissioner himself, actions have not always followed from these processes. Implementation problems also exist at the provincial level. Objectives and/or intermediate targets are not always clearly set in the various areas, for example fisheries and toxic substances management. While it is true that reconciling diverging views among the various departments and ministries concerned may be especially difficult in Canada, a rather loose federation with shared jurisdictions, it must be recognised that implementing no measures at all often implies environmental degradation (or resource depletion) to the detriment of current and future generations. Improving both the mechanisms for decision-making at each government level and the co-operation mechanisms between the two levels of government, in particular their accountability, would help in this respect.

The frequent recourse to voluntary agreements, partly as a result of reductions in funding of the government departments responsible, has not proved effective in dealing with the resource and environmental challenges, as shown by the management of toxic substances and in the policies to curb GHG emissions. Self-regulation faces the same limits as elsewhere. "No-cost" opportunities for pollution reduction are limited, and, by definition, self-regulation cannot be expected to correct for the external costs of pollution. In this respect, the project to introduce a tradable permit scheme for NO_x and SO_x emissions in Ontario should be pursued.

To put Canada on a more sustainable growth path, greater reliance on price signals is needed. Increasing the use of economic instruments will indeed prove necessary if Canada is to achieve significant cost-effective progress in terms of resource conservation, allocative efficiency and environmental performance. The benefits from greater recourse to economic instruments would be particularly welcome in a period in which competitive pressures are heightened and marginal costs of abatement are climbing.

Notes

1. The slowdown in inventory accumulation was accentuated by the effects of the US auto workers' strike in the third quarter of 1998.

2. In this regard, automobile purchase incentives offered by the manufacturers and their dealers have played a significant role.

3. Both headline and core CPI inflation are currently about 1 percentage point below US levels.

4. As in 1999-2000, when C$ 1¼ billion in real return bonds (RRBs) were issued, the government plans to issue up to C$ 2 billion in RRBs in the current year. The total outstanding amount of RRBs was C$ 5¼ billion in early April, about 1 per cent of total federal debt outstanding.

5. For instance, progressive cuts in the responsible minister's salary.

6. This reduces revenue as recorded in the public accounts. In addition, spending estimates are much higher on a public accounts basis.

7. The debt ratios shown in Figure 13 are based on the new definition adopted by Statistics Canada whereby government non-autonomous employer-sponsored pension plans are treated as government liabilities. To the extent that other countries do not apply the same accounting procedures, Canada's relative position is overstated.

8. In addition, Canada's R&D spending remains lower than the OECD average because of the economy's continuing orientation towards resource activity, where such spending is relatively low.

9. As noted in Trajtenberg's (1999) paper, patentable innovations are only a subset of all research outcomes, and not all innovations are patented in any case.

10. Indeed, the semi-conductor industry in Canada is relatively small compared with other computer-related production. As to how prices are calculated, Canada uses a number of sources to collect price information on computers and related equipment. For example, for telephone switching equipment, it uses the purchase prices of Canadian telephone companies, whereas the United States uses hedonic pricing techniques. For a number of other goods (for example computers, printers, displays, tape and hard drives) Canada uses hedonic pricing (both directly and indirectly by using prices derived from US series). In the area of semi-conductors, Canada uses the Bureau of Labor Statistics producer price indices, adjusted for exchange rate differences. See Elridge and Sherwood (2000).

11. Only software that is capitalised by businesses is included as investment.

12. In contrast to the 1980s when the self-employed typically hired staff, in the 1990s most were own-account workers with no employees.

13. Estimates of the decline in youth participation attribute about half to structural factors (Archambault and Grignon, 1999), including the concomitant rise in enrolment in education, but this should also strengthen the workforce attachment of these cohorts once schooling is complete.

14. Lin *et al.* (1999) find that self-employment growth is negatively related to the business cycle.

15. In 1998/99, 56 per cent of those affected by the intensity rule had their benefit rate reduced 1 percentage point and 34 per cent by 2 percentage points.

16. In addition, small weeks adjustment "projects" were implemented to exclude earnings that would lower the benefit rate to encourage participants to take all available work. This was directed towards those with varying work patterns, such as seasonal workers.

17. The latest monitoring report notes that the number of short-term claimants in receipt of the family supplement increased, possibly implying that this income top-up has had no adverse impact on work incentives. However, in the absence of this extra income, the number of short-term claims might have been even higher.

18. A potentially negative side-effect of the tightening of EI rules over the 1990s may have been a shifting of jobseekers to the social assistance rolls rather than improving work incentives. Evidence on this point is scarce. Studies on reforms introduced in the early 1990s indicate that both the number of welfare beneficiaries increased and re-entry by those who left the rolls rose as a result of UI changes (OECD, 1999*a*; Fortin *et al.*, 1999), although it is likely that such effects would be dampened somewhat under the current robust labour-market conditions. Indeed, the latest monitoring report notes that take-up rates of social assistance decreased for claimants after EI reform. Another area where evidence is scarce is whether provinces have attempted to shift welfare recipients back onto employment insurance, for example via the use of wage subsidies. These could allow welfare recipients to re-qualify for EI benefits.

19. Thus, the current 10 weeks of parental leave would be extended to 35 weeks. That plus 15 weeks maternity leave gives a total of 50 weeks of benefits.

20. Note that this figure captures only the federal spending component on active labour market programmes. Provinces also run schemes (independent of those under the LMDAs), but data on their expenditures are not available.

21. Impact evaluations examine the outcome of programme participants and determine whether they were better off after having participated in a programme than they otherwise would have been.

22. They are: Alberta, British Columbia, New Brunswick, Newfoundland/Labrador, Nova Scotia, Quebec and Ontario. The latter was included even though an LMDA has not been signed because it has significant control over ALMPs.

23. The indicators monitored are the number of EI claimants returning to work, costs savings realised and the number of claimants served.

24. The percentage of children less than 18 years of age living in families with income below Statistics Canada's low income cut-off increased by 4 percentage points between 1989 and 1997 to 15.8 per cent. This is consistent with an observed (albeit small) rise in family earnings inequality in the early 1990s (Picot and Heisz, 2000*b*; Rashid, 1998 and 1999). The Gini coefficient increased from 0.359 to 0.373 between 1985 and 1995 (although transfers and the progressive tax system served to reduce it; that is, the coefficient would have been 0.458 in 1995 without them).

25. The federal and provincial-territorial governments have created a series of indicators to monitor progress of the NCB (such as depth of low income, percentage of low-income parents employed, average weeks worked and average earnings) and is in the process of developing a comprehensive framework to evaluate outcomes.

26. While Brazil has agreed to no longer provide subsidies for future aircraft sales, it has refused to remove subsidies from undelivered aircraft under current contracts. Brazil has announced it will appeal the WTO panel ruling.

27. Specifically, the duty exemption provision applies only to the qualified manufacturers under the Auto Pact of 1965, which were grandfathered under NAFTA. The Auto Pact requires them to build as many cars in Canada as they sell. They are then exempted from paying a 6.1 per cent duty when they import cars for sale in Canada from anywhere else in the world (typically the United States). Competing vehicle manufacturers that have also invested in Canada to a significant extent do not benefit from this exemption.

28. Market power mitigation involves short-, medium- and long-term measures. In the short term (beginning with open access slated to come into effect in late 2000), Ontario Power Generation will be subject to a revenue cap on a fixed quantity of energy (price cap/rebate mechanism). In the medium term (by 42 months after open access), Ontario Power Generation is required to relinquish control over at least 4 000 megawatts of specific types of generation. In the long term (within 10 years of open access), Ontario Power Generation is required to reduce its capacity in Ontario to 35 per cent of total supply.

29. The American authorities have argued that allowing mergers would encourage rail companies to avoid making difficult decisions on how to organise their operations. Still, mergers could also help to resolve some of these operational problems.

30. The foundation was established in 1997 to help universities and colleges, research hospitals and not-for-profit institutions modernise their research infrastructure.

31. Under the infrastructure programme, C$ 100 million will be used for a municipal component with priority funding going to green infrastructure. Projects will be cost-shared among all levels of government. The remaining C$ 200 million will be used for federal infrastructure, mainly federally-owned buildings and bridges. Funding for provincial highways (up to C$ 150 million per year) will only become available in 2002-03.

32. They are: the Mutual Life Assurance Company of Canada (now known as Clarica), Manufacturers Life Insurance Company, the Canada Life Assurance Company, Sun Life of Canada and Industrial Alliance (Quebec Charter).

33. Foreign banks are allowed to set up as either a lending branch or a full-service branch. A lending branch is not allowed to accept retail deposits and are restricted to borrowing from other financial institutions, while a full-service branch is able to accept deposits above C$ 150 000.

34. Federally regulated financial institutions include banks, trust and loan companies, co-operative credit institutions, life insurance companies, fraternal benefit societies, property and casualty insurance companies and pension plans.

35. The Ontario Securities Commission reports that a federally chartered financial institution, operating in every province and territory with deposit-taking, securities and insurance subsidiaries would be forced to deal with separate regulators for each.

36. The CSA is comprised of the twelve provincial and territorial securities regulatory authorities that administer the Canadian Securities Regulatory System.

37. Banks and other regulated financial institutions would continue to be fully regulated, which would help to reduce the risk of self-dealing.

38. Note that while these are the statutory tax rates, the burden may be quite different due to exemptions, allowances and subsidies.

39. An additional factor distorting the corporate tax environment between Canada and the United States is the latter's partial exemption of company taxation on certain export sales, through the use export corporations (Foreign Sales Corporations, FSC). A WTO panel has ruled that these are inconsistent with US commitments, and the United States has since then agreed to abide by the decision. The elimination of the FSC tax relief to US exporters will improve the relative competitiveness of Canada's 21 per cent rate in the manufacturing and processing areas.

40. Since 1994, the EI premium rate has been reduced from C$ 3.07 to C$ 2.40 per C$ 100 in insurable earnings, but the EI account continues to be in surplus because the extent of the reductions has not matched the additional net revenues arising from favourable labour market conditions and cost reductions from EI reform.

41. The CPP is one of the cornerstones of social security in Canada. It provides earnings-linked benefits to about 3 million retired workers who meet a minimum level of contributions, financed by a combined employer/employee payroll charge (split equally) and contributions from the self-employed, with payments indexed annually to the consumer price index. CPP benefits amount to about 25 per cent of the average wage in Canada. In addition, individuals are eligible for Old Age Security (OAS), a taxable entitlement offered to most elderly Canadians, and a Guaranteed Income Supplement (GIS), targeted on the low-income elderly and tested against family income, with benefits reduced by 50 cents for each additional dollar of non-OAS earnings. Workers also receive tax incentives to save in private plans for their retirement.

42. Traditionally, CPP funds have been lent to provinces in the form of non-marketable bonds yielding federal government bond rates. Provinces will have the option to roll over their existing CPP borrowings at a maturity of another 20-year term. However, they will be forced to pay the same rate of interest as they do on their other market borrowings, thus eliminating the subsidy they have benefited from heretofore.

43. The indices are those which replicate the TSE 300 Composite Index, the Standard and Poor's 500 Index and the Morgan Stanley EAFE (Europe, Australia, New Zealand and Far East) Index. Foreign holdings are limited to 20 per cent of the stock portfolio.

44. These are the fertility rate, net annual migration, mortality, incidence of disability, employment/unemployment rates, real wages, price increases and rates of return on new fund investments.

45. Indeed, the scarcity of MRI scanners and the resulting waiting lists have led to a growing number of private MRI clinics, despite criticism that they may violate the provisions of the Canada Health Act.

46. Indeed, the capping of costs may have induced some physicians to schedule additional patient visits to boost income (at the expense of the income of other physicians).

47. Regionalisation has involved the consolidation of hospitals and hospital boards to fewer regional health authorities, which has led to some centralisation of costs and budgets while allowing some intraprovincial variation to meet more localised needs.

48. Still, while primary-care reform is clearly necessary, there are indications that emergency-room overcrowding, particularly during holiday periods, has resulted from poor hospital planning since many hospitals have been able to avoid this problem (Gray, 2000).

49. Specifically, the legislation would allow regional authorities to contract out services to private facilities requiring overnight stays that would normally be provided in a hospital setting.

50. Although forestry is an important activity in a number of Canadian provinces, and there are periodic public debates about the sustainability of this activity, this section does not review forest policy. At the national level, the annual growth in wood stock is larger than the annual harvest (OECD, 1998*b*), so that in quantitative terms the intensity of forest resource use seems sustainable. There are important and more complex issues at the intersection of economics and the environment associated with forest exploitation, but these go beyond the time and space available for this chapter.

51. For a more comprehensive survey of institutions and the governance of sustainable development see OECD (2000*e*).

52. The federal government has just introduced a draft bill for protecting species at risk.

53. Incidentally, it could be noted that tax breaks provided by the federal government to resource-based sectors presumably result in increasing the royalties provinces can extract, thereby constituting an implicit transfer to these provinces.

54. These rates take into account all federal and provincial tax provisions related to investment (corporate income taxes, capital taxes and sales tax on business inputs) except for royalties, which are considered as a cost rather than a tax. If royalties paid to provincial governments are treated as a tax, the marginal effective tax rate for the upstream activities of the oil and gas industry is 18.2 per cent, which is close to the average for all industries.

55. The 2000 Report of the Commissioner of the Environment and Sustainable Development confirms the result found in "The Level Playing Field Study", released in 1996 by Natural Resources Canada, which concluded that the variation in tax assistance between renewable and non-renewable energy projects was not large. There are some important exceptions, however, including oil sands and coal mines, nuclear technology, alternative fuels and certain energy efficiency investments.

56. In the federal corporate income tax system, exploration costs can generally be immediately deducted against income at 100 per cent, and development expenditures at a 30 per cent rate on a declining balance basis. Accelerated capital-cost allowances have also been provided.

57. The introduction of flow-through shares resulted in large amounts of financing being raised for mineral exploration in Canada, especially in the late 1980s (Brewer and Lemieux, 1997).

58. On the contrary, provinces introduced new preferential tax provisions for the minerals and metals sector in 1998, for example through increases in prospecting grants and in various tax allowances, and exemption of fuel taxes in the mining process (Natural Resources Canada, 1999).

59. The primary issuer of flow-through shares are those companies that cannot take immediate advantage of the allowable write-offs available through the tax system. Such companies would tend to be small or in a start-up phase, with limited access to other forms of financing.

60. Oil and natural gas sub-surface rights are systematically auctioned in Alberta. In the case of metals and non-metallic minerals, a competitive bidding process is implemented if there are several applications for the rights.

61. Fresh water supply is measured as precipitation less losses due to evaporation and out-flows to neighbouring countries or to the sea, plus inflows from neighbouring countries. Canada has about 9 per cent of the world's renewable fresh water, but also 7 per cent of the world's landmass. A large part of that water drains northward, though, and is not available to the Canadian population living near the southern border.

62. Water abstraction is the volume of water taken out from waterways or aquifers.

63. The intensity of use is measured by the ratio of gross abstractions to available freshwater resources.

64. Water is sometimes in short supply during summer and drought periods in southern Alberta, which accounts for about 60 per cent of Canadian irrigated land, and also in the southern parts of the Great Lakes basin, where urban needs have come into conflict with rural and agricultural demands.

65. Initially, water rights were riparian, that is vested in the owner of a body of water or neighbouring land. Provinces have reformed this system at various times, as far back as the end of last century in Alberta for example, and only in the early 1960s in Ontario.

66. Renzetti and Dupont (1999) indicate that charges applied to water withdrawal vary from a simple one-time payment when the license is issued (Manitoba) to a rather complex fee schedule depending on the use of water, the location and characteristics of the firm or agency withdrawing the water, and the quantity of water.

67. While it is certainly legally possible to make users pay for the costs of supplying water and the environmental costs of extraction, this is less clear for the scarcity rent. Water rights have been initially granted for free in Canada, and taxing the rent *ex post* may raise legal issues similar to those experienced in the United States under the heading "takings" (see OECD, 2000a).

68. Figures from a report of the National Round Table on the Environment and the Economy (1996) indicate that subsidies covered more than one-third of the operational costs of Canadian water and wastewater services in 1994, and about two-thirds of capital expenditure.

69. On average, agricultural water prices ranged between $0.0017 and $0.002 per cubic meter in 1996, against $0.7 for households in 1994.

70. Calculations of implicit values of water rights in southern Alberta, using market prices of different types of land (irrigated or not) show that the availability of irrigation water adds approximately 35 per cent to land values (Veeman *et al.*, 1997).

71. Metering is more prevalent in Ontario and the Prairies than in other regions of the country.

72. In Ontario, the charge is 0.39 cents per kWh, corresponding to one tenth of the average wholesale price.

73. The projects in question were subsequently cancelled, and all three jurisdictions have adopted regulations or laws that prohibit the bulk removal of water.

74. See, for example, the websites of the Canadian Environmental Law Association (*http://www.web.net/cela/*) and the Council of Canadians (*http://www.canadians.org/*).

75. The report is available on the IJC website (*www.ijc.org*).

76. This is the case in particular for the groundwater system, about which relatively little is known.

77. The IJC, an independent bi-national panel, also investigated the issue of trade consider-
    ations. After hearing from various citizens groups, and government and independent
    trade law experts representing every point of view, the IJC came to the same conclusion
    as Canada and the USA that trade agreements do not apply to water in its natural state.

78. A recent poll indicated that Canadians would agree to water exports as long as the
    government "controls the tap" (*The Globe and Mail*, 15 December 1999).

79. As environmental effects depend in large parts on the scale of the removals, they
    could be controlled in a licensing system (as they are currently at the domestic level).
    Permits could, for example, be provided on a one-off or fixed-term basis.

80. The failure of the proposal to tanker water from British Columbia to the Californian city
    of Santa Barbara at the start of the 1990s may be illustrative in this regard. There were
    several reasons why Canadian firms were not competitive, but one was the lack of
    credible seller commitment (Smith, 1994).

81. In fact, another problem associated with water removals is the absence of prices
    reflecting its "true" value, which makes it difficult to assess the opportunity costs of
    exports and to make projections on future values, since even today's value is not
    known.

82. The circumstances of the Atlantic groundfishery is not illustrative of the entire indus-
    try, which comprises about 160 distinct fisheries. Stocks are also diminishing in the
    Pacific salmon fisheries. However, the situation results from different factors, and
    overfishing has probably played less of a role. In addition, the consequences of the
    salmon crisis there are less acute than in the Atlantic region, because the economy is
    more diversified. Adjustment policies have resulted in the Pacific salmon fleet being
    reduced by 50 per cent since 1995.

83. Changes occurred in the natural environment. Temperatures fell and ice coverage
    expanded. The water also became more saline. This has affected the survival capacity
    of fish as well as the predator-prey balance (reducing the number of prey available for
    groundfish but increasing the number of predators such as seals). These factors are
    probably still at play, as no substantial increase in stocks has been observed in the
    eight years of closure.

84. The others were: the Atlantic Fisheries Adjustment Program (AFAP) and the Quebec
    Federal Fisheries Development Program (QFFDP) in 1990, and the Atlantic Groundfish
    Adjustment Program (AGAP) in 1993.

85. In fact, when the sum available for income support turned out to be insufficient for the
    number of eligible individuals, all the non-income support measures contained in the
    TAGS were cut.

86. Regarding inshore ground fisheries, and IQ management, there is no example of a
    country that would have converted inshore fisheries with 10 000 users with small boats.
    Moreover, the only large and profitable fishery that is not an IQ in Canada is lobster
    and it would be most difficult to put lobster under IQ.

87. The decision whether to use property rights management is left to fishers, with in
    general a two-thirds majority rule required for implementation.

88. Charges are currently calculated as 2 per cent of landed value.

89. Greater involvement of the industry is important to achieve effective management.
    This is particularly the case for the fisheries comprising a large number of small
    vessels as it reduces the monitoring and enforcement costs.

90. Employment insurance legislation has a specific section for fishers.

91. Total benefits paid to fishers declined in the fiscal year 1996/97 due to the reduction in maximum insurable income. However, they increased in the following year, mainly as a result of increased multiple claims for winter and summer seasons (amounting to C$ 215 million in 1997-98 only 1 per cent less than two years earlier).

92. Claims for the under-25 age group decreased 20 per cent between 1995/96 and 1998/99.

93. The example referred to is that of the Newfoundland snow crab fishery. Another example where scientists' recommendations were not followed is that of the Bay of Fundy scallop fishery (Report of the Auditor General, 1999).

94. In 1997, the Fisheries Resource and Conservation Council estimated that in some instances, capacity was two to three times larger than needed. Estimating over-capacity, though, is not a simple task as it involves biological, technical and economic judgements.

95. The Atlantic Fisheries Policy Review is part of the "Fishery of the Future" strategy, which also includes policy guidelines for the Pacific coast salmon fisheries.

96. The index measures the extent to which a country achieves environmental sustainabil-ity by looking at five areas: the extent to which environmental systems are maintained at healthy levels, and improving rather than deteriorating; the level of anthropogenic environmental stress and risks; human vulnerability to environmental impact; social and institutional capacity to deal with environmental challenges; and environmental co-operation with other countries (World Economic Forum, 2000).

97. The Polluter Pays Principle (PPP), adopted by OECD countries in 1972, has evolved over time. Initially, it meant that the polluter should bear the costs of pollution prevention and control. Since then, it has been extended to cover administrative costs, and the costs of damage when the measures ordered by the authorities have not been taken, or those resulting from accidental discharge. Gradually, the PPP has tended to move towards the full internalisation of the external costs of pollution.

98. A policy measure proves effective if it meets its target. It is cost-effective if the target is achieved at minimum cost.

99. For example, in 1998, the federal enforcement capacity of the Yukon and Pacific region was reduced by more than one third. And in 1997, the job of public pest-inspectors was eliminated by the Ontario government.

100. One of the examples provided by the 1998 report of the Standing Committee on Environment and Sustainable Development, is that of a firm in Quebec, along with two individuals, who had been charged with 15 counts of polluting the St. Lawrence River contrary to provisions of the Fisheries Act. However, as the firm was acting under authorisation given by the Quebec government, it could not be prosecuted.

101. Seven federal-provincial agreements have been negotiated in relation to the CEPA and the provisions of the Fisheries Act relating to toxic substances, which have the advantage of providing the industry with a "single window". Matters covered by these agreements include research, training, monitoring, inspections and investigations. As a rule, however, both parties retain the authority to act under their respective legislation.

102. It includes only 10 of the 25 substances listed as top priority in the CEPA and covers only large companies.

103. The first package was announced in September 1999 and the second in the 2000 budget. After the initial three years, incremental annual enforcement funding will continue at C$ 9 million.

104. The Canada Wide Standards sub-agreement, signed in January 1998, aims at developing and attaining standards for substances that have general significance across the country and present significant human health or ecosystem risk. For more information, see www.mbnet.mb.ca/ccme.

105. Smog, or high concentration of tropospheric ozone, is also a problem in the Vancouver area, where a substantial share of emissions comes from the Seattle area.

106. Canada has succeeded in meeting its domestic, bilateral and international reduction targets for sulphur dioxide and nitrogen oxide. Targets (national or concerning only the seven eastern provinces) for SO2 were set in the 1985 Eastern Canada Acid Rain Program, in the 1991 Air Quality Accord with the United States, and in the two sulphur protocols of the UN-ECE Convention on Long-Range Transboundary Air Pollution (CLRTAP). Targets for NOx were set in the UN-ECE CLRTAP Sofia protocol and in the 1991 NOx/VOCs Management Plan (cf. OECD, 1995).

107. The multi-stakeholder Acidifying Emissions Task Group concluded in 1997 that sulphur dioxide emissions should be reduced by 75 per cent below their 1997 cap (actual emissions were already about 25 per cent below their cap at that time), to reach the critical load – the deposition level that will not cause any harm to the eco-system. In fact, the reductions already achieved have had a smaller effect than expected on the eco-system.

108. Emission reduction credits created by sources outside the capped entities should be: 1) real; 2) quantifiable; 3) surplus, that is not otherwise required by current regulations or voluntary obligations; 4) verifiable; and 5) unique.

109. Emissions could be valued with a distance-related discount factor according to the damage they cause.

110. Annex B to the Protocol lists the countries accepting emissions targets, that is OECD countries with the exception of Korea, Mexico, and Turkey, plus Russia and a number of economies in transition.

111. Canada signed the Kyoto Protocol on the understanding that it would have access to a number of "flexibility mechanisms", such as joint mitigation projects with other developed as well as developing countries, international emissions trading and soil sequestration ("sink" activities) in order to achieve its target.

112. The estimates for the price of permit per tonne of carbon provided by GREEN, the model developed by the OECD Secretariat, is $90 per tonne when trade takes place only among Annex B countries and $10 to $20 in the unlikely event that all developing countries were to participate. GREEN does not provide estimates for Canada of GDP losses and permit prices with no trade, as it is a sub-part of one of the regions considered by the model. In this latter case, the corresponding increase in the price of gasoline would be about 2 cents per litre (around 3 per cent of the current price in Ontario). If trading occurs among Annex B countries only, the increase in the price of gasoline would range between 6 and 10 cents (i.e. about 9 to 15 per cent of current Ontario price).

113. Regarding hydropower production, there are not many sites left, and opposition to the construction of new dams for environmental reasons has been mounting over the last decade.

114. Compared with a national average of about 23 tonnes of GHG emissions per person, Alberta produces about 71 tonnes per person, Saskatchewan 59, New Brunswick 25, Nova Scotia 21, Ontario 17, Newfoundland 16, British Columbia 14, and Quebec and Manitoba 12 (IEA, 2000).

115. The extent of the cost to fossil fuel-producing provinces very much depends on the ease with which natural gas can displace coal in the US electricity sector. As for provinces exporting non-fossil-fuel-based electricity, they will partly benefit from Kyoto implementation, as this will increase the export price.

116. Some regulatory measures were also used, such as energy efficiency standards for lighting (estimated to reduce greenhouse gas emissions by 5 megatonnes annually by 2000), household appliances and electric motors.

117. The 2000 budget provides about C\$ 625 million in additional funds over the next five years for programmes related to climate change.

118. As far as average consumption standards are concerned, this makes sense in an integrated North American automobile market, as it minimises the costs of meeting those standards through economies of scale.

119. Trucking is a major source of greenhouse gas emissions, representing 27 per cent of the emissions from transport, of which they are the most rapidly growing component.

120. The federal tax rate is 10 cents per litre of gasoline and 4 cents per litre of diesel. Provincial tax rates range from 9 cents for both diesel and gasoline in Alberta to 16.5 cents in Newfoundland.

121. The environmental costs are estimated based on estimates of the costs of emissions of various gases per tonne or passenger-kilometre.

122. The price of urban public transit increased by 69 per cent in the decade to 1999, a 36 per cent rise in real terms.

123. See the option paper of the issue table on transportation on the website of the National Climate Change Process [www.nccp.ca]. The cost-effectiveness of an increase in fuel taxes is recognised, but the magnitude of the increase required is considered incompatible with "the value that Canadians place on the convenience, necessity and pleasure of transportation".

124. The competitiveness issue has been dealt with at length in previous OECD Economic Surveys' chapters on the same subject. For example, see OECD (1999f), OECD (2000a) and OECD (2000d).

125. Just as significantly lower sales tax in the United States does not result in Canadians living in the border area doing all their shopping in the United States, it would probably not do so in the case of fuel.

126. There are also probably ways to partly address the problem, by for example introducing a graduated tax based on the distance from the border, provided that the administrative costs associated with such a tax do not offset the "retained" tax receipts (cf. OECD, 2000a).

127. Municipalities are increasingly aware of these problems, and some, such as Greater Vancouver, are launching initiatives to reverse this trend and reduce associated emissions of GHGs and other air pollutants. However, the effective implementation of changes in land use faces strong resistance from people that have already invested (in houses or commercial buildings), and creates a number of transition problems.

128. As a matter of fact, public transport services require subsidies even in densely populated areas.

129. See, for example, Pollution Probe (1999).

130. Programmes such as Energy Innovators and the Canadian Industry Program for Energy Conservation (CIPEC) set sectional targets and get member companies to comply. CIPEC's 21 task forces representing a total of 3 000 companies, achieved an overall decrease in energy intensity of 0.9 per cent per year between 1990 and 1997, while their value added increased by 2.3 per cent annually over the same period.

131. For a discussion of what they call the "rebound" effect, see Birol and Keppler (2000).

132. Three Canadian projects have been accepted as having met the criteria for registration under the GERT Pilot, and there six more projects currently being reviewed. One project is being registered in the GERT process as a trade matched project – one where there is both a buyer and seller of emission reductions: Ontario Power Generation Inc. purchasing almost 90 000 tonnes of CO_2 emission reductions that were expected to be generated during 1999 by the Star Lake Partnership. GHG emission reductions are being created because the hydroelectrically-generated power at Star Lake is displacing fossil fuel-based power currently generated on the Avalon Peninsula in Newfoundland.

133. Ontario Power Generation has purchased credits of 2.5 million tonnes of carbon dioxide from Zahren Alternative Power, a small American firm that captures methane from landfills. A coalition of Canadian energy companies has also bought 3.3 million tonnes of carbon dioxide credits from Iowa farmers that are generating the credits from not tilling the soil.

134. The National Climate Change Process, the current federal government strategy, includes a requirement that "no region of the country should be asked to bear an unreasonable burden".

Bibliography

Abare (1999),
Economic Impacts of the Kyoto Protocol – Accounting for the three major gases, Research Report 99.6, Canberra.

Archambault, R. and L. Grignon (1999),
"Decline in the Youth Participation Rate Since 19990: Structural or Cyclical?", W-99-1E, Applied Research Branch, Strategic Policy, Human Resources Development Canada, January.

Atta-Mensah, J. (2000),
"Recent Developments in the Monetary Aggregates and Their Implications", Bank of Canada Review, spring.

Birol, F. and J.H. Keppler (2000),
"Technology, Prices and Energy Efficiency", STI Review No. 25, Special Issue on Sustainable Development.

Boston Consulting Group (2000),
Fast Forward: Accelerating Canada's Leadership in the Internet Economy, Report of the Canadian E-Business Opportunities Roundtable, January.

Brean, D.J.S., D.P. Dungan and S. Murphy (1999),
"The Industrial and Economic Consequences of Removing The Canadian Tariff on Imported Vehicles", University of Toronto, mimeo, September.

Brewer K.J. and A. Lemieux (1997),
"Canada's Global Position in Mining", Natural resource Canada, Ottawa [http://nrn1.nrcan.gc.ca:80/mms/efab/invest/metals/title.htm].

Brewer, K.J. (1996),
"Canada's Mining Industry: A Global Perspective", Natural resource Canada, Ottawa [http://nrn1.nrcan.gc.ca/mms/efab/mmsd/mining_report/].

Charles River Associates (1999),
Analysis of the Impact on the Canadian Upstream Oil and Gas Industry of the Global Implementation of the Kyoto Protocol, prepared for the Canadian Upstream Oil and Gas Working Group of the Industry Issues Table, September, mimeo.

Copeland, B.R. (1998),
"Economics and the environment: the recent Canadian experience and prospects for the future", in Canada in the 21st century, II. Resources and technology, Industry Canada Research Publications Program, Paper Number 8, November.

Department of Fisheries and Oceans (1999),
Canada's Strategy for Fisheries Reform and Renewal, October.

Dupont, D.P. (1996),
    "Limited Entry Fishing Programs", in D.V. Gordon and G.R. Munro (eds), *Fisheries and Uncertainty – A Precautionary Approach to Resource Management*, University of Calgary Press.

Elridge, L. and M. Sherwood (2000),
    Investigating the Canada-US Productivity Gap: BLS Methods and Data, Centre for the Study of Living Standards, Conference on the Canada- US Manufacturing Productivity Gap, January.

Fisheries Resource Conservation Council (1997),
    A *Groundfish Conservation Framework for Atlantic Canada*, Report to the Monister of Fisheries and Oceans, FRCC 97.3, July.

Fortin, B., G. Lacroix and J.F. Thibault (1999),
    "The Interaction of UI and Welfare, and the Dynamics of Welfare Participation of Single Parents", *Canadian Public Policy*, Vol. XXV Supplement, 1999.

Fortin, P. (1999),
    The Canadian Standard of Living, Is There a Way Up? C.D. Howe Institute Benefactors Lecture, Montreal, October, C.D. Howe Institute.

Fortin, P. and M. Van Audenrode (2000),
    "The Impact of Experience Rating on Unemployed Workers", Human Resources Development Canada, mimeo.

Frank, J. and E. Belair (2000),
    "Are We Losing Our Best and Brightest to the US?" *Canadian Journal of Policy Research*, Spring.

Grafton, R.Q. and D. Lane (1998),
    "Canadian Fisheries Policies: Challenges and Choices", *Canadian Public Policy – Analyse de Politiques*, Vol. XXIV, No. 2.

Gray, C. (2000),
    "Hospital Crisis? What Crisis?", *Canadian Medical Association Journal*, April.

Gu, W. and M. Ho (2000),
    A *comparison of Productivity Growth in Manufacturing between Canada and the United States*, 1961-95, Centre for the Study of Living Standards, Conference on the Canada- US Manufacturing Productivity Gap, January.

Harrison, K. (1996),
    Passing the Buck – Federalism and Canadian Environmental Policy, UBC Press, Vancouver.

Health Canada (1997),
    Drug Costs in Canada, Submitted to the House of Commons Standing Committee on Industry, Ministry of Health, March.

Helliwell, J.F. (1999),
    "Checking the Brain Drain: Evidence and Implications", *Policy Study* 99-3, Policy and Economic Analysis Program, University of Toronto, June.

Hessing, M. and M. Howlett (1997),
    Canadian Natural Resource and Environmental Policy – Political Economy and Public Policy, UBC Press, Vancouver.

Horbulyk, T.M, and L.J. Lo (1998),
    Welfare Gains from Potential Water Markets in Alberta, Canada", in K.W. Easter, M.W. Rosegrant and A. Dinar (eds), *Markets for Water: Potential and Performance*, Natural resource management and policy series, Kluwer.

Horbulyk, T.M. and L.J. Lo (1998),
    "Welfare Gains from Potential Water Markets in Alberta, Canada".

HRDC (1998),
Evaluation of the Transition Jobs Fund (Phase I) Final Report, Human Resources Development Canada, October.

HRDC (1999),
Overview of the Evaluation of the Labour Market Development Agreements, Human Resources Development Canada, mimeo, December.

HRDC (2000),
Employment Insurance 1999 Monitoring and Assessment Report, Canada Employment Insurance Commission, Human Resources Development Canada.

IBI Group and Boon, Jones and Associates Inc. (1995),
Full costs Transportation and Cost-Based Pricing Strategies, November.

Johnson, J.R. (1994),
"Canadian Water and Free Trade", in T.L. Anderson (ed.), Continental Water Marketing, Pacific Research Institute for Public Policy, San Fransisco.

Krarup, S. (1999),
"Voluntary agreements in energy policy", mimeo.

Lin, Z., J. Yates and G. Picot (1999),
"Rising Self-Employment in the Midst of High Unemployment: An Empirical Analysis of Recent Developments in Canada", Working Paper No. 133, Statistics Canada.

May, D. and A. Hollett (1995),
The Rock in a Hard Place – Atlantic Canada and the UI Trap, C.D. Howe Institute, Toronto.

Ministry of National Revenue (1998),
Electronic Commerce and Canada's Tax Administration A Response by the Minister of National Revenue to his Advisory Committee's Report on Electronic Commerce, Ministry of National Revenue, September.

Munro, G.R. and S. McCorquodale (1981),
"The Northern Cod Fishery of Newfoundland", in Public Regulation of Commercial Fisheries in Canada, Case Study No. 3, Ottawa: Economic Council of Canada.

Nadeau, S., L. Whewell and S. Williamson (1999),
"Beyond the Headlines on the 'Brain Drain'", Industry Canada, mimeo, September.

National Round Table on the Environment and the Economy (1996),
Water and Wastewater services in Canada, Ottawa.

Natural Resource Canada (1996),
"The Level Playing Field – The Tax Treatment of Competing Energy Investment".

Natural Resource Canada (1999),
Summary of mining-related measures announced in 1998, http://nrn1.nrcan.gc.ca:80/mms/efab/tmrd/budget_summary98.htm.

Naylor, C.D. (1999),
"Health Care in Canada: Incrementalism Under Fiscal Duress", Health Affairs, May/June 1999.

OECD (1996a),
Enhancing the Effectiveness of Active Labour Market Policies, OECD, Paris.

OECD (1996b),
Economic Survey of Canada, OECD, Paris.

OECD (1998a),
Economic Survey of Canada, OECD, Paris.

OECD (1998b),
Towards Sustainable development – Environmental Indicators, Paris.

OECD (1999a),
  The Battle against Exclusion, Social Assistance in Canada and Switzerland, Vol. 3, OECD, Paris.
OECD (1999b),
  Economic Survey of Canada, OECD, Paris.
OECD (1999c),
  Implementing Domestic Tradable Permits for Environmental Protection, OECD Proceedings, Paris.
OECD (1999d),
  The Price of Water, Paris.
OECD (1999e),
  Voluntary Approaches for Environmental Policy – An Assessment, Paris.
OECD (1999f),
  Economic Survey of Finland, Paris.
OECD (2000a),
  Economic Survey of the United States, Paris.
OECD (2000b),
  Science, Technology and Industry Scoreboard 1999: Benchmarking Knowledge-Based Economies, OECD, Paris.
OECD (2000c),
  Energy Policies of IEA Countries, Canada 2000 Review, Paris.
OECD (2000d),
  Economic Survey of Denmark, Paris.
OECD (2000e),
  Case study of the governance for sustainable development, Paris (forthcoming).
Oliner, S.D. and D.E. Sichel (2000),
  "The Resurgence of Growth in the Late 1990s: Is Information Technology the Story?", Federal Reserve Board, February.
Pearse, P.H. (1988),
  "Property rights and the Development of Natural Resource Policies in Canada", *Canadian Public Policy – Analyse de Politiques*, XIV:3:307-320.
Picot, G. and A. Heisz (2000a),
  "The Labour Market in the 1990s", *Canadian Economic Observer*, Statistics Canada, January.
Picot, G. and A. Heisz (2000b),
  "The Labour Market in the 1990s Part II: Distributional Outcomes: Who is Winning and Losing", *Canadian Economic Observer*, Statistics Canada, February.
Rashid, A. (1998),
  "Family income inequality, 1970-1995", *Perspectives On Labour and Income*, Winter 1998, Vol. 10, No. 4, Statistics Canada.
Rashid, A. (1999),
  "Family income: 25 years of stability and change", *Perspectives on Labour and Income*, Spring 1999, Vol. 11, No. 1, Statistics Canada.
Renzetti (1999),
  "Municipal water supply and sewage treatment: costs, prices and distorsions", *Canadian Journal of Economics, Revue canadienne d'Économique*, Vol. 32, No. 3.
Renzetti, S. and D. Dupont (1999),
  "An Assessment of the Impact of Charging for Provincial Water Use Permits", *Canadian Public Policy – Analyse de Politiques*, Vol. XXV, No. 3.

Resources Future International (1996),
    Transportation grants and subsidies: their environmental implications, Transport Canada Discussion Paper 5, September.

Retail Council of Canada (1999),
    The Race Is On: Who Will Win Canada's Internet Shoppers? The Comprehensive Report on E-Retail in Canada, Retail Council of Canada, June.

Schrank, W.E. (1996),
    "Origins of Atlantic Canada Fishing Crisis", in D.V. Gordon and G.R. Munro (eds), *Fisheries and Uncertainty – A Precautionary Approach to Resource Management*, University of Calgary Press.

Schreyer, P. (2000),
    "The Contribution of Information and Communication Technology to Output Growth: A Study of the G7 Countries", STI *Working Paper* 2000/2, OECD.

Schwanen, D. (2000),
    Putting the Brain Drain in Context: Canada and the Global Competition for Scientists and Engineers, C.D. Howe Institute Commentary No. 140, April.

Smith. R.T. (1994),
    "The Economic Structure of Contracts for International Water Trades", in T.L. Anderson (ed.), *Continental Water Marketing*, Pacific Research Institute for Public Policy, San Fransisco.

Stanford, J. (2000),
    A Success Story: Canadian Productivity Performance in Auto Assembly, Centre for the Study of Living Standards, Conference on the Canada- US Manufacturing Productivity Gap, January.

Trajtenberg, M. (1999),
    Is Canada Missing the Technology Boat? Evidence from Patent Data, Centre for the Study of Living Standards-Industry Canada, Conference on Canada in the 21st Century, September.

Tupulé, V., S. Brown, J. Lim, C. Polidano, H. Pant and B.S. Fisher (1998),
    "An economic assessment of the Kyoto Protocol using the Global Trade and Environment Model", in OECD Workshop Report, *Economic Modelling of Climate Change*.

Van Kooten, G.C. and A. Scott (1995),
    "Constitutional Crisis, The Economics of Environment, and Resource Development in Western Canada", *Canadian Public Policy – Analyse de Politiques*, XXI:2:233-249.

Veeman, T.S. and M.M. Veeman, with W.L. Adamovicz, S. Royer, B. Viney, R. Freeman and J. Baggs (1997),
    Conserving Water in Irrigated Agriculture: The Economics and Valuation of Water Rights, Project Report No. 97-01, Department of Rural Economy, University of Alberta.

Wolff, E. (2000),
    Has Canada Specialised in the Wrong Manufacturing Industries? Centre for the Study of Living Standards, Conference on the Canada- US Manufacturing Productivity Gap, January.

World Economic Forum (2000),
    Pilot Environmental Sustainability Index, An Initiative of the Global Leaders for Tomorrow Environment Task Force, Annual meeting 2000, Davos.

Zhao, J., D. Drew and T.S. Murray (2000),
    "Knowledge workers on the move", *Perspectives on Labour and Income*, Summer 2000, Vol. 12, No. 2, Statistics Canada.

Annex I

Agreement on Internal Trade: major outstanding obligations

Chapter (No.)	Obligations	Status
Procurement (5)	By June 1995, extend coverage to municipalities, academic institutions, social service agencies and hospitals (the MASH sector).	February 1998, agreed (except for British Columbia and the Yukon) to include the MASH sector under a new annex to the AIT. Provisions of this annex came into force in July 1999.
	By June 1996, accelerate and conclude negotiations to move government entities (mainly crown corporations) off the exclusion list.	Negotiations are well advanced. Federal, provincial and territorial ministers responsible for internal trade matters are scheduled to review outstanding issues this spring.
	By July 1996, further negotiate reduction of excluded services (including professional, transportation, financial, health and advertising).	Negotiations have been suspended.
	By July 1998, review, harmonise, reconcile bid protest procedures.	No action taken.
	Review the Chapter.	No action taken.
Investment (6)	By December 1996, make recommendations as to the retention, removal or replacement of local presence and residency requirement measures.	Recommendations approved in February 1998. Some local presence and residency requirements remain (Annex 604.4).
	Reconcile extra-provincial corporate registration and reporting requirements. Establish arrangements to have this information available electronically by 1 July 1999.	Parties are examining the feasibility and costs of developing an electronic system.
	Examine matters as directed by ministers. In particular, ministers are pursuing a suggestion of provincial premiers to clarify and improve the Code of Conduct on Incentives.	Negotiations on the Code of Conduct on Incentives are ongoing. Ministers are to review outstanding issues this spring.

Chapter (No.)	Obligations	Status
Labour mobility (7)	In a "reasonable time", seek compliance of regional, local and other forms of municipal governments or governmental and non-governmental bodies.	Consultations ongoing.
	Mutual recognition of qualifications and reconciliation of occupational standards	Occupational regulatory bodies have been invited to initiate work towards compliance with the Agreement. More than 20 draft mutual recognition agreements covering professionals, such as registered nurses, teachers, engineers and chiropractors, have been reached and are being reviewed by governments.
		In February 1999, in the context of the Social Union Framework Agreement, all provinces (except Quebec) set a deadline of 1 July 2001 for full compliance of the mobility provisions of the AIT, including the requirements for mutual recognition of occupational qualifications and elimination of residency requirements for access to employment opportunities. Quebec, nonetheless, has indicated its willingness to work towards meeting this deadline for the AIT's labour mobility obligations.
Consumer-related measures and standards (8)	Reconcile consumer-related measures and standards.	With respect to co-operative enforcement, all jurisdictions (except the Yukon) have signed a Cooperative Enforcement Agreement.
		Consumer ministers have agreed to co-operate in the following areas: electronic commerce; consumer redress; and vulnerable consumers.
	Develop dispute resolution mechanisms before the date of entry into force of the AIT (1 July 1995).	Consumer ministers have agreed on these mechanisms. Internal trade ministers are expected to endorse such mechanisms at their spring meeting so that they may be formally incorporated in the AIT.
	By 1 July 1996, adopt harmonised legislation respecting direct selling contracts.	In progress. Eleven jurisdictions have adopted such legislation.
	By 1 January 1997, adopt harmonised legislation concerning disclosure for the cost of consumer credit.	In progress. One party has passed such legislation while three others have drafted bills.
Agriculture and food goods (9)	By September 1997, review the scope and coverage of the chapter.	Agriculture ministers undertook the required review and, based on public consultations, which reaffirmed the importance of, and support for, liberalising internal trade, have decided to pursue negotiations to revise the scope and coverage of the chapter.

Chapter (No.)	Obligations	Status
	Review supply management.	With respect to supply management of poultry and eggs, in July 1999, agriculture ministers reaffirmed their aim for greater flexibility and better adaptation to changing market conditions. The National Association of Agri-Food Supervisory Agencies continues to work towards a revised federal-provincial agreement consistent with this direction.
	Review agricultural safety nets.	Agriculture ministers also agreed to decide on a new framework agreement for farm income stabilisation and the phasing in of implementation by the spring of 2000.
Alcoholic beverages (10)	Review a host of non-conforming measures.	A working group annually reviews such measures with a view to their elimination. Implementation of the chapter has now been largely completed. However, New Brunswick and Quebec continue to maintain a reservation to apply differential costs while Newfoundland continues its reservation respecting beer distribution in the province.
		Quebec requires that any wine sold in its grocery stores must be bottled in Quebec as long as alternative outlets are provided in Quebec for the sale of wine of other parties. As a result, British Columbia reserves the right to invoke measures against the distribution of wine from Quebec.
		Agreement has been reached to eliminate the differential markups between wine produced from 100 per cent Canadian grapes and products from the European Community. Internal trade ministers are expected to endorse this change so that it may be formally deleted from the AIT.
		The Canadian Wine Standard was approved as a voluntary regulation under the Canadian General Standards Board (CGSB) in 1996, but its implementation has been delayed pending clarification of certain requirements. A CGSB national quality wine standard is currently under development as well. The Canadian Association of Liquor Jurisdictions continues to examine several packaging/case marking issues to determine possible harmonisation implications. This Association also has a National Quality Assurance Committee which meets regularly to harmonise technical standards for alcoholic beverages in Canada.
National resource processing (11)	By July 1998, review the achievement of objectives, identify and resolve implementation issues and make necessary revisions to the chapter.	No action items identified from reviews to date.

Chapter (No.)	Obligations	Status
Energy (12)	By July 1995, include energy under the Agreement.	Energy ministers have approved a text to come into effect upon satisfactory resolution of issues relating to the treatment of certain obligations of project sponsors embedded in the energy legislation of some jurisdictions. Internal trade ministers are scheduled to address the remaining issues this spring.
Telecommunications (13)	Telecommunications crown corporations in Saskatchewan not covered by certain sections of the Telecommunications Act (Canada) until the federal government passes an Order-in-Council.	Pursuant to an agreement between Saskatchewan and the federal government, an Order-in-Council was passed fixing 30 June 2000 as the date when certain provisions of the Telecommunications Act would apply. After this date telecommunications carriers in the province of Saskatchewan will be fully covered by the provisions of the AIT.
Transportation (14)	By July 1996, extend coverage to municipal governments.	Transportation ministers recommend deletion of obligation.
	By January 1996, reconcile regulations and standards-related measures.	Work ongoing (mostly completed).
	Phase-out non-conforming measures.	Ongoing negotiations.
Environmental protection (15)	Harmonise environmental measures.	In January 1998, provincial environment ministers (except Quebec) signed the Harmonisation Accord and related sub-agreements on standards, inspections and environmental assessment. In doing so, they agreed to work in partnership to achieve the highest level of environmental quality across Canada. Although not a signatory to this Accord, Quebec has indicated that it would work with other governments in meeting the Accord's provisions.
		Under Harmonisation, each government retains its existing powers and will use them collaboratively. In September 1998, those ministers approved an Annex to the Harmonisation Accord providing clarification on principles for stakeholders' involvement and public accountability. (Work is under way to develop Canada-wide standards, in six key areas: particulate matter; ozone; benzene; petroleum hydrocarbons in soil; dioxins and furans; and mercury.)
Institutional provisions (16)	By April 1996, report on the effects of the Agreement.	Not yet available.
Final provisions (18)	Annual review of the scope and coverage of the Agreement.	Ministers are expected to review issues respecting the future of the AIT at their spring meeting.

Annex II

Further information on the financial services sector in Canada

A. The proposed framework for the financial services sector

This framework discussed in Chapter III consists of four interrelated components designed to promote efficiency, foster competition, empower consumers and improve regulation. Within each of these broad areas, the government plans several initiatives, outlined below.

Promoting efficiency and growth with:

– A new definition of widely held ownership to allow strategic alliances and joint ventures with significant share exchanges.
– A new holding company regime to provide greater structuralflexibility.
– A transparent bank merger review process with a formal mechanism for public input.
– An examination of capital taxation policy with the provinces.

Fostering domestic competition by:

– Encouraging new entrants with liberalised ownership rules and lower capital requirements.
– Facilitating the ability of the credit unions to compete by allowing a restructuring of their system.
– Expanding access to the payments system to provide additional competition in deposit-like services.
– Allowing foreign banks to offer services to businesses and individual consumers via branches, in addition to subsidiaries.

Empowering and protecting consumers of financial services with:

– Measures to improve access to financial services regardless of income or place of residence, including a standard low-cost account and a process to govern branch closures.
– A Financial Consumer Agency of Canada to strengthen oversight of consumer protection measures and expand consumer education activities.
– An independent Canadian Financial Services Ombudsman.
– Measures to prevent coercive tied selling and improve the information consumers receive when purchasing services or making investments.
– Public Accountability Statements for financial institutions to report on their contributions to the Canadian economy and society.
– More and better statistics on, and analysis of, small and medium-sized business financing to provide a better understanding of their needs.

Improving the regulatory environment by:
- Bolstering the governance of the payments system.
- Reducing the reporting burden relating to Canadian Deposit Insurance Corporation Standards.
- Providing the Superintendent of Financial Institutions with new powers to deal with the potential risks arising from increased competition.
- Streamlining the Office of the Superintendent of Financial Institutions' regulatory approval process.

B. The regulatory framework

As noted in Chapter III, financial institutions must deal with a number of regulators, reflecting to some extent the different powers held by federal and provincial authorities as set out by the Canadian Constitution. This section briefly describes the recently introduced framework used by the Office of Superintendent of Financial Institutions as well as the risk-based system implemented by the Canada Deposit Insurance Corporation.

I. *Office of the Superintendent of Financial Institution's* (OSFI) *new supervisory framework*

The framework, introduced in August 1999, creates a risk-based supervisory approach that sets a composite risk rating and direction of risk for each regulated financial institution. This new approach assesses not only the "inherent" (see below) risk stemming from operations, but how it is mitigated by the quality of management, with the periodicity of each institution's examination depending upon its overall risk rating. This new framework allows regulators to channel their resources to where they are most needed, but also requires substantial judgement by staff. The examination follows a matrix approach, comprising: the *net risk* in each activity (low, moderate or high); a *direction of net risk* (decreasing, stable or increasing over an appropriate time horizon) and an *overall risk rating* and *direction of risk* for the all activities. A Risk Assessment Summary is then drawn up, compiling the institution's present financial condition, its prospective risk profile, key issues and past supervisory findings.

1.   The inherent risk faced by the institution is evaluated by examining a number of different factors:
- *Credit risk* which arises from a counterparty's inability or unwillingness to fully meet its on- or off-balance sheet obligations.
- *Market risk* that arises from changes in market rates or prices, including interest rates, foreign exchange rates, equity prices, commodity prices and real estate.
- *Insurance risk* that comprises product design and pricing risk.
- *Operational risk* that arises from problems in the performance of business function and processes such as the breakdown of internal controls, technology failures, human errors and so on.
- *Liquidity risk* which arises when an institution is unable to purchase or obtain necessary funds to meet its on and off balance sheet obligations as they come due without incurring unacceptable losses.
- *Legal and regulatory risk* that arises when an institution's non-conformance with laws, rules, regulations and other standards in jurisdiction in which the institution operates.
- *Strategic risk* which is inability of an institution to implement appropriate business plans, strategies, decision-making, resource allocation and adapt to changes in business environment.

2.   The criteria to measure the quality of management also span a number of categories, each of which are classified as strong, acceptable or weak.

-   *Operational management* is responsible for planning, directing and controlling the day to day operations of an institution's business activities.

-   *Financial analysis* is the function that performs in-depth analyses of the operational results of an institution and reports them to management.

-   *Compliance* is an independent function within an institution that: sets the policies and procedures for adherence to regulatory requirements in all jurisdictions where an institution operates; monitors the institution's compliance with these policies and procedures; and reports on compliance matters to senior management and the Board.

-   *Internal audit* is an independent function within the institution that assesses adherence to and effectiveness of operational and organisational controls.

-   *Risk management* is an independent function responsible for planning, directing and controlling the impact on the institution of risks arising from its operations.

-   *Senior management* is responsible for planning, directing and controlling the strategic direction and general operations of the institution.

-   *The Board of Directors* is responsible for providing stewardship and management oversight for the institution.

II.   Canada Deposit Insurance Corporation (CDIC) Standards of Sound Business and Financial Practices

In addition to meeting OSFI regulations, financial institutions covered by deposit insurance (or seeking coverage) are required to annually comply with CDIC standards* (Standards Assessment and Reporting Program or SARP), which set out requirements with respect to the risk management programmes that each member must have in place to manage their business activities and related risks. Results of the self-assessment are reported not only to the CDIC, but also to the main regulator (typically OSFI but the CDIC can also designate relevant provincial regulators), which is charged with ensuring that the member is actually following the standards. In its overall assessment of the financial health of the institution, the CDIC also uses a number of ancillary pieces of information, including OSFI examination reports, market information, reports from ratings agencies and so on. It then takes appropriate action, if necessary, which could include the closure of weak members or adjustment of premium rates. In this context, the CDIC introduced a new classification system for member institutions, commencing 1 May 1999. Since that time, each is assigned into one of four different premiums categories (formerly only one), based on a member's score related to a number of criteria, including capital adequacy, and other quantitative and qualitative factors (such as return on risk-weighted assets and real estate asset concentration). Those with the highest score (category 1) pay a premium rate of $1/24$ of 1 per cent of insured deposits while those with the lowest score pay $1/3$ of 1 per cent (except for the first 2 premium years during which the rate is set at $1/6$ th of 1 per cent). As compared with best practices for deposit insurance (as defined by the IMF), the CDIC is in compliance with each of the eleven areas identified.

---

*   A set of eight standards defines the minimum policies, procedures and criteria that member institutions must adhere to: liquidity management; interest rate risk management; credit risk management; real estate appraisals; foreign exchange risk management; securities portfolio management; internal control; capital management.

Annex III

Institutions and policies in the area of resources and the environment in historical perspective

Institutional responsibilities[1]

Canada's institutional set-up has played a major role in the definition of resource and environmental policies, as well as their evolution. It is a federal state in which each of the ten provinces and three territories has considerable autonomy, much more than in the United States, for example. The Canadian constitution gives responsibility to provincial and territorial institutions for everything that is not explicitly stated as federal. This gives them a major role in the policy area under consideration.

Provinces are the key players in resource policy. They own their natural resources such as coal, oil and gas, as well as the majority of the forests.[2] Moreover, they have the authority to legislate with respect to both publicly and privately owned resources within the province. The major exception to this rule concerns fisheries and migratory birds which, as a common property transcending provincial boundaries, fall under federal jurisdiction.[3] The federal government also exercises varying degrees of control over other resources through its sectoral power over agriculture and navigation, and through more general constitutional provisions – spending and taxing power, criminal law, interprovincial and international trade, and emergency powers falling under the "Peace, order and good government" clause of the Constitution. It has also jurisdiction over its own properties.

As the environment is not explicitly addressed in the Constitution, the division of powers regarding Canadian environmental policy between the various levels of government also flows to a great extent from jurisdiction over resources. Environmental management is thus shared between the various levels of government. A responsibility to protect fish provides the federal government with the opportunity to regulate water quality, in particular in coastal areas; federal authorities are charged with regulating pesticides in agriculture; navigation and shipping authority grants them a veto power over all developments that can affect the flow of water (such as dams and bridges on navigable waters); they are responsible for environmental protection of Aboriginal territories; and they undertake environmental monitoring and research. Apart from these sectoral responsibilities, federal regulatory activity in the environmental field is limited to international and interprovincial pollution, federal land developments and controlling toxic substances. Provinces, on the other hand, are responsible for pollution control on their territories. Municipalities are generally responsible for land-use functions such as the provision of water and sewerage services, zoning and the layout of roads. Together, the provinces and local governments (which are under their tutelage) are responsible for a large part of Canada's environmental regulation.

Development of policies

Royalties from the sale or lease of natural resources were (and still are in some cases) a very important source of revenues for the provinces, which have therefore strongly encouraged resource development. Progressively, though, the focus has shifted towards long-term resource conservation, and they have created institutions and established regulations and instruments for that purpose (such as long-term tenure in forest management). Initially, the role of the federal government was restricted to administering its own properties and trying to promote resource conservation through persuasion.[4] After the second world war, however, in its reconstruction efforts, the federal government started to rely on its spending power to support resource development. With the Canada Forestry Act (1949), for example, the federal government entered into shared-cost conditional grant programmes with the provincial governments. It also intervened more directly, notably in the energy sector. To support the development of oil production in western Canada, in the 1960s, the federal government prevented consumers west of the Ottawa River Valley from purchasing oil from foreign sources, thereby increasing prices significantly compared to the world market. Conversely, after the oil shock in 1973 and until the liberalisation of the energy market in the 1980s, the federal government froze the price of oil and subsidised oil imports in eastern Canada through taxes on exports and oil companies, heightening the tensions between the western provinces and the federal government. The latter also subsidised exploration outside the producing provinces. More generally, the federal government also provided grants to the resource sector through various regional development programmes.

In the environmental field, the main mechanisms to regulate pollution were established in the early 1970s, when a number of incidents both outside and inside Canada heightened public concern about environmental problems and brought them onto the policy agenda. Regulatory statutes for environmental licensing were passed in a number of provinces and bodies established to administer them. The federal government also started to get involved in environmental policy. The Canada Water Act (1970) and the Clean Air Act (1971) – two facilitating statutes – were essentially building on the need for federal-provincial co-operation in these areas. The federal department for the environment (Environment Canada) was also created in 1971. As in the United States, regulations adopted by the provinces relied mostly on standards based on best available technology.

Environmental policy activity slowed substantially from the mid-1970s to the mid-1980s, when Canada had to face two energy crises, rising inflation and unemployment, and a deep recession. It revived in the late 1980s when public concern about environmental issues re-emerged.[5] Both the federal government and the provinces passed a second round of environmental legislation, with the former taking a high profile on environmental issues in that period. The Canadian Environmental Protection Act (1988), which consolidated several pieces of environmental legislation, significantly strengthened the federal government's role in the control of toxic substances despite considerable resistance from some provinces. Resistance to the Canadian Environmental Assessment Act, originally introduced in 1990 but adopted only in 1995, has been even stronger. The provinces, which have their own environmental assessment legislation, felt that it would threaten their capacity to control economic development within their jurisdiction. In the early 1990s, two judicial decisions regarding large resource infrastructure projects brought to the Federal Court by environmental NGOs, had required the federal government to conduct environmental assessments. The new legislation provides the federal authorities with more discretion to decide on the necessity of conducting reviews in some areas, while at the same time strengthening their obligations in others.[6]

In 1990, the federal government also launched the Green Plan, a policy framework and action plan for sustainable development, in which it committed itself to substantial additional spending on the environment over the following five years (C$ 3 billion compared with annual federal environmental expenditure of about C$ 1.3 billion, which represented 1.2 per cent of overall budgetary expenditure at the time). The plan put an emphasis on environmental research, national parks and monitoring and education programmes, but also included quantitative targets on specific environmental issues. All provinces also established sustainable development plans in the early 1990s, some with associated special funds.

Subsequently, the impetus for strengthening environmental policies weakened at all government levels as a result of the fiscal consolidation effort, and only about 50 per cent of the sums programmed in the Green Plan were finally allocated. Cuts weighed heavily on environmental departments. Environment Canada's budgets stopped increasing in 1994/95 and had decreased by about 30 per cent in nominal terms by 1998/99 (compared to a 6 per cent reduction of overall federal budgetary expenditure).[7] In the face of these budgetary constraints, the federal government has reduced its transfers to provinces for "shared responsibility" in the environmental area[8] and has signed agreements with the provinces to carry out inspections, collect information and in cases where the provincial regulations had been considered equivalent, give priority of intervention to the provinces. The provinces, on the other hand, have also substantially reduced their environmental budgets: by up to about 60 per cent between 1994/95 and 1998/99 in Ontario, for example, a period when overall provincial expenditure was roughly stable.

Generally, the policy approach to environmental issues has been rather "co-operative". The regulatory standards have generally been developed through close co-operation among the federal government, the provincial government and industry, and the authorities have shown flexibility in cases of non-compliance operative (Harrison, 1995). Voluntary agreements have also become the cornerstone of federal policy on pollution control. Hence, in practice, there is a lot of self-regulation. Litigation, on the other hand, has played a relatively small role – in particular when compared with the United States – although it gained some importance in the 1990s. The use of economic instruments has been very limited at the various government levels, and, even though the issue has raised interest in the past decade, it is not significantly increasing.

Cost considerations have also played a role in shaping resource and environmental policies, in the sense that profit margins, the viability of the industry subject to regulation, employment patterns and international competitiveness issues have been taken into account. Yet, formal cost-benefit analysis has been relatively scarce, although its use would seem to have increased in the 1990s. Environmental legislation generally prescribes the examination of a measure's economic, environmental and social consequences, but cost-benefit analysis as such is not required. Under the more general framework of regulatory policy, a guide to cost-benefit analysis has been elaborated, but it is not prescriptive, and the authorities concerned have discretion to decide over whether such analysis is necessary.[9] Environment Canada has also developed models to estimate the environmental costs of air pollution, for example, and these models are being diffused to provincial and territorial governments, thereby enhancing their capacity to use cost-benefit analysis.

Administrative framework

Environment departments have been given responsibility for environmental protection at both levels of government, but substantial powers have been left in the hands of other departments, notably the agriculture, energy (and more widely natural resources) and transport departments, but also fisheries and health. As in other OECD countries, this division of responsibilities also reflects the fact that other goals occasionally override environmental objectives. To address co-ordination issues, various mechanisms have been put in place at the federal and provincial levels, as well as between the two levels (co-ordinating committees, interdepartmental research initiatives, interdepartmental networks and information sharing).

The shared nature of environmental jurisdiction also requires close co-operation between the different levels of government. The Canadian Council of Ministers of the Environment (CCME), composed of the environment ministers of the ten provinces, the three territories and the federal government, is the main forum through which federal/provincial co-ordination on environmental matters is negotiated and formalised. Over the last decade, it has developed substantive joint programmes, on contaminated sites and urban smog, for example. Bilateral agreements on specific issues have also been signed between the federal departments concerned and individual provinces (such as one with Quebec on pulp and paper regulation). More recently, in early 1998, all provinces (except Quebec) and the federal government signed a CCME Canada-Wide Accord on Environmental Harmonisation, which aims at clarifying the respective roles and responsibilities for environmental management.[10] Other federal-provincial-territorial ministerial councils have been established for natural resource issues, such as forests, agriculture, wildlife, and a joint one for energy and the environment.

At the federal level, since 1995, there has been a Commissioner of the Environment and Sustainable Development, a rather unique function among OECD countries. The Commissionner is in charge of auditing federal policies for sustainable development, reporting on the extent to which federal departments are implementing the sustainable development strategies they have elaborated since 1997, as well as on specific themes. The role of the yearly reports, which are delivered to the Auditor General and the Parliament, is to criticise things which are found wrong in the policy reviewed. Although they have no direct influence on policies, these reports play an important role in providing and disseminating information, raising public awareness, and providing recommendations for policy reform to the departments concerned. They have also provided valuable input to this chapter.

Environmental policy formulation relies quite heavily on consultation processes. For example, the National Roundtable on the Environment and the Economy, an independent agency of the federal government composed of leaders from all sectors of society, provides information and tries to clarify the state of the debate on emerging issues with both environmental and economic implications.[11] To prepare Canada's national strategy on climate change, a National Secretariat on Climate Change has also been established.

International context

Policies for natural resources and the environment are also bound by the various international agreements that Canada has signed. The North American Free Trade Agreement (NAFTA) has implications for resource policies, in particular for energy, since it specifies that export and domestic prices have to be equal – ruling out the possibility of implementing an energy export tax as existed in the 1970s – and provides rules for handling periods of shortage. By contrast, NAFTA seems to have had little effect on environmental policy-making. Canada also has long-standing experience of co-operation on transboundary environmental issues with the United States, including through a number of bilateral agreements on boundary waterways, such as the Great Lakes, air quality and acid rain, waterfowl management, and some animal species. Canada is also part to the 1994 Oslo Protocol on sulphur dioxide, which set quantitative targets for emissions reduction for the eastern provinces. Finally, Canada has signed, though not yet ratified, the Kyoto Protocol for reducing greenhouse gas emissions.

The federal government is responsible for negotiating these international agreements. However, Canada is one of the few federal countries in the OECD in which an international agreement in force in federal law is not necessarily binding on the provinces. Implementation of international agreements in matters of provincial competence is subject to assent by provinces. Here also, the CCME tries to harmonise procedures and views among the provinces and between the provinces and the federal government, but it works on a consensus basis. Hence, implementing common policies on global or regional issues may be particularly challenging.

Notes

1. The discussion of this section draws heavily on Hessing and Howlett (1997), Harrison (1996), OECD (1995) and Van Kooten and Scott (1995).

2. This is the case not only for resources under provincial land, but also under private land.

3. In the case of inland fisheries not crossing provincial boundaries, though, the rights of the provinces have been upheld by the courts (Hessing and Howlett, 1997).

4. At the end of the 19th century, the federal government made some attempts to take control of provincial resources and the associated revenues, but it lost the constitutional battle (Hessing and Howlett, 1997).

5. For an analysis of the relative salience of environmental and economic concern in public opinion, see Harrison (1996).

6. To avoid regulatory duplication in public consultation processes, it also allows the establishment of joint federal-provincial panel reviews.

7. Environment Canada budget does not account for all federal environmental expenditure; in 1990/91, it accounted for slightly more than half. More recent figures for overall federal environmental expenditure are not available.

8. Federal environmental expenditures are small in relation to those incurred by provincial and local governments (about 20 per cent in 1990/91), but in the poorest provinces federally supported activities are not negligible.

9. When cost-benefit analysis is conducted, it is not obligatory that the option ranking best be chosen; in the case where benefits do not exceed costs, a supplementary justification is required.

10. One of its main provisions is that specific roles and responsibilities will be attributed to one level of government only. This has important implications in the area of environmental assessment in particular, where provinces are likely to take the lead.

11. Such roundtables also exist at the provincial level.

Annex IV

Background material on the management of the Atlantic fishery

Factors underlying the fisheries collapse

Assessment of fisheries conservation standards is difficult, as the biology of stocks is not fully understood and stocks are subject to environmental shocks. The Canadian scientific estimations also suffered from data limitations. Stock assessments were based on data collected from research survey cruises and on commercial fishery landing statistics. Survey data indicated a decline for some species, but not the data on offshore commercial fishing, which reflected fishing with increasingly sophisticated technology in areas of high fish concentrations (Report of the Auditor General of Canada, 1997). As early as 1986 scientists had established that they had been greatly overestimating the size of the stock. Prediction errors were compounded by a decision-making process that allowed substantial flexibility *vis-à-vis* scientific recommendations (with for instance a rule specifying that the total allowable catch could be set halfway between the current fishing mortality level and the one corresponding to safe conservation standards).

To get the highest catch possible as quickly as possible, fishermen borrowed to invest in larger and better equipped vessels, which forced them to catch even more fish to repay their debts. This also made for more forceful resistance to controlling catches, not to say to shrinkage of the sector.

A consistent time series for subsidies to Atlantic fisheries is not available. According to Schrank (1996), total public financial outlays doubled over the 1980s, reaching C$ 1 billion in 1990/91, exceeding the value of the landed catch. Over the decade they amounted to C$ 8 billion, somewhat less than half being paid in the form of unemployment insurance. The figure seems particularly high, however, compared with that provided in the 1997 Auditor General's report of $270 million in unemployment insurance payments in 1988-89. In Newfoundland, the provincial government subsidised up to 35 per cent of the capital costs of vessel purchases (Munro and McCorquodale, 1981).

The centralised and top-down character of fisheries management in the 1970s and 1980s, whereby government regulations covered virtually every aspect of the harvesting operation, also played a significant part in the Atlantic fishery collapse (Charles, 1994).

Evaluation of the TAGS labour adjustment measures

Labour adjustment measures (as well as the other non-income support measures) were abandoned in 1996 when the sum available for income support turned out to be insufficient for the number of eligible individuals. Some of the key findings of the evaluation conducted in 1998 follow:*

- In 1996, 27 per cent of the TAGS clients had earned income from sources other than TAGS that was at least 80 per cent of their pre-closure earnings. In addition, 4 per cent had accepted early retirement or license retirement packages.
- However, of these so-called "adjusted" TAGS clients, 75 per cent were still relying on employment insurance or TAGS income support for up to 80 per cent of their income.
- In addition, 80 per cent of the TAGS clients who worked in 1996 still did so in the fishing or fish-processing sector.

The Canadian Fisheries Adjustment and Restructuring programme (CFAR)

This programme concerns both Atlantic and Pacific Fisheries.

Final cash payment is proposed to those enrolled in TAGS who did not opt for license retirement or early retirement, equal to the maximum amount they would have received if TAGS had continued to its original termination date of 15 May, 1999.

Adjustment measures include: related income support to assist individuals to become self-employed and to gain practical work experience and training to develop new skills; mobility assistance to help people willing to move to find new employment opportunities; changes to employment insurance (EI) regulations whereby weeks of paid TAGS income support count as labour force attachment in order to make it easier to requalify for EI.

Table A1. **The CFAR: sums programmed and spent**

C$ millions	Sums programmed	Sums spent as of March 2000
Licence retirement	250	162
Early retirement	65	79
Final cash payments	180	202
Adjusted measures	135	108
Economic development measures	100	3
Total	730	454

The Oceans Management Strategy

In Canada, there are more than 20 federal government departments and agencies with some degree of responsibility for activities in, or affecting, the oceans. In 1997, Parliament passed the Ocean Act. This legislation sets out an approach for oceans management, based on a sustainable development approach, integrated management and the precautionary approach, which calls for co-operation and collaboration in this sector, under the leadership of the Minister of Fisheries and Oceans. One of the key parts of the Act is the development and implementation of a national Oceans Management Strategy.

---

*For more details, see *http://www11.hrdc-drhc.gc.ca/edd/TAG_brf.shtml.*

The Ocean Management Strategy will focus on three main objectives: balancing economic, environmental and social goals; managing the increasing complexity and diversity of ocean use; and engaging communities and stakeholder in making decisions that affect them. Ecosystems are under stress due to rising and often competing demands among resource users (commercial fishing, transportation, oil and gas, telecom, recreation and tourism, etc.). The challenge therefore is to strike a balance between competing resource users and the need to conserve the resource. To this end, policy has to shift from a primarily fishery focus to a multi-use focus. In particular, the interface between land and water (for example, the impact of land-based pollution such as urban run-off, agricultural drainage and sewage discharges on fishing stocks) has to be taken into account. This involves dealing with a number of different players and using new and multiple regulatory instruments.

The implementation of the Oceans Act, and in particular the Ocean Management Strategy, is underway. Up to now, the main implementation activities have included initiating work on Marine Protected Area, Integrated Management projects and Marine Environmental Quality. An integral part of the development process for these initiatives is discussions with fishing groups and other oceans space interests. The scope of integrated management is very broad,taking into account all existing and potential coastal and marine activities, and presents challenges to institutions, organisations and individuals used to dealing bilaterally with their interest. Given the nature of the management challenge, raising public awareness and understanding is another key-element of the strategy.

Annex V
Chronology of economic events

1999

February

The federal government released its budget on 16 February, announcing that a balanced budget or better is expected for 1998/99 and that it is committed to a balanced budget or better for 1999/2000 and 2000/01. Highlights included increased provincial transfers for health care by C$ 11.5 billion over five years as well as money for health research and information; the elimination of employment insurance premiums for employers on new jobs created for youth aged 18-24; a C$ 300 million increase to the Canada Child Tax Benefit programme; and across-the-board tax cuts of C$ 16.5 billion (as a result of both the 1998 and 1999 budgets) over the next three years, including the elimination of the 3 per cent general surtax for all taxpayers effective 1 July. It was eliminated for low- and modest-income workers in the 1998 budget and completely eliminated in the 1999 budget.

March

Alberta released its budget plan with increased spending of C$ 1.7 billion over the next three years, mainly for health and education. As well, Alberta will move to a single provincial tax rate of 11 per cent of income in 2002, surtaxes will be phased out and the basic personal and spousal exemptions will be increased and indexed to inflation.

The Newfoundland government announced its budget with a forecast deficit of C$ 33 million in 1999/2000, after a small surplus for the 1998/99 fiscal year. Highlights included increased spending for health and for education, no tax increases, and a 25-cent rise in the provincial minimum wage.

Saskatchewan released its budget with a slight surplus forecast for 1999/2000. Highlights included increased spending for health care and a cut in the provincial sales tax rate from 7 to 6 per cent.

The Bank of Canada cut its Bank Rate by 25 basis points to 5 per cent at the end of March.

April

Quebec forecast a second consecutive balanced budget for this fiscal year. Highlights of the 1999 budget included personal income tax reductions of C$ 400 million annually (by July 2000) and additional health and education funding.

The British Columbia budget forecast a deficit of C$ 890 million in 1999/2000. Revenue measures included a personal income surtax reduction and a small business corporate income tax rate reduction. Expenditure initiatives focused on health and education.

The Prince Edward Island budget forecast a small surplus of C$ 4 million in 1999/2000. The personal income tax rate was reduced by 1 percentage point to 58.5 per cent, effective 1 January 1999. Expenditure initiatives mainly focused on health and economic development.

The Manitoba budget forecast a C$ 21 million surplus for 1999/2000. The personal income tax rate will be reduced in two steps: from 50 to 48.5 per cent for the 1999 taxation year and to 47 per cent as of 1 January 2000 The small business income tax rate was reduced to 8 per cent from 9 per cent with further one-percentage point cuts for the next three years. Spending initiatives focused on health, education and children and families.

The new territory of Nanavut came into being. Formerly part of the Northwest Territories, Nanavut is inhabited by approximately 25 000 people, 85 per cent of whom are Inuit, and stretches over 2.2 million square kilometres.

May

The Bank of Canada cut its Bank Rate by 25 basis points to 4¾ per cent at the beginning of the month.

The Ontario budget targeted a deficit of C$ 2.1 billion for 1999/2000, including a C$ 500 million reserve. Both personal income taxes and residential property taxes will be reduced by 20 per cent over the next five years. The personal income tax rate will be reduced from 40.5 to 38.5 per cent as of 1 July 1999. Expenditure measures focused on health (C$ 1.6 billion), education and infrastructure.

September

The Canadian Auto Workers union reached a three-year agreement with Ford, calling for wage increases of 3 per cent a year, an improved cost of living allowance that will add another 1.5 per cent a year, a signing bonus of C$1 000, child care and tuition subsidies and pension gains.

October

Nova Scotia tabled its 1999/2000 budget with a forecast C$497 million deficit, following a significant accounting reform. The province announced a review of all programmes and only two new spending initiatives.

Daimler Chrysler reached an agreement with the Canadian Auto Workers Union for pay increases of 3 per cent each year of a three-year contract, plus a cost-of-living increase of up to 4.5 per cent over the life of the contract. Each worker will also receive a C$ 1 000 signing bonus and an annual C$ 1 200 Christmas bonus. General Motors signed a similar agreement.

November

The Bank of Canada raised its key interest rate by one quarter of a percentage point to 5 per cent in mid-November, following a rise in US rates.

The port of Vancouver reopened after an eight-day lockout, affecting almost 11 000 workers including 2 200 longshoremen. Almost 25 per cent of Canadian marine trade goes through Vancouver.

December

The Federal Government agreed to allow the Canada Pension Plan Investment Board to actively invest in the stock market. The CCP previously was restricted to investments in 20-year provincial bonds.

2000

January

Air Canada took over Canadian Airlines in a C$ 92 million merger. Air Canada assumed Canadian's C$ 3 billion in liabilities and announced no layoffs but expects to reduce the combined workforce by 2 500 through attrition and buyouts.

The federal government approved a plan to provide an additional C$ 1 billion over the next two years of disaster assistance for farmers, many of whom have been hit by record low prices and floods.

February

The federal government delivered its budget on 28 February, with numerous tax cuts and a 4 per cent increase in programme spending. Highlights include: fully indexing tax brackets for inflation; increasing the threshold for the middle and highest tax brackets to C$ 35 000 and C$ 70 000 respectively and reducing the middle-income tax rate from 26 per cent to 23 per cent; a five year plan to level the corporate tax rate to 21 per cent and raising its threshold; reducing the capital gain tax; raising the Child Tax Benefit; and C$ 2.5 billion more over four years for post-secondary education and health.

The Alberta government tabled its budget, with a forecast surplus of C$ 1 035 million, of which C$ 500 million is allocated to the establishment of an endowment fund. Highlights include: a C$ 60 million reduction in user fees including the cost of registering land and mortgages, no tax changes other than the existing plan to switch to a flat tax rate of 11 per cent starting next year and increased base budgets for health and education spending over the next three years of 21 per cent and 19 per cent, respectively.

The federal government approved Toronto-Dominion Bank's C$ 8 billion takeover of Canada Trust. The plan will cut 4 900 jobs over three years and close about 275 branches out of a combined total of 1 323.

The Bank of Canada increased its Bank Rate in early February by one quarter of a percentage point to 5¼ per cent, matching a rise in US rates.

March

The Quebec government announced major new tax reductions and spending initiatives, while maintaining balanced budgets for 2000/01 and 2001/02. Personal income tax cuts will come into effect earlier than envisaged, retroactive to January 2000, and the tax system will be indexed to inflation from 2003. Businesses will benefit from a ten-year tax holiday for job-creating investment projects, a refundable tax credit for e-commerce support for SMEs, and the extension of an existing tax holiday for investments in manufacturing and computer equipment. Additional spending concerns health and social services, education and youth initiatives, and economic development and infrastructure projects.

Prince Edward Island forecast a balanced budget in 2000/01, following a small surplus expected for 1999/2000. The budget included a move to a tax-on-income system for personal taxation (de-linking it from basic federal tax) that provides some tax relief. New spending measures focused on health and education.

The British Colombia budget also announced a move to a tax-on-income system and provided some modest tax relief for low-and middle-income earners and small businesses while accommodating pressures for significant new spending, especially on health care and education. The province now reports its budgetary balance on a Summary Accounts basis, which combines the Consolidated Revenue Fund with the results of taxpayer-supported and self-supporting Crown corporations. The budget deficit was estimated at C\$ 1.3 billion in 2000/01 (including a C\$ 300 million forecast allowance), compared to a deficit of C\$ 1.1 billion in 1999/2000 (including a C\$ 100 million forecast allowance). Budget balance is envisaged only by 2004/05. On the positive side, the introduction of a new Budget Transparency and Accountability Act aims at restoring policy credibility following budget shortfalls associated with unrealistic economic and fiscal assumptions.

Newfoundland forecast a deficit of C\$ 35 million for 2000/01, including a contingency reserve of C\$ 30 million. The budget reiterated the previously announced plan to move to a tax-on-income system for personal taxation while providing tax cuts over three years. Investments were made in the priority programmes: health, education, social services and municipal infrastructure.

The Saskatchewan government, forecasting its seventh consecutive surplus , unveiled a tax-on- income structure for personal income taxation which will be indexed to inflation, in an attempt to remain competitive with neighbouring Alberta. The province will establish a new C\$ 400 million Fiscal Stabilisation Fund with the proceeds from a one-time transfer of retained earnings from the Saskatchewan Liquor and Gaming Authority. New spending initiatives focus on health, education, roads and infrastructure.

Following an accounting review in 1999/2000, the New Brunswick government projected a move back into slight budget surplus position, while offering income tax cuts for individuals and small businesses.Modest spending increases on health care and education will be offset by expenditure reductions in other areas resulting from a programme and service review.

The Bank of Canada increased its Bank Rate by 25 basis points to 5½ per cent, following a similar move by the US Federal Reserve.

April

In Nova Scotia, the new government slashed expenditures to reduce the budget deficit to C\$ 268 million in 2000/01, following an estimated deficit of C\$ 765 million in 1999/2000. The province offered some tax relief with its move to a tax-on-income structure for personal income taxation. Overall, the budget targets C\$ 295 million in expenditure reductions. Contained programme spending is expected to put the budget into balance by 2002/03.

May

The Ontario government announced the achievement of a budget surplus of C\$ 654 billion in 1999/2000, the first one in a decade. A balanced budget was projected for the current fiscal year, including an increased contingency reserve of C\$ 1 billion. The budget provided additional funds for healthcare and education and delivered substantial tax cuts for business and low-and middle-income earners (including a special C\$ 1 billion tax rebate in 1999/2000).

Manitoba forecast its sixth consecutive surplus, despite an accounting review in 1999/2000. The province provided some tax relief with its transition to a tax-on-income system which will be fully implemented in 2002. New spending initiatives were targeted towards health, education and families and communities.

Shortly after tabling its 2000 budget, the Alberta government announced a decrease in its tax rate for the 2001 tax year to 10.5 per cent from the previously announced 11 per cent and an increase in the basic personal and spousal exemptions to C$ 12 900 from C$ 11 620.

The Bank of Canada increased its Bank Rate by ½ percentage point to 6 per cent, matching a rise in US rates.

Statistical annex

Table A. **Selected background statistics**

	Average 1990-99	1990	1991	1992	1993	1994	1995	1996	1997	1998	1999
A. Percentage change											
Private consumption[1]	2.2	1.3	-1.4	1.8	1.8	3.1	2.1	2.5	4.4	2.9	3.5
Gross fixed capital formation[1]	2.7	-3.6	-3.5	-1.3	-2.7	7.4	-1.9	5.8	15.4	3.4	10.1
Public investment[1]	2.6	6.8	7.0	-0.3	-2.0	7.4	-2.9	-3.1	-2.4	1.4	15.9
Private investment[1]	2.7	-5.1	-5.1	-1.4	-2.8	7.4	-1.7	7.4	18.2	3.7	9.4
Residential[1]	-1.0	-10.2	-14.5	7.2	-3.5	4.2	-15.1	9.7	12.6	-2.0	6.6
Non residential[1]	4.7	-1.6	0.5	-5.9	-2.4	9.2	5.7	6.4	20.7	6.1	10.5
GDP[1]	2.3	0.3	-1.9	0.9	2.3	4.7	2.8	1.5	4.4	3.3	4.5
GDP price deflator	1.6	3.1	2.7	1.3	1.5	1.1	2.3	1.7	1.0	-0.6	1.6
Industrial production[1]	2.3	-2.8	-3.8	1.1	4.5	6.4	4.5	1.7	5.5	2.3	4.5
Employment	1.1	-0.0	-1.8	-0.7	0.8	2.0	1.9	0.8	2.3	2.6	2.8
Compensation of employees (current prices)	3.6	5.2	2.8	2.3	1.8	2.6	3.4	2.4	5.7	4.7	5.1
Productivity per worker (real GDP/employment)	1.3	0.4	-0.0	2.1	1.8	3.0	0.8	0.6	2.0	0.5	1.9
Unit labour costs	1.3	4.9	4.7	1.4	-0.5	-2.1	0.6	0.8	1.2	1.4	0.5
B. Percentage ratios											
Gross fixed capital formation as per cent of GDP[1]	18.5	18.9	18.6	18.2	17.3	17.7	16.9	17.7	19.5	19.5	20.6
Stockbuilding as per cent of GDP[1]	0.2	-0.3	-0.8	-0.9	-0.1	0.2	1.1	0.3	1.2	0.7	0.5
Foreign balance as per cent of GDP[1]	1.3	-0.5	-0.8	-0.4	0.6	1.9	2.9	3.0	1.2	2.2	2.5
Compensation of employees as per cent of GDP	53.2	54.4	55.5	55.5	54.5	52.8	51.9	51.5	51.6	52.6	52.1
Direct taxes on households as per cent of GDP	16.3	16.4	16.0	15.7	15.2	15.5	15.8	16.5	16.9	17.3	17.3
Household saving ratio as per cent of disposable income	9.1	13.3	13.5	13.2	12.1	9.6	9.3	7.1	4.8	4.5	3.7
Unemployment rate as per cent of labour force	9.5	8.1	10.3	11.2	11.4	10.3	9.4	9.6	9.1	8.3	7.6
C. Other indicator											
Current balance (million US dollars)	-12.3	-19.8	-22.4	-21.1	-21.7	-13.0	-4.4	3.3	-10.3	-11.1	-2.9

1. In constant 1992 prices.
Source: Statistics Canada and OECD.

Table B. **Supply and use of resources**
Million Canadian dollars, current prices

	1990	1991	1992	1993	1994	1995	1996	1997	1998	1999
Private consumption	386 913	399 932	412 940	430 162	447 748	462 865	482 367	512 454	532 926	558 567
Public consumption	151 977	162 765	169 262	171 630	172 073	172 947	171 644	171 744	175 864	179 999
Gross fixed investment	140 996	130 343	127 045	126 095	139 290	137 327	143 651	167 876	174 082	186 554
Final domestic demand	679 886	693 040	709 247	727 887	759 111	773 139	797 662	852 074	882 872	925 120
(Annual growth rate, per cent)	(4.4)	(1.9)	(2.3)	(2.6)	(4.3)	(1.8)	(3.2)	(6.8)	(3.6)	(4.8)
Stockbuilding	-2 660	-5 882	-6 562	-951	449	8 913	2 339	10 595	5 740	3 884
(Contribution to GDP growth, per cent)	(-1.0)	(-0.5)	(-0.1)	(0.8)	(0.2)	(1.1)	(-0.8)	(1.0)	(-0.6)	(-0.2)
Total domestic demand	677 226	687 158	702 685	726 936	759 560	782 052	800 001	862 669	888 612	929 004
(Annual growth rate, per cent)	(8.3)	(3.3)	(1.5)	(2.3)	(3.5)	(4.5)	(3.0)	(2.3)	(7.8)	(3.0)
Exports of goods and services	175 513	172 161	189 784	219 664	262 127	302 480	321 248	346 513	373 184	414 291
Imports of goods and services	174 624	176 093	192 393	219 673	253 014	276 618	287 553	331 509	360 359	385 941
Foreign balance	889	-3 932	-2 609	-9	9 113	25 862	33 695	15 004	12 825	28 350
(Contribution to GDP growth, per cent)	(0.1)	(-0.7)	(0.2)	(0.4)	(1.3)	(2.2)	(1.0)	(-2.2)	(-0.2)	(1.7)
Statistical discrepancy	20	13	-1 532	-1 967	-1 167	-826	-626	248	368	557
GDP (market prices)	678 135	683 239	698 544	724 960	767 506	807 088	833 070	877 921	901 805	957 911
(Annual growth rate, per cent)	(3.3)	(0.8)	(2.2)	(3.8)	(5.9)	(5.2)	(3.2)	(5.4)	(2.7)	(6.2)

Source: Statistics Canada.

Table B. **Supply and use of resources** (*cont.*)
Million Canadian dollars, constant 1992 prices

	1990	1991	1992	1993	1994	1995	1996	1997	1998	1999
Private consumption	411 343	405 783	412 940	420 442	433 649	442 941	453 983	473 895	487 866	504 763
Public consumption	162 937	167 541	169 262	169 362	167 263	166 380	164 104	162 053	164 725	166 905
Gross fixed investment	133 392	128 682	127 045	123 657	132 780	130 301	137 911	159 124	164 584	181 208
Final domestic demand	707 672	702 006	709 247	713 461	733 692	739 622	755 998	795 072	817 175	852 876
(Annual growth rate, per cent)	(0.9)	(−0.8)	(1.0)	(0.6)	(2.8)	(0.8)	(2.2)	(5.2)	(2.8)	(4.4)
Stockbuilding	−1 926	−5 806	−6 562	−907	1 373	8 195	2 015	9 928	5 833	4 454
(Contribution to GDP growth, per cent)	(−0.9)	(−0.5)	(−0.1)	(0.8)	(0.3)	(0.9)	(−0.8)	(1.0)	(−0.5)	(−0.2)
Total domestic demand	705 746	696 200	702 685	712 554	735 065	747 817	758 013	805 000	823 008	857 330
(Annual growth rate, per cent)	(−0.0)	(−1.4)	(0.9)	(1.4)	(3.2)	(1.7)	(1.4)	(6.2)	(2.2)	(4.2)
Exports of goods and services	171 977	175 926	189 784	210 537	238 141	259 667	275 021	299 157	325 652	358 272
Imports of goods and services	175 482	181 120	192 393	206 575	223 710	237 606	251 499	289 366	306 992	335 859
Foreign balance	−3 505	−5 194	−2 609	3 962	14 431	22 061	23 522	9 791	18 660	22 413
(Contribution to GDP growth, per cent)	(0.6)	(−0.2)	(0.4)	(0.9)	(1.5)	(1.0)	(0.2)	(−1.8)	(1.1)	(0.4)
Statistical discrepancy	3 223	1 241	−1 532	−1 933	−1 146	−796	−619	222	334	511
GDP (market prices)	705 464	692 247	698 544	714 583	748 350	769 082	780 916	815 013	842 002	880 254
(Annual growth rate, per cent)	(0.3)	(−1.9)	(0.9)	(2.3)	(4.7)	(2.8)	(1.5)	(4.4)	(3.3)	(4.5)

Source: Statistics Canada.

Table C. **Industrial production, employment and other business indicators**

Seasonally adjusted

	1995	1996	1997	1998	1999	Q1 99	Q2 99	Q3 99	Q4 99	Q1 2000
Indices of industrial production (1990 = 100)										
Total	113.1	115.0	121.3	124.1	129.7	126.6	128.0	131.5	132.9	134.6
Durable manufactures	118.7	121.5	132.2	138.7	150.9	145.6	148.5	154.1	155.4	158.3
Non-durable manufactures	103.9	104.8	109.4	112.2	115.3	113.7	114.1	116.0	117.3	117.0
New residential construction (annual rates)										
Building permits (million C$)	13 242	15 716	18 317	17 953	19 957	18 404	19 651	19 908	21 864	21 281
Starts (thousand units)	112.6	123.3	148.2	138.4	149.6	146.2	147.0	148.2	157.0	162.7
Employment and unemployment (thousands, monthy averages)										
Labour force	14 750	14 902	15 151	15 416	15 722	15 631	15 714	15 754	15 787	15 907
Non-agricultural employment	12 933	13 039	13 356	13 710	14 122	13 976	14 070	14 155	14 287	14 426
Employees										
Mining	134	131	143	143	137	137	136	134	139	143
Manufacturing	1 697	1 737	1 800	1 873	1 914	1 896	1 885	1 916	1 958	1 986
Durables	931	963	1 004	1 053	1 077	1 068	1 064	1 077	1 101	1 115
Non-durables	766	775	796	821	836	828	824	836	856	871
Transportation, communication, utilities[1]	857	839	852	873	886	884	881	884	894	902
Unemployment (thousands)	1 392	1 437	1 377	1 278	1 189	1 236	1 230	1 191	1 098	1 081
Unemployment (percentage of labour force)	9.4	9.6	9.1	8.3	7.6	7.9	7.9	7.6	6.9	6.8
Average weekly hours worked in manufacturing	38.5	38.4	39.3	38.6	38.7	38.6	38.8	38.9	38.7	38.9
Retail sales (C$ million, monthly averages)	17 814	18 406	19 820	20 553	21 724	21 243	21 414	22 079	22 161	22 580
Orders and inventories in manufacturing (C$ million)										
New orders (monthly averages)[2]	33 033	33 736	37 162	38 046	41 234	39 548	40 021	42 314	43 053	43 463
Unfilled orders (end of period)	34 256	32 266	43 177	50 978	54 938	51 736	51 461	53 457	54 938	53 728
Total inventories (end of period)	45 569	46 892	49 129	51 229	55 520	51 424	52 427	54 206	55 520	57 396

1. Includes storage, electric power, gas and water utilities.
2. 3-month averages for quarters
Source: Statistics Canada; OECD, *Main Economic Indicators.*

Table D. **Prices, wages and finance**

	1995	1996	1997	1998	1999	Q1 99	Q2 99	Q3 99	Q4 99	Q1 2000
Prices (1990 = 100)										
Consumer prices, all items	100.0	101.6	103.2	104.2	106.1	104.8	105.9	106.6	107.0	107.5
of which:										
Food	100.0	101.3	102.9	104.6	105.9	106.0	106.3	105.7	105.7	106.0
Non-food	100.0	101.7	103.3	102.9	105.0	103.1	104.6	105.7	106.7	107.9
Producer prices, manufactured goods	100.0	100.4	101.2	101.2	103.1	101.1	102.0	104.2	105.0	106.6
Wages and profits										
Hourly earnings in manufacturing (1990 = 100)	100.0	103.2	104.1	106.3	106.4	106.6	106.1	106.0	107.1	110.0
Corporate profits before taxes (C$ million, annual rates)	75 309	79 135	86 512	81 671	101 032	89 844	94 724	106 504	113 056	121 072
Banking (C$ million, end of period)										
Chartered banks :										
Canadian dollar deposits	433 558	449 541	490 148	489 113	521 527	492 468	500 962	504 222	521 527	581 903
of which: Personal savings deposits	297 559	292 444	289 697	289 752	298 524	291 029	293 286	294 137	298 524	338 600
Liquid assets	91 788	87 099	78 257	77 632	79 666	85 473	86 441	79 695	79 666	83 312
Holdings of Government of Canada direct and guaranteed securities	49 284	55 361	51 073	57 727	53 975	58 537	65 634	55 018	53 975	59 102
Total loans	417 947	468 017	538 428	535 090	548 176	542 634	549 125	550 054	548 176	584 898
Currency outside banks	26 160	27 188	28 699	30 615	34 281	31 265	31 788	32 443	34 281	33 227
Interest rates (per cent, end of period)										
3-month commercial paper rate	5.7	3.1	4.8	5.0	5.3	4.8	4.9	4.8	5.3	5.5
Over-10-year Government bond yield	7.5	6.8	5.8	5.1	6.2	5.3	5.7	5.9	6.2	5.9
Miscellaneous										
Share prices Toronto stock exchange (1990 = 100)	129.6	154.0	188.8	197.5	206.3	191.4	203.3	204.7	226.0	263.8

Source: Statistics Canada; OECD, *Main Economic Indicators.*

Table E. Balance of payments

Million US dollars

	1990	1991	1992	1993	1994	1995	1996	1997	1998	1999
Merchandise exports	130 322	128 888	135 236	147 441	167 072	193 329	205 271	217 668	217 230	242 713
Merchandise imports	120 847	122 768	127 764	137 295	152 213	167 538	174 487	200 569	204 516	219 870
Trade balance	9 475	6 120	7 474	10 147	14 860	25 791	30 784	17 098	12 715	22 843
Services credit	19 183	20 357	20 783	21 883	23 982	26 082	29 199	30 484	30 941	33 087
Services debit	28 299	30 325	30 813	32 432	32 521	33 468	35 623	37 029	35 630	37 551
Services, net	-9 116	-9 967	-10 030	-10 550	-8 539	-7 386	-6 425	-6 546	-4 689	-4 463
Investment income, credits	15 068	12 935	11 392	10 687	15 450	18 870	19 205	21 845	20 559	20 977
Investment income, debits	34 459	30 341	28 877	31 485	34 407	41 597	40 761	43 280	40 174	43 012
Investment income, net	-19 390	-17 406	-17 484	-20 799	-18 957	-22 727	-21 556	-21 435	-19 615	-22 035
Official transfers, net	-755	-1 111	-997	-711	-549	-325	391	534	394	621
Private transfers, net	-41	-6	55	136	204	201	130	46	150	114
Current account	-19 828	-22 369	-20 981	-21 776	-12 983	-4 445	3 322	-10 303	-11 045	-2 920
Capital account	5 316	5 595	7 093	8 296	7 498	4 943	5 847	5 446	3 355	3 426
Direct investment, assets	-5 237	-5 835	-3 590	-5 700	-9 295	-11 463	-12 880	-22 050	-26 567	-17 362
Portfolio investment, assets	-2 225	-10 182	-9 720	-13 860	-6 537	-5 342	-14 045	-8 111	-14 987	-15 445
Other investment, assets	-9 422	2 811	1 387	-1 323	-20 070	-11 171	-26 604	-13 413	7 125	5 951
Total assets, net flows	-16 883	-13 204	-11 923	-20 885	-35 901	-27 975	-53 529	-43 576	-34 430	-26 857
Direct investment, liabilities	7 582	2 880	4 722	4 731	8 205	9 256	9 407	11 469	16 494	24 269
Portfolio investment, liabilities	15 928	27 493	20 436	40 927	17 070	18 386	13 384	11 850	16 856	2 827
Other investment, liabilities	9 627	-255	-2 218	-6 353	16 133	-3 666	16 242	27 877	7 457	-9 198
Total liabilities, net flows	33 138	30 122	22 938	39 304	41 409	23 975	39 033	51 194	40 807	17 898
Change in reserves	-1 069	1 835	4 757	-935	358	-2 753	-5 499	2 448	-5 023	-5 935
Financial account	16 253	16 917	11 017	18 420	5 507	-3 999	-14 496	7 620	6 377	-8 959
Errors and omissions	-1 742	-141	2 872	-4 941	-23	3 501	5 326	-2 764	1 313	8 453

Source: Statistics Canada; OECD Secretariat.

Table F. **Public sector**

	A. Budget indicators General government accounts Per cent of GDP					
	1961	1970	1980	1990	1998	1999
Current receipts[1]	27.8	35.6	37.4	43.1	44.4	44.0
Non-interest current expenditure[1]	22.9	28.0	32.6	36.1	34.0	32.6
Primary budget balance	−0.2	2.1	0.3	1.3	7.0	8.5
Net interest payments	2.5	2.4	4.3	7.1	6.8	6.3
General government budget balance	−2.8	−0.4	−4.1	−5.8	0.2	2.1
of which:						
Federal	−1.7	−0.5	−4.0	−4.9	0.5	0.6
Provincial-local	−1.1	−1.2	−1.0	−1.2	−0.2	1.5
Pension plans[2]	0.0	1.3	1.0	0.3	−0.1	0.1
General government debt						
Gross debt	71.0	61.1	57.2	93.3	116.6	111.6
Net debt	29.0	19.6	26.1	61.5	81.4	75.3
of which: Federal	21.2	13.4	23.5	54.2	62.3	58.2

	B. The structure of outlay and capital accounts Per cent of GDP					
Outlay						
Total general government expenditure	25.8	31.7	38.0	45.5	42.5	40.4
Current consumption[1]	15.9	20.7	21.7	23.3	20.8	20.0
Current transfers	7.0	7.3	11.0	12.7	13.2	12.6
Persons	5.9	6.1	7.9	10.8	11.7	11.1
Business (subsidies)	0.9	0.9	2.7	1.5	1.2	1.1
Non-residents	0.2	0.3	0.3	0.4	0.3	0.3
Total current program expenditure	22.9	28.0	32.6	36.1	34.0	32.6
Gross interest payments	2.9	3.7	5.4	9.5	8.4	7.8
Capital						
Net capital transfers[3]	−0.1	−0.2	−0.4	−0.4	0.3	0.4
Non-financial capital acquisition[4]	4.7	4.0	3.0	2.9	2	1.8

	C. General government expenditure by function, financial management system basis Per cent of GDP, fiscal years					
	1965-66	1970-71	1980-81	1990-91[5]	1996-97[5]	1997-98[5]
Social services	4.8	6.0	7.4	10.9	11.7	n.a.
Education	4.6	6.2	5.0	6.3	6.7	n.a.
Health	2.6	4.3	4.4	6.1	6.4	n.a.
Transport and commmunication	3.3	2.8	2.6	2.6	2.4	n.a.
National defence	2.7	1.9	1.6	1.7	1.4	1.3
General services	1.5	2.3	2.4	1.5	1.5	n.a.

1. Exclude capital consumption allowances.
2. Canada and Quebec Pension Plans.
3. Includes net capital formation assistance to persons, businesses and non-residents, and other net capital transfers.
4. Includes fixed capital formation, inventories and existing assets.
5. Based on the new Statistics Canada's FMS universe.
Source: Department of Finance; OECD Secretariat.

Table G.   **Financial markets**

	1970	1980	1993	1998	1999
Size of the financial sector (percentages)[1]					
Sector employment/total employment	4.8	5.7	6.5	6.0	5.9
Net financial assets/GDP	6.3	4.3	7.3	11.1	9.8
Structure of financial assets and liabilities					
Financial institutions' share in domestic financial assets					
(per cent)	33.1	38.6	41.5	42.0	44.7
Government securities in NFB[2] total financial assets					
(per cent)	0.3	0.1	2.2	1.1	1.1
Structure of NFB liabilities					
Debt to equity ratio[3]	1.13	1.44	1.61	1.49	1.48
Short-term:					
Securities and mortgages ($ billion)	8.6	32.4	117.7	135.7	146.3
Trade payables ($ billion)	12.4	54.9	111.6	143.4	157.4
Long-term					
Bonds ($ billion)	13.7	28.7	97.5	149.2	155.8
Loans and corporate claims ($ billion)	22.8	109.0	272.1	364.4	374.5
Internationalisation of markets					
Share of foreign currency assets and liabilities					
in the banking sector[4]					
Assets	28.9	39.1	30.8	46.4	40.2
Liabilities	28.6	40.2	33.3	47.7	42.3
Foreign purchases of Canadian securities[5]	12.4	18.2	68.5	49.1	4.9
Canadian purchases of foreign securities[5]	−1.2	0.6	23.2	43.6	26.9
Debt (per cent of GDP)					
Private non-financial sector					
NFB[2, 6]	70.3	77.4	89.2	96.8	96.0
Households[7]	38.8	48.3	57.2	61.2	60.0

1. Public and private financial institutions and insurance.
2. NFB = non-financial corporate business, excluding farms.
3. (Liabilities − shares)/shares.
4. Per cent of consolidated balance sheet of chartered banks; excludes other deposit-taking institutions.
5. Per cent of net issues on dosmestic securities market. Data include new issues as well as secondary market transactions.
6. Liabilities less shares.
7. Persons and unincorporated business liabilities less trade payables, other loans and other Canadian bonds.
Source: Bank of Canada.

Table H. **Labour market indicators**

	A. Labour market performance			
	1976	1980	1990	1999
Standardised unemployment rate	7.0	7.5	8.2	7.6
Unemployment rate:				
Total	7.0	7.5	8.2	7.6
Male	6.4	7.0	8.2	7.8
Female	8.1	8.2	8.1	7.3
Youth[1]	12.2	12.8	12.4	14.0
Share of long-term unemployment in total unemployment[2]	2.5	3.8	7.5	11.6
Dispersion of regional unemployment rates[3]	3.0	3.0	3.4	3.6

	B. Structural or institutional characteristics			
	1976	1980	1990	1999
Participation rate:[4]				
Total	61.5	64.2	67.4	65.6
Male	77.7	78.3	76.1	72.5
Female	45.7	50.4	58.5	58.9
Employment/population (15-64 years)	57.2	59.4	61.7	60.6
Average hours worked (manufacturing)	. .	. .	36.9	37.9
Part-time work (as per cent of dependent employment)	19.6	22.2	26.3	28.7
Non-wage labour costs[5] (as per cent of total compensation)	8.0	8.3	9.6	12.1
Government unemployment insurance replacement ratio[6]	44.8	41.4	45.4	43.2
Unionisation rate	31.5	30.9	29.6	26.7

	Average percentage changes (annual rates)		
	1979/1977	1989/1980	1999/1990
Labour force	3.1	2.0	1.1
Employment			
Total	2.9	2.0	1.1
Goods-producing	. .	. .	−0.1
Services	. .	. .	1.6

1. People between 15 and 24 years as a percentage of the labour force of the same age group.
2. People looking for a job since one year or more.
3. Measured by standard deviation for 10 provinces.
4. Labour force as a percentage of relevant population group, aged between 15 and 64 years.
5. Supplementary labour income (including contributions to social security, pension funds and other forms of SLI).
6. Average weekly benefits (regular)/average weekly earnings (including overtime).
Source: Canadian authorities.

Table I. **Production structure and performance indicators**

	A. Production structure					
	Per cent share of GDP at factor costs (constant prices)[1]			Per cent share of total employment[2]		
	1979	1989	1999	1979	1989	1999
Agriculture	1.7	1.6	1.8	..	3.4	2.8
Mines, quarries and oil wells	4.2	3.5	3.6	..	1.5	1.1
Manufacturing	18.7	17.5	18.2	..	16.2	14.9
of which:						
Food and beverages	3.4	2.5	2.4	..	..	..
Paper and paper products	1.3	1.0	0.9	..	..	..
Primary metal industries	1.0	0.9	0.9	..	..	..
Fabricated metal products, machinery						
and equipment	3.0	2.3	2.2	..	..	..
Chemicals and chemical products	1.3	1.4	1.5	..	..	..
Construction	7.2	7.1	5.6	..	6.5	5.5
Market services	63.1	65.5	66.7	..	68.9	71.6
of which:						
Transport, storage and communication	6.8	7.2	8.2	..	5.0	4.9
Wholesale and retail trade	10.0	11.4	12.3	..	15.6	15.0
Finance, insurance and real estate	15.5	14.6	16.1	..	6.0	5.6
Community, business social and personal services	24.1	25.3	24.0	..	36.4	40.9
Government services	8.0	7.0	6.1	..	6.0	5.1

	B. Labour productivity		
	Real output per hour worked, annual per cent growth		
	1970s	1980s	1990s
Business sector industries	2.5	1.0	1.1
Business sector excluding agriculture	2.2	0.8	1.0
Goods sector industries	2.8	1.6	1.8
Service sector industries	2.3	0.7	0.8
Manufacturing sector industries	2.7	2.3	2.1

1. Industrial structure of GDP at factor cost series on the SIC 1980 basis.
2. Industrial structure of employment series on the NAICS basis.
Source: Canadian authorities.

BASIC STATISTICS:

INTERNATIONAL COMPARISONS

	Units	Reference period[1]	Australia	Austria
Population				
Total	Thousands	1997	18 532	8 07
Inhabitants per sq. km	Number	1997	2	9
Net average annual increase over previous 10 years	%	1997	1.3	0.
Employment				
Total civilian employment (TCE)[2]	Thousands	1997	8 430	3 68
of which:				
Agriculture	% of TCE	1997	5.2	6.
Industry	% of TCE	1997	22.1	30.
Services	% of TCE	1997	72.7	63.
Gross domestic product (GDP)				
At current prices and current exchange rates	Bill. US$	1997	392.9	206.
Per capita	US$	1997	21 202	25 54
At current prices using current PPPs[3]	Bill. US$	1997	406.8	186.
Per capita	US$	1997	21 949	23 07
Average annual volume growth over previous 5 years	%	1997	4.1	1.
Gross fixed capital formation (GFCF)	% of GDP	1997	21.5	24.
of which:				
Machinery and equipment	% of GDP	1997	10.3 (96)	8.8 (96
Residential construction	% of GDP	1997	4.4 (96)	6.2 (96
Average annual volume growth over previous 5 years	%	1997	7.3	2.
Gross saving ratio[4]	% of GDP	1997	18.4	2
General government				
Current expenditure on goods and services	% of GDP	1997	16.7	19.
Current disbursements[5]	% of GDP	1996	34.8	4
Current receipts	% of GDP	1996	35.4	47.
Net official development assistance	% of GNP	1996	0.28	0.2
Indicators of living standards				
Private consumption per capita using current PPP's[3]	US$	1997	13 585	12 95
Passenger cars, per 1 000 inhabitants	Number	1995	477	44
Telephones, per 1 000 inhabitants	Number	1995	510	46
Television sets, per 1 000 inhabitants	Number	1994	489	48
Doctors, per 1 000 inhabitants	Number	1996	2.5	2.
Infant mortality per 1 000 live births	Number	1996	5.8	5.
Wages and prices (average annual increase over previous 5 years)				
Wages (earnings or rates according to availability)	%	1998	1.5	5.
Consumer prices	%	1998	2.0	1.
Foreign trade				
Exports of goods, fob*	Mill. US$	1998	55 882	61 75
As % of GDP	%	1997	15.6	28.
Average annual increase over previous 5 years	%	1998	5.6	
Imports of goods, cif*	Mill. US$	1998	60 821	68 01
As % of GDP	%	1997	15.3	31.
Average annual increase over previous 5 years	%	1998	7.5	
Total official reserves[6]	Mill. SDR's	1998	10 942	14 628 (97
As ratio of average monthly imports of goods	Ratio	1998	2.2	2.7 (97

* At current prices and exchange rates.
1. Unless otherwise stated.
2. According to the definitions used in OECD Labour Force Statistics.
3. PPPs = Purchasing Power Parities.
4. Gross saving = Gross national disposable income minus private and government consumption.

EMPLOYMENT OPPORTUNITIES

Economics Department, OECD

The Economics Department of the OECD offers challenging and rewarding opportunities to economists interested in applied policy analysis in an international environment. The Department's concerns extend across the entire field of economic policy analysis, both macro-economic and microeconomic. Its main task is to provide, for discussion by committees of senior officials from Member countries, documents and papers dealing with current policy concerns. Within this programme of work, three major responsibilities are:

- to prepare regular surveys of the economies of individual Member countries;
- to issue full twice-yearly reviews of the economic situation and prospects of the OECD countries in the context of world economic trends;
- to analyse specific policy issues in a medium-term context for the OECD as a whole, and to a lesser extent for the non-OECD countries.

The documents prepared for these purposes, together with much of the Department's other economic work, appear in published form in the *OECD Economic Outlook, OECD Economic Surveys, OECD Economic Studies* and the Department's *Working Papers* series.

The Department maintains a world econometric model, INTERLINK, which plays an important role in the preparation of the policy analyses and twice-yearly projections. The availability of extensive cross-country data bases and good computer resources facilitates comparative empirical analysis, much of which is incorporated into the model.

The Department is made up of about 80 professional economists from a variety of backgrounds and Member countries. Most projects are carried out by small teams and last from four to eighteen months. Within the Department, ideas and points of view are widely discussed; there is a lively professional interchange, and all professional staff have the opportunity to contribute actively to the programme of work.

Skills the Economics Department is looking for:

a) Solid competence in using the tools of both microeconomic and macroeconomic theory to answer policy questions. Experience indicates that this normally requires the equivalent of a Ph.D. in economics or substantial relevant professional experience to compensate for a lower degree.

b) Solid knowledge of economic statistics and quantitative methods; this includes how to identify data, estimate structural relationships, apply basic techniques of time series analysis, and test hypotheses. It is essential to be able to interpret results sensibly in an economic policy context.

c) A keen interest in and extensive knowledge of policy issues, economic developments and their political/social contexts.

d) Interest and experience in analysing questions posed by policy-makers and presenting the results to them effectively and judiciously. Thus, work experience in government agencies or policy research institutions is an advantage.

e) The ability to write clearly, effectively, and to the point. The OECD is a bilingual organisation with French and English as the official languages. Candidates must have excellent knowledge of one of these languages, and some knowledge of the other. Knowledge of other languages might also be an advantage for certain posts.

f) For some posts, expertise in a particular area may be important, but a successful candidate is expected to be able to work on a broader range of topics relevant to the work of the Department. Thus, except in rare cases, the Department does not recruit narrow specialists.

g) The Department works on a tight time schedule with strict deadlines. Moreover, much of the work in the Department is carried out in small groups. Thus, the ability to work with other economists from a variety of cultural and professional backgrounds, to supervise junior staff, and to produce work on time is important.

General information

The salary for recruits depends on educational and professional background. Positions carry a basic salary from FF 318 660 or FF 393 192 for Administrators (economists) and from FF 456 924 for Principal Administrators (senior economists). This may be supplemented by expatriation and/or family allowances, depending on nationality, residence and family situation. Initial appointments are for a fixed term of two to three years.

Vacancies are open to candidates from OECD Member countries. The Organisation seeks to maintain an appropriate balance between female and male staff and among nationals from Member countries.

For further information on employment opportunities in the Economics Department, contact:

Management Support Unit
Economics Department
OECD
2, rue André-Pascal
75775 PARIS CEDEX 16
FRANCE

E-Mail: eco.contact@oecd.org

Applications citing ''ECSUR'', together with a detailed *curriculum vitae* in English or French, should be sent to the Head of Personnel at the above address.

Did you Know?

This publication is available in electronic form!

Many OECD publications and data sets are now available in electronic form to suit your needs at affordable prices.

CD-ROMs

For our statistical products we use the powerful software platform Beyond 20/20™ produced by Ivation. This allows you to get maximum value from the data. For more details of this and other publications on CD-ROM visit our online bookshop **www.oecd.org/bookshop** or **www.oecdwash.org.**

STATISTICS VIA THE INTERNET

During 2000 we are launching SourceOECD/statistics. Whilst some statistical datasets may become available on the Internet during the second half of 2000 we anticipate that most will not be available until late 2000 or early 2001. For more information visit **www.oecd.org/sourceoecd** or **www.ivation.com.**

BOOKS AND PERIODICALS IN PDF

Most of our printed books are also produced as PDF files and are available from our online bookshop **www.oecd.org/bookshop.** Customers paying for printed books by credit card online can download the PDF file free of charge for immediate access.

We are also developing two new services, SourceOECD/periodicals and SourceOECD/studies, which will deliver online access to all printed publications over the Internet. These services are being developed in partnership with ingenta. For more information visit **www.oecd.org/sourceoecd or www.ingenta.com.**

OECD DIRECT

To stay informed by e-mail about all new OECD publications as they are published, why not register for OECD Direct?

OECD Direct is a free, opt-in, e-mail alerting service designed to help you stay up to date with our new publications. You've a choice of different themes so you can adapt the service to your fields of interest only. Registration is free of charge and there is no obligation. To register, simply follow the instructions at the top of the online bookshop's home page **www.oecd.org/bookshop.** We don't use your e-mail address for any other purpose and we won't give them to anyone else either – you'll just get what you registered for, e-mails announcing new publications as soon as they are released.

Le saviez-vous ?

Cette publication est disponible en version électronique !

Pour répondre aux besoins de ses clients, l'OCDE a décidé de publier un grand nombre d'études et de données sous forme électronique à des prix très abordables.

CD-ROM

Nos bases de données statistiques fonctionnent avec le logiciel Beyond 20/20™ produit par Ivation. Ce logiciel, convivial et très simple d'utilisation, vous permet d'utiliser au mieux les données.
Pour plus de détails et pour consulter la liste des publications sur CD-ROM, visitez notre librairie en ligne : **www.oecd.org/bookshop.**

STATISTIQUES SUR INTERNET

SourceOECD/statitics sera lancé au cours de l'an 2000. Ce nouveau service commencera à être opérationnel à partir du second semestre de l'an 2000 et nous envisageons de diffuser la totalité de notre catalogue de statistiques pour la fin de l'an 2000/début 2001.
Pour plus d'information : **www.oecd.org/sourceoecd** ou **www.ivation.com.**

LIVRES ET PÉRIODIQUES EN VERSION PDF

La plupart de nos publications sont également disponibles en format PDF. Vous pouvez les trouver dans notre librairie en ligne : **www.oecd.org/bookshop.**
Les clients de notre librairie en ligne, qui font l'acquisition d'un ouvrage imprimé en utilisant une carte de crédit, peuvent télécharger gratuitement la version électronique, pour une lecture immédiate.

Nous développons actuellement deux nouveaux services, SourceOECD/periodicals et SourceOECD/studies, qui vous permettront d'accéder en ligne à toutes nos publications. Ces services, qui sont actuellement en voie de développement en association avec ingenta, ne seront dans un premier temps disponibles que pour les versions en langue anglaise. Une étude est en cours pour élargir ce service aux publications en langue française. Pour plus d'information, visitez les deux sites **www.oecd.org/sourceoecd** ou **www.ingenta.com.**

OECD DIRECT

Pour être informé par e-mail de la parution de nos toutes dernières publications, enregistrez dès maintenant votre nom sur **www.oecd.org/bookshop.**
OECD Direct est notre service « Alerte » gratuit qui permet aux lecteurs qui le souhaitent de recevoir par e-mail des informations sur la sortie de nos nouvelles publications. Une série de thèmes est proposée et chacun pourra choisir en fonction de ses propres centres d'intérêt. L'inscription est gratuite et sans obligation. Pour enregistrer votre nom, il vous suffit de suivre les instructions figurant en haut de la page d'accueil de notre librairie en ligne **www.oecd.org/bookshop.** Soyez assurés que nous n'utiliserons pas votre adresse e-mail à d'autres fins et ne la transmettrons en aucun cas. Vous ne recevrez par e-mail que des informations vous annonçant nos nouvelles publications dès lors qu'elles sont parues.

www.oecd.org/sourceoecd

For more information about all OECD publications contact your nearest OECD Centre, or visit **www.oecd.org/bookshop**

Pour plus d'informations sur les publications de l'OCDE, contactez votre Centre OCDE le plus proche ou visitez notre librairie en ligne : **www.oecd.org/bookshop**

Where to send your request:
Où passer commande :

In Central and Latin America / En Amérique centrale et en Amérique du Sud

OECD MEXICO CENTRE / CENTRE OCDE DE MEXICO
Edificio INFOTEC
Av. San Fernando No. 37 Col. Toriello Guerra
Tlalpan C.P. 14050, Mexico D.F.
Tel.: +525 528 10 38   Fax: + 525 606 13 07
E-mail: mexico.contact@oecd.org   Internet: www.rtn.net.mx/ocde

In North America / En Amérique du Nord

OECD WASHINGTON CENTER / CENTRE OCDE DE WASHINGTON
2001 L Street N.W., Suite 650
Washington, DC 20036-4922
Tel.: +1 202 785-6323
Toll free / Numéro vert : +1 800 456-6323   Fax: +1 202 785-0350
E-mail: washington.contact@oecd.org   Internet: www.oecdwash.org

In Japan / Au Japon

OECD TOKYO CENTRE / CENTRE OCDE DE TOKYO
Landic Akasaka Bldg.
2-3-4 Akasaka, Minato-ku
Tokyo 107-0052
Tel.: +81 3 3586 2016   Fax: +81 3 3584 7929
E-mail : center@oecdtokyo.org   Internet: www.oecdtokyo.org

In the rest of the world / Dans le reste du monde
DVGmbH
Birkenmaarsstrasse 8
D-53340 Meckenheim
Germany
Tel.: +49 22 25 9 26 166/7/8   Fax: +49 22 25 9 26 169
E-mail: oecd@dvg.dsb.net

OECD Information Centre and Bookshop/
Centre d'information de l'OCDE et Librairie
OECD PARIS CENTRE / CENTRE OCDE DE PARIS
2 rue André-Pascal, 75775 Paris Cedex 16, France
Enquiries / Renseignements : Tel: +33 (0) 1 45 24 81 67
E-mail: sales@oecd.org

ONLINE BOOKSHOP / LIBRAIRIE EN LIGNE : **www.oecd.org/bookshop**
(secure payment with credit card / paiement sécurisé par carte de crédit)

OECD PUBLICATIONS, 2, rue André-Pascal, 75775 PARIS CEDEX 16
PRINTED IN FRANCE
(10 2000 01 1 P) ISBN 92-64-17501-6 – No. 51393 2000
ISSN 0376-6438